TAKE A ...
THE ...
W...

Enter Sydney Omarr's star-studded world of accurate day-by-day predictions for every aspect of your life. With expert readings and forecasts, you can chart a course to romance, adventure, good health, or career opportunities while gaining valuable insight into yourself and others. Offering a daily outlook for 18 full months, this fascinating guide shows you:

• The important dates in your life
• What to expect from an astrological reading
• The initials of people who will be influential in your life
• How the stars can help you stay healthy and fit
• Your lucky lottery numbers
• And more!

Let this expert's sound advice guide you through a year of heavenly possibilities—for today and for every day of 1998!

SYDNEY OMARR DAY-BY-DAY ASTROLOGICAL GUIDE FOR

ARIES—March 21–April 19
TAURUS—April 20–May 20
GEMINI—May 21–June 20
CANCER—June 21–July 22
LEO—July 23–August 22
VIRGO—August 23–September 22
LIBRA—September 23–October 22
SCORPIO—October 23–November 21
SAGITTARIUS—November 22–December 21
CAPRICORN—December 22–January 19
AQUARIUS—January 20–February 18
PISCES—February 19–March 20

IN 1998

SYDNEY OMARR'S DAY-BY-DAY ASTROLOGICAL GUIDES
18 Months of Daily Horoscopes From
July 1997 to December 1998

Let America's most accurate astrologer show you what the signs of the zodiac will mean for you in the coming year! Sydney Omarr gives you invaluable tips on your love life, your career, your health—and your all-round good fortune.

SYDNEY OMARR'S

DAY-BY-DAY ASTROLOGICAL GUIDE FOR

CANCER

June 21—July 22

1998

A SIGNET BOOK

SIGNET
Published by the Penguin Group
Penguin Books USA Inc., 375 Hudson Street,
New York, New York 10014, U.S.A.
Penguin Books Ltd, 27 Wrights Lane,
London W8 5TZ, England
Penguin Books Australia Ltd, Ringwood,
Victoria, Australia
Penguin Books Canada Ltd, 10 Alcorn Avenue,
Toronto, Ontario, Canada M4V 3B2
Penguin Books (N.Z.) Ltd, 182–190 Wairau Road,
Auckland 10, New Zealand

Penguin Books Ltd, Registered Offices:
Harmondsworth, Middlesex, England

First published by Signet, an imprint of Dutton Signet,
a division of Penguin Books USA Inc.

First Printing, July, 1997
10 9 8 7 6 5 4 3 2

Sydney Omarr is syndicated worldwide by *Los Angeles Times* Syndicate.
Cover art by Faranak

 REGISTERED TRADEMARK—MARCA REGISTRADA

Printed in Canada

CONTENTS

INTRODUCTION

Astrology
Your Link to the Millennium

We're now in an exciting time of transition between this
century and the next, as our personal universe opens
up with possibilities we never imagined. Thanks to the
Internet, our favorite comfortable chair can be a command control center from which we can travel the globe
at warp speed. Information from a distant library can be
at our fingertips in moments. New friends and new lovers can meet in cyberspace. But though our lifestyle is
changing, our longings haven't. We are still searching for
the same things that have always made life worth living—love, meaningful work, and fulfilling personal
relationships.

Astrology is an age-old tool that can guide us in our
search, one that works as well today as it has for several
millennia. Like "links" in the Internet, astrological clues
can speed you from where you are now to where you'd
like to be. But if you're new to astrology, you may feel
just as bewildered as you did when you got a new PC.
Though you have a marvelous tool available, it takes
some practice and familiarity to operate effectively in
your life. Fortunately, a little knowledge can get you up
and running quickly. We give you basic information to
help you understand the scope of astrology. We tell you
what you need to know about your sun sign. Then you
can look up other planets in your horoscope, to find out
how each contributes to your total personality.

Many readers are fascinated by astrology's insights
into relationships. This year, we give you ways to rate
your relationship, to find out who you're most likely to

get along with and why. You'll learn the upsides and downsides of possible partners, and how to handle each sign.

For those who are connected to the Internet, we've added a special chapter this year, so you can surf the many astrology sites to download programs, connect with other astrology fans, even find someone who is born on your birthday—your astro-twin.

It's fitting that Jupiter, the planet of expansion, will be moving into the astrology-friendly sign of Pisces this year. What better portent for using this ancient art every day. Let our daily forecasts guide you to having the happiest, most successful year ever!

CHAPTER 1

What's Hot for '98!

This year's picks and predictions—
the worldwide trends that
can influence your life.

The Year of Interactivity

Welcome to the world of cyberspace, where you can reinvent yourself. Who's to know if you have the dazzling form of Cindy Crawford or you're fifty pounds overweight? It makes no difference if you're a beauty or a beast, a grandma or a teenager. In the electronic world of Neptune and Uranus in 1998, you can be who you want to be with no one the wiser! Expect this year's high-tech innovations to play a new theme that could send you dashing through cyberspace as wild, wonderful, or wacky as you want to be. You create your own character, then interact with others in whatever way you choose. It's all in the mind, aided and abetted by the imagination.

The action starts in late February, when Neptune makes its big move into Aquarius. Get ready for a new kind of fun and games. You'll have your choice between watching TV or "doing" TV, actively participating in shows by offering your instant opinion via the phone or a special gadget connected to your TV. Or you'll interact through a tiny screen popping up on your computer. If you've been a couch potato, you'll now be jockeying new kinds of remote controls that can propel you right into the action.

Neptune, the planet of illusion, dissolves boundaries

between reality and fantasy. Uranus, the planet of high tech, has already been setting the stage in Aquarius, its natural home space. So when these two planets get together again in the same sign, watch out!

Spiritual Revival

The slow-moving planet Pluto is our guide to the hottest trends. Pluto is the planet of transformation, and while traveling through a sign, it brings about a heightened consciousness and the transformation of matters related to that sign. While traveling through Scorpio in the Eighties, we saw Scorpio-type "hotness" everywhere—black clothing, radical kinds of sexual issues, tattoos, transvestites, police dramas. Now traveling through Sagittarius, Pluto's task is to eliminate outworn belief systems to prepare us philosophically for the future. All that is ruled by Sagittarius is sure to be emphasized and transformed—religion, advertising, banking, higher education, the travel industry, the legal professions, publishing, gambling, outdoor sports, pets. At this writing, we've become a pet-happy nation, with pigs, Dalmatians, and St. Bernards playing leading roles in hit films. Color has come back into fashion, pushing black to the sidelines. Rugged, sporty four-wheel drive vehicles are in, as are pick-up trucks. Legs (Sagittarius-ruled) are exposed in fashion, emphasized by eye-catching hosiery.

The old, intrusive commercials and print ads are being replaced by a more subtle, well-disguised motivational message. Books, magazines, and newspapers are experimenting with new electronic publishing methods.

Along with an emphasis on spirituality, look for new insights and interpretations of ancient manuscripts, such as the Dead Sea Scrolls. We astrologers are reclaiming our own roots, by retranslating ancient manuscripts in a more astrology-friendly way. These writings are now published and circulating in professional astrology circles and they're eye-openers.

The Sagittarius bow and arrow now greets visitors to one of the gambling casinos on Native American reservations. Because Sagittarius rules gambling and sporting events, expect these to translate into the electronic Aquarian world. By the time this is published, gambling via your PC may be a reality.

Pisces Is Lucky

Good fortune and big money are always associated with Jupiter, the planet that embodies the principle of expansion. Jupiter has a 12-year cycle, staying in each sign for approximately one year. When Jupiter enters a sign, the fields governed by that sign usually provide excellent investment opportunities. Areas of speculation governed by the sign Jupiter is passing through will have the hottest market potential—they're the ones that currently arouse excitement and enthusiasm.

This year, Jupiter is traveling through Pisces, so sun-sign Pisceans, or those with strong Pisces influence in their horoscopes, will have abundant growth opportunities. On the other hand, those born under Virgo, the sign opposite Pisces, will need to make adjustments because this particular Pisces expansive atmosphere is opposed to their natural tendencies. For example, Virgo prospers in an atmosphere of order, efficiency, and precision, where skills and techniques are emphasized. While Jupiter is in Pisces, the expansive emphasis is ongoing with the flow, breaking rules and boundaries, appreciating chaos, imagination, escape. Though these qualities promote creativity and are excellent for artistic expansion, those who prefer a regimented atmosphere might feel uncomfortable and out of sync.

Some of the Pisces-blessed areas that should prosper this year are the oil industry, fishing and ocean-related industries, shipping, perfume, cosmetics, theater, poetry, dance, pharmaceuticals, alcohol, hospitals, prisons, monastic life (wherever we escape the world), footwear, and spiritual counseling. It's a great year for dancers and those involved with theatrical arts and filmmaking of all kinds. Expect a revival of all kinds of issues related to the petroleum industry.

If you're planning a vacation, consider a Pisces place: Portugal, Scandinavia, Vermont, north Africa, southern Asia, Normandy, Polynesia, Florida, or Chicago.

Pisceans are especially lucky this year. However, the principle of expansion also applies to your waistline. This is one of your most difficult times to diet! So focus on providing yourself with an abundance of fruits and vegetables and avoid fats and sugar.

Tests for Taurus, Unfinished Business for Aries

The emphasis so far has been on the idealistic, spiritual, philosophical areas governed by Aquarius, Sagittarius, and Pisces. It is interesting that, when there is so much emphasis on the idealistic, there is always some force in astrology that brings us back to earth and makes us face reality. This year, and for the next two years, it will be Saturn passing through the earth sign of Taurus.

Saturn keywords are focus, time, commitment, accomplishment, discipline, restriction. If Jupiter steps on the gas, Saturn applies the brakes. It's always a good idea to find the houses of your horoscope where Saturn and Jupiter are passing at any given time. It should help you to focus your time and energy on what is of value. But in Saturn areas, be sure to finish what you start. Saturn rewards responsible actions, hard work, and persistence.

Talk to an Aries and chances are, you'll be hearing about the trials and tribulations of the past two years, when Saturn was transiting this sign. Aries is a sign that facilitates fast action, rather than the slow, methodical, thorough approach, which Saturn demands. Most Aries will be heaving a sigh of relief when Saturn leaves their sign in June. However, "it's not over 'til it's over." Saturn retrogrades back to Aries to clear up unfinished business until March 1999, so Aries, as well as the other cardinal signs (Cancer, Libra, Capricorn) will still be feeling the restrictive, disciplinary influence of Saturn.

The brief stay of Saturn in Taurus from June to October should give the fixed signs (Taurus, Leo, Scorpio, Aquarius) a preview of challenges ahead. Saturn is quite powerful in the fixed signs, which are more focused and methodical by nature. It will facilitate the more stubborn, tyrannical forces over the next two years, building up to a meeting of Saturn and Jupiter in Taurus in the year 2000. The last time this conjunction happened in Taurus was in 1941, with ominous results. We can only hope that the wisdom and maturity of Saturn will be manifested this time around.

Taurus rules financial matters, the earning and spending of money, possessions of all kinds, and our attitude toward them. Retailing, land development, the territorial attitudes of nations, and wealth and poverty issues are areas to watch for Saturn's restrictive influence.

CHAPTER 2

Your Astro-Agenda
Plan Ahead for Perfect Timing

From the stacks of best-selling books on how to become more effective, gain control of our time, and set goals and priorities, we could say that the Nineties have become the Decade of the Agenda. Whether you use a computer program to schedule your activities or simply pencil activities in your calendar, chances are, you're more conscious of how you spend your time than ever before. Astrology has a different perspective on time management, as you become more sensitive to the cycles of the moon and planets and relate these celestial movements to your own life. If you become attuned to the natural rhythms of these cycles, you may find that certain activities go more smoothly if done at the most advantageous time.

The next step is to harmonize your schedule with the astrological cycles. If you know that three times a year, the tricky planet Mercury will be creating havoc with communications, you'll back up that vital fax with a duplicate by Express Mail; you'll read between the lines of contracts and put off closing that deal until Mercury is in a better mood.

Why not find out for yourself if there's truth to the saying "timing is everything," by marking your own calendar for love, career moves, vacations, and important events, using the following information and lists in this chapter and the one titled "Look Up Your Planets," as well as the moon sign listings under your daily forecast.

Here are some special times to note on your calendar:
• Dates of your sun sign (high-energy period)

- The month previous to your sun sign (low-energy period)
- Dates of planets in your sign this year
- Full and new moons (pay special attention when these fall in your sun sign)
- Eclipses
- Moon in your sun sign every month, as well as moon in the opposite sign (listed in your daily forecast)
- Mercury retrogrades

Check Your Vital Sign

Each birthdate recharges your energy with a powerful surge of vitality as the sun enters your sign. Take advantage of this time, when the predominant energies are most favorable to you to start new projects and make your big moves. You're more likely to get support and recognition now, when everyone is naturally attuned to your sun sign. Look in the tables in this book to see if other planets will also be passing through your sun sign at this time. Venus will activate your social and love life, making you the flavor of the month. Mars fuels your energy and drive, while Mercury turns on your brain power and helps you communicate, and Jupiter signals an especially lucky period of expansion.

There are two "down" times related to the sun. During the month before your birthday period, when you are completing your annual cycle, you could be feeling more vulnerable and depleted. It's a time when you may need extra rest and an especially nutritious diet. Cut back on stressful activities while you prepare for a big push when the sun enters your sign.

Another "down" time is when the sun is passing through the opposite sign (six months from your birthday) and the prevailing energies are very different from yours. You may feel at odds with the world, and things might not come easily. You'll have to work harder for recognition, because people are not on your wavelength. However, this could be a good time to work on a team, in cooperation with others or behind the scenes.

Phasing In and Out
With the Moon

Working with the phases of the moon is as easy as looking up at the night sky. At the new moon, when both sun and moon are in the same sign, it's the best time to begin new ventures, especially the activities that are favored by that sign. You'll have powerful energies pulling you in the same direction. You'll be focused outward, toward action. Postpone breaking off, terminating, deliberating, or reflecting activities that require introspection and passive work.

Get your project under way during the first quarter, then go public at the full moon, a time of high intensity, when feelings come out into the open. This is your time to shine, so express yourself. Be aware, however, that because pressures are being released, other people are also letting off steam and confrontations are possible. So try to avoid arguments. Traditionally, astrologers often advise against surgery at this time, which could produce heavier bleeding.

During the last quarter until the next new moon, you'll be most controlled. This is a winding-down phase, a time to cut off unproductive relationships and to do serious thinking and inward-directed activities.

You'll feel some new and full moons more strongly than others, especially those new moons that fall in your sun sign and full moons in your opposite sign. Because that full moon happens at your low-energy time of year, it is likely to be an especially stressful time in a relationship, when any hidden problems or unexpressed emotions could surface.

1998 Full and New Moons

January 12	Full Moon in Cancer
January 28	New Moon in Aquarius
February 11	Full Moon in Leo
February 26	New Moon/Solar Eclipse in Pisces

March 12	Lunar Eclipse/Full Moon in Virgo
March 27	New Moon in Aries
April 11	Full Moon in Libra
April 26	New Moon in Taurus
May 11	Full Moon in Scorpio
May 25	New Moon in Gemini
June 10	Full Moon in Sagittarius
June 23	New Moon in Cancer
July 9	Full Moon in Capricorn
July 23	New Moon in Leo
August 7	Full Moon/Lunar Eclipse in Aquarius
August 21	New Moon/Solar Eclipse in Leo
September 6	Full Moon/Lunar Eclipse in Pisces
September 20	New Moon in Virgo
October 5	Full Moon in Aries
October 20	New Moon in Libra
November 4	Full Moon in Taurus
November 19	Full Moon in Scorpio
December 3	Full Moon in Gemini
December 18	New Moon in Sagittarius

Forecasting With the Daily Moon Sign

The daily moon sign listed under your forecast in this book can be a powerful tool when scheduling your activities. To forecast the daily emotional weather, to determine your monthly high and low days, or to prioritize your time, note the activities favored and the moods you are likely to encounter as the moon passes through each sign.

Moon in Aries

Get moving! The new moon in Aries is an ideal time to start new projects. Everyone is pushy, raring to go, impatient, and short tempered. Leave the details and the follow-up for later. Competitive sports or martial arts are great ways to let off steam. Quiet types could use some assertiveness, but it's a great day for dynamos. Be careful not to step on too many toes.

Moon in Taurus

Stick to solid, methodical tasks, and tackle follow-through or backup work, laying the foundations for later success. Make investments, buy real estate, do appraisals, bargain hard. Attend to your property or get out in the country and spend some time in your garden. Enjoy creature comforts—your favorite music, a delicious dinner, sensual lovemaking. Forget about starting a diet at this time.

Moon in Gemini

Talk means action today, so telephone, write letters, fax! Make new contacts, and stay in touch with steady customers. you can handle lots of tasks at once. It's a great day for mental activity of any kind. Don't try to pin people down, for they too are feeling restless, so it helps to keep it light. Flirtations and socializing are good, but watch the gossip—and don't give away secrets.

Moon in Cancer

This is a moody, sensitive, emotional time. People respond to personal attention and mothering, and some may feel insecure and in need of extra TLC. Stay at home, have a family dinner, call your mother at a time when nostalgia, memories, and psychic powers are heightened. You'll want to hang on to people and things (don't clean out your closets now). You could have some insights into what others really need and want, so pay attention to dreams, intuition, and your own gut reactions.

Moon in Leo

Everybody is in a much more confident, warm, generous mood. It's a good day to ask for a raise, show what you can do, and dress up for your audience. People will respond to flattery and even enjoy a bit of drama. You may be more extravagant, so treat yourself royally and show off a bit—but don't break the bank! Be careful not to promise more than you can deliver!

Moon in Virgo

Do practical, down-to-earth chores—review your budget, make repairs, be an efficiency expert. This is not a day to ask for a raise. Have a health checkup, revamp your diet, or buy vitamins or health food. Be a demon house cleaner, taking care of details and piled-up chores. Reorganize your work and life so they run more smoothly and efficiently and save money too. Be prepared for others to be in a critical, fault-finding mood.

Moon in Libra

Attend to legal matters, negotiating contracts and arbitrating disputes. Do things with your favorite partner, socializing and being very romantic. Buy a special gift or a beautiful object and decorate yourself or your surroundings. Buy new clothes and then throw a party— make it an elegant, romantic evening. Smooth over any ruffled feathers. Avoid confrontations by sticking to civilized discussions.

Moon in Scorpio

This is a day to do things with passion, for you'll have excellent concentration and focus. Try not to get too intense emotionally, however, and avoid sharp exchanges with your loved ones. Others may tend to go to extremes, getting jealous and overreacting. Today is great for troubleshooting, problem-solving, research, scientific work—and making love. Pay attention to psychic vibes.

Moon in Sagittarius

It's a great time for travel and philosophical discussions. Set long-range career goals. Work out, do sports, or buy athletic equipment. Others will be feeling upbeat, exuberant, and adventurous. Risk taking is favored—you may feel like taking a gamble, betting on the horses, visiting a local casino, or just buying a lottery ticket. Teaching, writing, and spiritual activities also get the green light. Relax outdoors, taking care of animals.

Moon in Capricorn

You can accomplish a lot today, so get on the ball! Issues concerning your basic responsibilities and duties, and those involving your family and parents could crop up. You'll be expected to deliver on promises now. Weed out the dead wood from your life. Get a dental checkup.

Moon in Aquarius

It's a great day for doing thing with groups—clubs, meetings, outings, politics, parties. Campaign for your candidate or work for a worthy cause, dealing with larger issues that affect humanity, such as the environment or metaphysical questions. Buy a computer or electronic gadget. Watch TV. Wear something outrageous. Try something you've never done before—present an original idea and refuse to stick to a rigid schedule. Go with the flow. Take a class in meditation, mind control, or yoga.

Moon in Pisces

This can be a very creative day, so let your imagination work overtime. Film, theater, music, or ballet could inspire you. Spend some time alone, resting and reflecting, reading or writing poetry. Daydreams can also be profitable. Help those less fortunate or lend a listening ear to someone who may be feeling blue. Don't overindulge in self-pity or escapism, however. People are especially vulnerable to substance abuse now. Turn your thoughts to romance and someone special.

How to Handle Eclipses

One of the most amazing phenomena in the cosmos, which many of us take for granted, is the spatial relationship between the sun and the moon. How many of us have ever noticed or marveled that, relative to our viewpoint here on earth, both the largest source of energy (the sun) and the smallest (the moon) appear to be almost exactly the same size. This is most evident to us at the time of the solar eclipse, when the moon is directly aligned with the sun and so nearly covers it that scientists use the moment of eclipse to study solar flares.

When the two most powerful forces in astrology—the sun and the moon—are lined up, we're sure to feel the effects, both in world events and in our personal lives. It might help us to learn how best to cope with the periods around eclipses. Both solar and lunar eclipses are times when our natural rhythms are changed, depending on where the eclipse falls in your horoscope. If it falls on or close to your birthday, you're going to have important changes in your life, and perhaps even come to a turning point.

Lunar eclipses happen when the earth is on a level plane with the sun and moon and lines up exactly between them during the time of the full moon, breaking

21

the opposition of these two forces. We might say the earth short-circuits the connection between them. The effect can be either confusion or clarity, as our subconscious energies, which normally react to the pull of opposing sun and moon, are turned off. As we are temporarily freed from the subconscious attachments, we might have objective insights that could help us change any destructive emotional patterns, such as addictions, which normally occur at this time. This momentary turnoff could help us turn our lives around. On the other hand, this break in the normal cycle could cause a bewildering disorientation that intensifies our insecurities.

The solar eclipse occurs during the new moon, when the moon blocks the sun's energies as it passes exactly between the sun and the earth. Symbolically, this means the objective, conscious force, represented by the sun, will be temporarily darkened and subconscious lunar forces, activating our deepest emotions, will now dominate, putting us in a highly subjective state. Emotional truths can be revealed or emotions can run wild, as our objectivity is cut off and hidden patterns surface. If your sign is affected, you may find yourself beginning a period of work on a deep inner level; you may have psychic experiences or a surfacing of deep feelings.

You'll start feeling the energies of an upcoming eclipse a few days after the previous new or full moon. The energy continues to intensify until the actual eclipse, then disperses for three or four days. So plan ahead at least a week or more before an eclipse, and allow several days afterward for the natural rhythms to return. Try not to make major moves during this period—it's not a great time to get married, change jobs, or buy a home.

Eclipses in 1998:

February 26	Solar Eclipse in Pisces
March 12	Lunar Eclipse in Virgo
August 7	Lunar Eclipse in Aquarius
August 21	Solar Eclipse in Leo
September 6	Lunar Eclipse in Pisces

When the Planets Go Backward

All the planets, except for the sun and moon, have times when they appear to move backward—or retrograde—in the sky, or so it seems from our point of view on earth. At these times, planets do not work as they usually do, so it's best to take a break from that planet's energies in our life and do some work on an inner level.

Mercury Retrograde

Mercury goes retrograde most often, and its effects can be especially irritating. When it reaches a short distance ahead of the sun three times a year, it seems to move backward from our point of view. Astrologers often compare retrograde motion to the optical illusion that occurs when we ride on a train that passes another train traveling at a different speed—the second train appears to be moving in reverse.

What this means to you is that the Mercury-ruled areas of your life—analytical thought processes, communications, scheduling, and such—are subject to all kinds of confusion. So be prepared for people to change their minds and renege on commitments. Communications equipment can break down; schedules must be changed on short notice; people are late for appointments or don't show up at all. Traffic is terrible. Major purchases malfunction or don't work out in some way, or they get delivered in the wrong color. Letters don't arrive or might be delivered to the wrong address. Employees tend to make errors that have to be corrected later, and contracts might not work out or must be renegotiated.

Since most of us can't put our lives on hold for nine weeks every year (three Mercury retrograde periods), we should learn to tame the trickster and make it work for us. The key is in the prefix "re." This is the time to go back over things in your life, reflecting on what you've done during the previous months and looking for deeper insights. Try to spot errors you may have missed and then take time to review and reevaluate what has happened. This time is very good for inner spiritual work and meditations. REst and REward yourself—it's a good time to take a vacation, especially if you revisit a favorite place. REorganize your work and finish up projects that are backed up. Clean out your desk and closets. Throw away what you can't REcycle. If you must sign contracts or agreements, do so with a contingency clause that lets you reevaluate the terms later.

Postpone major purchases or commitments. Don't get married—unless you're re-marrying the same person. Try not to rely on other people keeping appointments, contracts, or agreements to the letter—have several alternatives. Double-check and read between the lines, and don't buy anything connected with communications or transportation (if you must, be sure to cover yourself). Mercury retrograding through your sun sign will intensify its effect on your life.

If Mercury was retrograde when you were born, you may be one of the lucky people who don't suffer the frustrations of this period. If so, your mind probably works in a very intuitive, insightful way.

The sign that Mercury is retrograding through can give you an idea of what's in store—as well as the sun signs that will be especially challenged.

Mercury Retrograde Periods in 1998

Mercury Retrograde in Aries	March 27–April 20
Mercury Retrograde in Leo	July 30th–August 23
Mercury Retrograde in Sagittarius	November 21–December 11

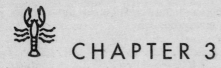

CHAPTER 3

Have Mouse . . . Will Travel!
An Astrologer's Guide to Surfing the Internet

If you have a personal computer and access to the Internet, you're connected to a global community of astrologers. This brings you instant access to atlases, programs, charts, databases, and personal contacts that could only be dreamed about just a few years ago. Since the Internet is buzzing with new astrology sites, its astrology resources will probably be much more extensive when this guide is published.

Here are some of the things you can do on the Internet: Find a pen pal who's interested in astrology at your level; get a hard-to-find book on any aspect of astrology; get information on your moon sign or the exact location and time zone of your birthplace from an online atlas; find your astro-twin, someone who shares your birthday; look for the perfectly compatible romantic partner in an astro-dating area. So click your mouse and travel the worldwide astrology community. Here are our picks from the hundreds of sites now open to "surfers."

Newsgroups:

Of the many newsgroups, there are several devoted to astrology. The most popular is "alt.astrology." Here's your chance to connect with astrologers worldwide, exchange information, and answer some of the skeptics who frequent this newsgroup.

Mailing Lists

Want to fill your e-mail box with astrology-related notes? Subscribe to a list and get e-mail sent directly to your address. The following lists are especially for astrology fans.

Festival

To subscribe, send e-mail to: srozhon@cybergate.net with the message: "Subscribe festival," plus your e-mail address, and you will receive further instructions.

Oracle-a

To subscribe, send e-mail to: oracle-a-request@idirect.com, with the message: "subscribe," and you will receive all details.

AAmail

This is the mailing list of the Astrological Association of Great Britain. To subscribe, send e-mail to: listserver @astrologer.com with the message: "subscribe AAmail end."

Online Services

The top online services offer areas devoted to astrology that include chat rooms, daily forecasts, special interest groups, articles, lectures, and links to other interesting astrology sites. They're an easy place to begin surfing.

America Online

This huge service offers ASTRONET, with an Astrology Newsstand, software reviews, horoscopes, featured guests, and a shopping area for books, reports, and software. A popular feature is "Astromates," where you can browse profiles of prospective partners under their zodiac sign. There are lots of links to other sites.

An Astrological Calendar

Download a calendar for each month, with Moon sign changes and important aspects.
  Address: http://users.aol.com/zodiactime

Dates of Important Events

Find out what important events happened on any date in history.
  Address: http://www.scopsys.com/today

Great Places to Visit

Metalog Yellow Pages

This offers an extensive list of international sites, as well as an agenda of astrology conferences and seminars all over the world. If you'll be traveling and you'd like to take in an astrology conference in, say, England or New Zealand, check out this site.
  Address: http://www.astrologer.com/

The Urania Trust Guide

Here's another great list of astrologers, from Kansas to Kazakstan.
  Address: http://www.astrologer.com/utguide/index

Internet Atlas

Get the geographic longitude and latitude and the correct time zone for cities worldwide.
   Address: http://www.astro.ch/atlas/

The Zodiacal Zephyr

This is a great place to start out. It has a U.S. and World Atlas, Celebrity Birthdata, an Ephemeris, and information on conferences, software, and tapes. There is also a link to an Astrology Compatibility Service, where you can meet potential soulmates from around the world.
   Address: http://metro.turnpike.net/S/SRozhon/index.html

TMA Communications

Here you'll find articles and astroweather.
   Address: http://www.lightworks.com

Astrology Alive

This site features Barbara Schermer's creative approach to astrology, along with a great list of links.
   Address: http://www.lightworks.com/Astrology/Alive/

National Council for Geocosmic Research (NCGR)

This site contains information on membership and testing programs, and updates on conferences. Order conference tapes and get complete lists of conference topics. There's also a list of astrology Websites to visit and links to resources. This is an easy place to find chapters and conferences near you.
   Address: http://www.geocosmic.org/

Astrology Software: Freeware and Shareware

Magitech

Download *Astrolog,* a terrific astrology program, here.
   Address: http://www.magitech.com/pub/astrology/software/pc

The Widening Gyre

This is a good source for software.
   Address: http://www.prairienet.org/rec/gyre/widegyre.html

Software Search Engine: Shareware.Com

Select DOS or Windows and type "astrol" in the search input.
   Address: http://www.shareware.com

Best General Search Engine: Yahoo!

This is an excellent search engine that enters your input into other popular search engines.
   Address: http://www.yahoo.com

Astrolabe

Preview some of Astrolabe's terrific astrology programs. You can download a demo version of their top-rated Solar Fire III at this site.
   Address: http://www.alabe.com

Astrolog

Walter Pullen's freeware program has fascinating graphics and lots of features used by professional astrologers. An excellent program for serious students. You'll enjoy it most if you have a basic knowledge of astrology and can read astrology symbols. Get a preview before you download.

Address: http://www.speakeasy.org/~cruiser1/astrolog.htm

Matrix Software

Connect here to Matrix Software's innovative programs. Check out the easy-to-learn Winstar and the colorful fun-to-use Kaleidoscope.

Address: http://www.theNewAge.com

ACS Software and Services

Here is the online headquarters of Astro Computing Services, with a bookstore, software demos, chart services, and lots of features.

Address: http://www/astrocom.com

Astrology Books

National Clearinghouse for Astrology Books

Here is a wide selection of books on all aspects of astrology, from basics to advanced, and including many hard-to-find books.

Address: http://www.astroamerica.com

Your Astrology Questions Answered

ASTROLOGY FAQ (Frequently Asked Questions)
    Address: http://magitech.com/pub/astrology/info/faq.txt

Who was born on your Birthday?

Find out who was born on any day you specify. You can also get biographies of your choice at this site.
   Address: http://www.eb.som/bio.html

Online Astrology Magazines:

Welcome to Planet Earth

Get the astrology slant on fast-breaking news and the latest trends. A great site for links, articles, celebrity profiles.
   Address: http://alive.mcn.org/greatbear/tofc.html

The Mountain Astrologer

Read articles by top astrologers. Good material for beginning students.
   Address: http://www.jadesun.com/tma

A Terrific Link to the Astrology Community:

Web First

A comprehensive astrology site well worth a visit. Features a list of teachers, a link to homepages of professional astrologers on the "Festival" mailing list, plus lots of interesting links.
   Address: http://hudson.idt.net/~motive/

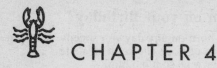

CHAPTER 4

Sydney Omarr's Yellow Pages
The Top Astrological Clubs, Conferences, Organizations, and More

Ever wondered where the astrologers are in your area, where you can get a basic astrology program for your new computer, or where to take a class with a professional astrologer? Look no further. In this chapter we'll give you the information you need to locate the latest products and services available.

There are very well-organized groups of astrologers all over the country who are dedicated to promoting the image of astrology in the most positive way. The National Council for Geocosmic Research (NCGR) is one nationwide group that is dedicated to bringing astrologers together, promoting fellowship and high-quality education. They have an accredited course system, with a systematized study of all the facets of astrology. Whether you'd like to know more about such specialties as financial astrology or techniques for timing events, or if you'd prefer a psychological or mythological approach, you'll find the leading experts at NCGR conferences.

Your computer can be a terrific tool for connecting with other astrology fans at all levels of expertise. If you do not yet own a computer and are thinking about buying a new or used one, have no fear. In spite of the breakneck pace of technology, there will still be plenty of software available for your computer. Even if you are using a "dinosaur" from the early Eighties, there are still calculation and interpretation programs available. They may not have all the bells and whistles or exciting graphics, but they'll still get the job done!

If you are a newcomer to astrology, it is a good idea to learn the glyphs (astrology's special shorthand language) before you purchase a computer program. Use Chapter 7 to help you learn the symbols easily. That way, you'll be able to read the charts without consulting a book. One program, however, Astrolabe's Solar Fire for Windows, has pop-up definitions—just click your mouse on the glyph and a definition appears.

Astrology programs are available at all price levels, from under $20 CD's in your local software chain, to more sophisticated and expensive astrology programs from specialized dealers (approximately $200–250 at this writing). But before you make a serious investment, download or order some demo disks from the company. If you just want to have fun, investigate some of the lower-priced programs—there are many available for under $100. Most of the companies on our list will be happy to help you find the right program for your needs.

If you live in an out-of-the-way place or are unable to fit classes into your schedule, study-by-mail courses are available from several astrological computing services. Some courses will send you a series of tapes; others use workbooks or computer printouts.

Nationwide Astrology Organizations and Conferences

The astrology world has been buzzing this year in preparation for one of its most exciting events, the United Astrology Conference, to take place May 21–26, 1998 at the Hyatt Regency Hotel in Atlanta, GA. Get updated on the latest conference news via the NCGR Website listed below. If you are visiting the Atlanta area, plan to attend and meet astrologers from around the world. The trade show is sure to be a treasure trove of all the latest astrological tools. If you can't attend the conference, you can purchase tapes of the lectures from Bulldog Audio, P.O. Box 127, Coeur D'Alene, Idaho 83814; (208)664–9885. They also have tapes available from previous UAC conferences.

Contact these organizations for information on conferences, workshops, local meetings, conference tapes, referrals:

National Council for Geocosmic Research
Educational workshops, tapes, and conferences; a directory of professional astrologers is available. For questions about NCGR membership, contact:
Pamela Huang
102 Deborah Dr.
Lynchburg, VA 24501–5112
(804)239–8643
http://www.geocosmic.org

American Federation of Astrologers (A.F.A.)
One of the oldest astrological organizations in the U.S., the A.F.A. was established 1938, and it offers conferences and conventions. The federation will refer you to an accredited astrologer.
P.O. Box 22040
Tempe, AZ 85382
(602)838–1751
Fax (602)838–8293

Association for Astrological Networking (A.F.A.N.)
They offer networking and legal issues. Did you know that astrologers are still being arrested for practicing in some states? AFAN provides support and legal information, and works toward improving the public image of astrology.
8306 Wilshire Blvd
Berkeley Hills, CA 90211

ARC Directory
This provides a listing of astrologers worldwide.
2920 E. Monte Vista
Tucson, AZ 85716
(602)321-1114

Conference and Lecture Tapes

National Council for Geocosmic Research
Class, lecture, and conference tapes are available.
Margie Herskovitz
5826 Greenspring Ave.
Baltimore, MD 20754-9998
(410)257-2824

Pegasus Tapes
Lectures and conference tapes are available.
P.O. Box 419
Santa Ysabel, CA 92070

International Society for Astrological Research
Lectures, workshops, and seminars are provided.
P.O. Box 38613
Los Angeles, CA 90038

ISIS Institute
P.O. Box 21222
El Sobrante, CA 94820-1222

Astrol-Analytics Productions
P.O. Box 16927
Encino, CA 91411-6927

Computer Programs

Astrolabe
Check out their powerful Solar Fire Windows software—
it's a breeze to use. This company also markets a variety

of programs for all levels of expertise, as well as a wide selection of computer astrology readings and MAC programs. It's also a good resource for innovative software and programs for older computers.
P.O. Box 1750–R
Brewster, MA 02631
(800)843–6682

Matrix Software
Find a wide variety of software in all price ranges and demo disks at student and advanced level, with lots of interesting readings.
315 Marion Ave.
Big Rapids, MI 49307
(800)PLANETS

Astro Communications Services
They offer books, software for MAC and IBM compatibles, individual charts, and telephone readings. It's a good resource for those who do not have computers, as they will calculate charts for you.
Dept. AF693, P.O. Box 34487
San Diego, CA 92163–4487
(800)888–9983

Air Software
115 Caya Avenue
West Hartford, CT 06110
(800)659–1247
http://www.alphee.com
A free program is available to download at Website.

Time Cycles Research
Beautiful graphic IO Series programs are available for the MAC.
375 Willets Avenue
Waterford, CT 06385
Fax (869)442–0625
astrology@timecycles.com
http://www.timecycles.com

Astro-Cartography
Charts for location changes are available.
Astro-Numeric Service Box 336-B
Ashland, OR 97520
(800)MAPPING

Microcycles
The "world's largest astrological software dealer," they
offer catalogs, demo diskettes, and professional help in
choosing software.
P.O. Box 2175
Culver City, CA 90231
(800)829–2537

Astrology Magazines

Most have listings of conferences, events, and local happenings.

American Astrology
475 Park Avenue South
New York, NY 10016

Dell Horoscope
P.O. Box 53352
Boulder, CO 89321–3342

Planet Earth
The Great Bear
P.O. Box 5164
Eugene, OR 97405

Mountain Astrologer
P.O. Box 11292
Berkeley, CA 94701

Aspects
Aquarius Workshops
P.O. Box 260556
Encino, CA 91426

CHAPTER 5

Clueless About Astrology?
Here's the Least You
Need to Know

Want to know how astrology really works, but you're clueless when it comes to knowing the difference between a sign and a constellation or deciphering those strange looking symbols all over the horoscope? Not to mention sorting out zodiacs, planets, houses, and aspects.

You've come to the right place. Here's a user-friendly guide to help you find your way around the fascinating world of astrology.

The Basics—Signs, Houses, Charts

Where the Signs Are

First, let's get our sign language straight, because for most readers, that's the starting point of astrology.

Signs are located on the *zodiac*, an imaginary 360-degree belt circling Earth. This belt is divided into 12 equal 30-degree portions, which define the boundaries of the *signs*. There's a lot of confusion about the difference between the signs and the *constellations* of the zodiac, patterns of stars that originally marked the twelve divisions, like signposts. Though a sign is named after the constellation that once marked the same area, the constellations are no longer in the same place relative to the Earth that they were centuries ago. Over hundreds of years, Earth's orbit has shifted, so that from our point of view here on Earth, the constellations moved, but the signs remain in place. (Most Western astrologers use the 12-equal-part division of the zodiac; however, there are some methods of astrology that still do use the constellations instead of the signs.)

Most people think of themselves in terms of their sun sign. A *sun sign* refers to the sign the sun is orbiting through at a given moment, from our point of view here on Earth. For instance, "I'm an Aries" means that the sun was passing through Aries when that person was born. However, there are nine other planets (plus asteroids, fixed stars, and sensitive points) that also form our total astrological personality, and some or many of these will be located in other signs. No one is completely "Aries," with all their astrological components in one sign! (Please note that, in astrology, the sun and moon are usually referred to as "planets," though of course they're not.)

What Makes a Sign Special?

What makes Aries the sign of go-getters and Taureans savvy with money? And Geminis talk a blue streak and Sagittarians footloose? Definitions of the signs are not accidental; they are derived from different combinations of four concepts—a sign's element, quality, polarity, and place on the zodiac.

Take the element of *fire:* It's hot, passionate. Then add the active cardinal mode. Give it a jolt of positive energy and place it first in line. And doesn't that sound like the active, me-first, driving, hot-headed, energetic Aries?

Then take the element of *earth,* practical and sensual. Add the fixed, stable mode. Give it energy that reacts to its surroundings and settles in. Put it after Aries. Now you've got a good idea of how sensual, earthy Taurus operates.

Another way to grasp the idea is to pretend you're doing a magical puzzle based on the numbers that can divide into twelve (the number of signs)—4, 3, and 2.

There are four building blocks or *elements*, three ways a sign operates *(qualities)*, and two *polarities*. These alternate in turn around the zodiac, with a different combination coming up for each sign.

The four elements. Here's how they add up. The *four elements* describe the physical concept of the sign. Is it fiery (dynamic), earthy (practical), airy (mental), watery (emotional)? There are three zodiac signs of each of the four elements: fire (Aries, Leo, Sagittarius), earth (Taurus, Virgo, Capricorn), air (Gemini, Libra, Aquarius), water (Cancer, Scorpio, Pisces). These are the same elements that make up our planet: earth, air, fire, and water. But astrology uses the elements as *symbols* that link our body and psyche to the rhythms of the planets. Fire signs spread warmth and enthusiasm. They are able to fire up or motivate others, and they have hot tempers. These are the people who make ideas catch fire and spring into existence. Earth signs are the builders of the zodiac, who follow through after the initiative of fire signs to make things happen. These people are solid, practical realists who enjoy material things and sensual pleasures. They are interested in ideas that can be used to achieve concrete results. Air signs are mental people, great communicators. Following the consolidating earth signs, they'll reach out to inspire others through the use of words, social contacts, discussion, and debate. Water signs complete each four-sign series, adding the ingredients of emotion, compassion, and imagination. Water-sign people are nonverbal communicators who attune themselves to their surroundings and react through the medium of feelings.

Quality. The second consideration when defining a sign is how it will operate. Will it take the initiative, or move slowly and deliberately? Will it adapt easily? Its *quality* (or modality) will tell. There are three qualities and four signs of each quality: cardinal, fixed, and mutable.

Cardinal signs are the start-up signs that begin each season (Aries, Cancer, Libra, Capricorn). These people love to be active and involved in projects. They are usually on the fast track to success, impatient to get things under way. *Fixed signs* (Taurus, Leo, Scorpio, Aquarius) move steadily, always in control. They happen in the middle of a season, after the initial character of the season is established. Fixed signs are naturally more centered, tending to move more deliberately and do things more slowly but more thoroughly. They govern parts of your horoscope where you take root and integrate your experiences. *Mutable signs* (Gemini, Virgo, Sagittarius, Pisces) embody the principle of distribution. These are the signs that break up the cycle, preparing the way for a change by distributing the energy to the next group. Mutables are flexible, adaptable, and communicative. They can move in many directions easily, darting around obstacles.

Polarity. In addition to an element and a quality, each sign has a polarity, either a positive or a negative electrical charge that generates energy around the zodiac, like a giant battery. Polarity refers to opposites, which you could also define as masculine/feminine, yin/yang, or active/reactive. Alternating around the zodiac, the six fire and air signs are positive, active, masculine, and yang in polarity. These signs are open, expanding outward. The six earth and water signs are reactive, negative and yin— they are nurturing and receptive in polarity, which allows the energy to develop and take shape. All positive energy would be like a car without brakes. All negative energy would be like a stalled vehicle, going nowhere. Both polarities are needed in balanced proportion.

Order. Finally we must consider the order of the signs. This is vital to the balance of the zodiac and the transmission of energy throughout the zodiac. Each sign is quite different from its neighbors on either side. Yet each seems to grow out of its predecessor like links in a chain, transmitting a synthesis of energy gathered along the chain to the following sign, beginning with the fire-powered active, positive, cardinal sign of Aries and ending with watery, mutable, reactive Pisces.

The Layout of a Horoscope Chart

A horoscope chart is a map of the heavens at a given moment in time. It looks somewhat like a wheel divided with twelve spokes. In between each of the "spokes" is a section called a "house." Each house deals with a different area of life and is influenced (or "ruled") by a special sign and a planet. In addition, the house is governed by the sign passing over the spoke (or cusp) at that particular moment. The houses start at the left-center spoke (or the 9 position if you were reading a clock) and are read counter-clockwise around the chart.

The first house, home of Aries and the planet Mars. This is the house of "firsts"—the first impression you make, how you initiate matters, the image you choose to project. This is where you advertise yourself. Planets that fall here will intensify the way you come across to others. Often the first house will project an entirely different type of personality than the sun sign. For instance, a Capricorn with Leo in the first house will come across as much more flamboyant than the average Capricorn. The sign passing over this house at the time of your birth is known as your ascendant, or rising sign.

The second house, home of Taurus and Venus. This refers to how you experience the material world and what you value. Here is your contact with the material world—your attitudes about money, possessions, finances, whatever belongs to you, as well as your earning and spending capacity. On a deeper level, this house reveals your sense of self-worth, the inner values that draw wealth in various forms.

The third house, home of Gemini and Mars. This concerns how well you communicate with others. Are you understood? This house shows how you reach out to others nearby and interact with the immediate environment. Here is how your thinking process works; here is the way you communicate. Here are your first relationships, your experiences with brothers and sisters, as well as the ways you deal with people close to you, such as neighbors or pals. It's also where you take short trips, write letters, or use the telephone. It shows how your mind works in terms of left-brain logical and analytical functions.

The fourth house, home of Cancer and the moon. This house relates to how you are nurtured and made to feel secure—your roots! At the bottom of the chart, the fourth house, like the home, shows the foundation of your life, your psychological underpinnings. Here is where you have the deepest confrontations with who you are, and how you make yourself feel secure. It shows your early home environment and the circumstances at the end of your life—your final home—as well as the place you call home now. Astrologers look here for information about the primary nurturers in your life.

The fifth house, home of Leo and the sun. This refers to how you express yourself creatively and to your idea of play. The Leo house is where the creative potential develops. Here you express yourself and procreate, in the sense that children are outgrowths of your creative ability. But this house most represents your inner child-like self, who delights in play. If inner security has been established by the time you reach this house, you are now free to enjoy fun, romance, and love affairs—to give of yourself. This is also the place astrologers look for playful love affairs, flirtations, and brief romantic encounters (rather than long-term commitments).

The sixth house, home of Virgo and Mercury. This shows how you function in daily life. The sixth house has been called the "repair and maintenance" department. Here is where you get things done and where you determine how you will look after others and fulfill service duties, such as taking care of pets. Here is your daily survival, your job (as opposed to your career, which is the domain of the tenth house), your diet, and your health and fitness regimens. This house shows how well you take care of your body and organize yourself so you can perform efficiently in the world.

The seventh house, home of Libra and Venus. This house has to do with how you form a partnership. Here is the way you relate to others, including close, intimate, one-on-one relationships (even open enemies—those you face off with). This house shows your attitude toward partners and those with whom you enter commitments, contracts, or agreements. Open hostilities, lawsuits, divorces, and marriages happen here. If the first house is the "I," the seventh or opposite house is the "Not-I," the complementary partner you attract by the way you come across. If you are having trouble with relationships, consider what you are attracting by the interaction of your first and seventh houses.

The eighth house, home of Scorpio, Pluto, and Mars. This refers to how you merge with something, or handle power and control. This is one of the most mysterious and powerful houses, where your energy transforms itself from "I" to "we." As you give up your personal power and control by uniting with something or someone else, these two kinds of energies merge and become something greater, leading to a regeneration of the self on a higher level. Here are your attitudes toward sex, shared resources, and taxes (what you share with the government). Because this house involves what belongs to others, you face issues of control and power struggles, or undergo a deep psychological transformation as you bond with another. Here you transcend yourself with the occult, dreams, drugs, or psychic experiences that reflect the collective unconscious.

The ninth house, home of Sagittarius and Jupiter. This house rules how you search for wisdom and higher knowledge—your belief system. While the third house represents the lower mind, its opposite on the wheel, the ninth house is the higher mind—the abstract, intuitive, spiritual mind that asks big questions like "Why are we here?" The ninth house shows what you believe in. After the third house explored what was close at hand, the ninth stretches out to expand horizons with higher education and travel, or to stretch spiritually with religious activity. Here is where you write a book or an

44

extensive thesis, where you pontificate, philosophize, or preach.

The tenth house, home of Capricorn and Saturn. This house rules your public image and how you handle authority. This house is located directly overhead at the high noon position. This is the most visible house in the chart, the one where the world sees you. It deals with your public image, your career (but not your routine job), and your reputation. Here is where you go public and take on responsibilities (as opposed to the fourth house, where you stay home). This will affect the career you choose and your public relations. This house is also associated with your father figure or whoever else was the authority figure in your life.

The eleventh house, home of Aquarius and Uranus. This refers to your support system, how you relate to society and your goals. Here you extend yourself to a group, a goal, or a belief system. This house is where you define what you really want, the kinds of friends you have, your political affiliations, and the kind of groups you identify with as an equal. Here is where you could become a socially conscious humanitarian—or a partygoing social butterfly. It's where you look to others to stimulate you and discover your kinship to the rest of humanity. The sign on this house can help you understand what you gain and lose from friendships.

The twelfth house, home of Pisces and Neptune. This determines how you become selfless. Here is where the boundaries between yourself and others become blurred. In your trip around the zodiac, you've gone from the "I" of self-assertion in the first house to the final house symbolizing the dissolution of the self that happens before rebirth; it's where accumulated experiences are processed in the unconscious. Spiritually oriented astrologers look to this house for your past lives and karma. Places where we go to be alone and do spiritual or reparatory work belong here, such as retreats, religious institutions, hospitals. Here is also where we withdraw from society—or are forced to withdraw because of antisocial activity. Selfless giving through charitable acts is part of this house. In your daily life, the twelfth house reveals your deepest intimacies and your best-kept secrets, especially those you hide from yourself and keep repressed deep in the unconscious. It is where we surrender the sense of a separate self to a deep feeling of wholeness, such as selfless service in religion or any activity that involves merging with the greater whole. Many sports stars have important planets in the twelfth house that enable them to find an inner, almost mystical, strength that transcends their limits.

Who's Home in Your Houses?

Houses are stronger or weaker depending on how many planets are inhabiting them. If there are many planets in a given house, it follows that the activities of that house will be especially important in your life. If the planet that rules the house is also located there, this too adds power to the house.

CHAPTER 6

The Planets in Your Life and What They Mean

The ten planets in your chart will play starring or supporting roles, depending on their position in your horoscope. A planet in the first house, particularly one that's close to your rising sign, is sure to be a featured player. Planets that are grouped together usually operate together like a team, playing off each other, rather than expressing their energy singularly. A planet that stands alone, away from the others, is usually outstanding and sometimes steals the show.

Each planet has two signs where it is especially at home. These are called its *dignities*. The most favorable place for a planet is in the sign or signs it rules; the next best place is in a sign where it is *exalted,* or especially harmonious. On the other hand, there are places in the horoscope where a planet has to work harder to play its role. These places are called the planet's detriment and fall. The sign opposite a planet's rulership, which embodies the opposite area of life, is its *detriment.* The sign opposite its exaltation is its *fall.* Though the terms may suggest unfortunate circumstances for the planet, that is not always the case. In fact, a planet that is debilitated can actually be more complete, because it must stretch itself to meet the challenges of living in a more difficult sign. Like world leaders who've had to struggle for greatness, this planet may actually develop great strength and character.

The Planets and the Signs They Rule

Here's a list of the best places for each planet to be, in the signs they rule. Note that as new planets were discovered in this century, they replaced the traditional rulers of signs that best complimented their energies.

Aries	Mars
Taurus	Venus in its most sensual form
Gemini	Mercury in its communicative role
Cancer	the Moon
Leo	the Sun
Virgo	Mercury in its critical capacity
Libra	Venus in its aesthetic, judgmental form
Scorpio	Pluto, replacing its original ruler, Mars
Sagittarius	Jupiter
Capricorn	Saturn
Aquarius	Uranus, replacing its original ruler, Saturn
Pisces	Neptune, replacing its original ruler, Jupiter

Exalted Signs

A person who has many planets in exalted signs is lucky indeed, for here is where the planet can accomplish the most, be its most influential and creative

Sun	exalted in Aries, where its energy creates action
Moon	exalted in Taurus, where instincts and reactions operate on a creative level
Mercury	exalted in Virgo, which it also rules, where it reaches analytical heights
Venus	exalted in Pisces, whose sensitivity encourages love and creativity
Mars	exalted in Capricorn, which puts energy to work
Jupiter	exalted in Cancer, where it encourages nurturing and growth
Saturn	at home in Libra, where it steadies the scales of justice and promotes balanced, responsible judgment
Uranus	powerful in Scorpio, where it promotes transformation
Neptune	favored in Cancer, where it gains the security

	to transcend to a higher state
Pluto	exalted in Pisces, where it dissolves the old cycle to make way for transition to the new.

The Sun Is Always Top of the List

Your sun sign is the part of you that shines brightest. But the other planets add special coloration that make you different from other members of your sign. When you know a person's sun sign, you already know some very useful generic qualities. But when you know all a person's planets, you have a much more accurate profile of that person and you'll be much more able to predict how that individual will act in a given situation. The sun's just one card in your hand—when you know the other planets, you can really play to win!

Since the sun is always the first consideration, it is important to treat it as the star of the show. It is your conscious ego and it is always center stage, even when sharing a house or a sign with several other planets. This is why sun-sign astrology works for so many people. In chart interpretations, the sun can also play the parental role.

The sun rules the sign of Leo, gaining strength through the pride, dignity, and confidence of the fixed-fire personality. It is exalted in "me-first" Aries. In its detriment, Aquarius, the sun-ego is strengthened through group participation and social consciousness, rather than through self-centeredness. Note how many Aquarius people are involved in politics, social work, and public life, following the demands of their sun sign to be spokesperson for a group. In its fall, Libra, the sun needs the strength of a partner—and "other"—to enhance balance and self-expression.

Like your sun sign, each of the other nine planets' personalities are colored by the sign it is passing through at the time. For example, Mercury, the planet that rules the way you communicate, will express itself in a dynamic, headstrong Aries way if it was passing through the sign of Aries when you were born. You would communicate in a much different way if it were passing through the slower, more patient sign of Taurus. And so on through the list. Here's a rundown of the planets and how they behave in every sign.

The Moon—The Inner You

The moon can teach you about the inner side of yourself and about your needs and secrets, as well as those of others. It is your most personal planet, the receptive, reflective, female, nurturing side of you. And it reflects who you were nurtured by—the "Mother" or mother figure in your chart. In a man's chart, the moon position also describes his female, receptive, emotional side, as well as the woman in his life who will have the deepest effect. (Venus reveals the kind of woman who attracts him physically.)

The sign the moon was passing through at your birth reflects your instinctive emotional nature and what appeals to you subconsciously. Since accurate moon tables are too extensive for this book, check through these descriptions to find the moon sign that feels most familiar—or, better yet, have your chart calculated by a computer service to get your accurate moon placement.

The moon rules maternal Cancer and is exalted in Taurus, both comforting, home-loving signs where the natural emotional energies of the moon are easily and productively expressed. But when the moon is in the opposite signs—in its Capricorn detriment and its Scorpio fall—it leaves the comfortable nest and deals with emotional issues of power and achievement in the outside world. Those of you with the moon in these signs will find your emotional role more challenging in life.

Moon in Aries

You are an idealistic, impetuous person who falls in and out of love easily. This placement makes you both independent and ardent. You love a challenge, but could cool once your quarry is captured. You should cultivate patience and tolerance—or you might tend to gravitate toward those who treat you rough, just for the sake of challenge and excitement.

Moon in Taurus

You are a sentimental soul who is very fond of the good life and gravitates toward solid, secure relationships. You like displays of affection and creature comforts—all the tangible trappings of a cozy, safe, calm atmosphere. You are sensual and steady emotionally, but very stubborn and determined. You can't be pushed and tend to dislike changes. You should make an effort to broaden your horizons and to take a risk sometimes.

Moon in Gemini

You crave mental stimulation and variety in life, which you usually get through either an ever-varied social life, the excitement of flirtation, or multiple professional involvements. You may marry more than once and have a rather chaotic emotional life due to your difficulty with commitment and settling down. Be sure to find a partner who is as outgoing as you are. You will have to learn at some point to focus your energies because you tend to be somewhat fragmented. You do two things at once and you may have two homes or even two lovers. If you can find a creative way to express your many-faceted nature, you'll be ahead of the game.

Moon in Cancer

This is the most powerful lunar position, which is sure to have a deep imprint on your character. Your needs are very much associated with your reaction to the needs of others. You are very sensitive and self-protective, though some of you may mask this with a hard shell. This placement also gives an excellent memory and an uncanny ability to psych out the needs of others. All of the lunar phases will affect you, especially full moons and eclipses, so you would do well to mark them on your calendar. You are happiest at home and may work at home or turn your office into a second home, where you can nurture and comfort people; you may tend to mother the world. This psychic, intuitive moon might draw you to occult work in some way, or you may get professionally involved with providing food and shelter to the needy.

Moon in Leo

This is a warm, passionate moon that takes everything to heart. You are attracted to all that is noble, generous, and aristocratic in life, and you may be a bit of a snob. You have an innate ability to take command emotionally, but you do need strong support, loyalty, and loud applause from those you love. You are possessive of your loved ones and your turf and will roar if anyone threatens to take over your territory.

Moon in Virgo

You are rather cool until you decide if others measure up. But once someone or something meets your ideal standards, you hold up your end of the arrangement perfectly. You may, in fact, drive yourself too hard to attain some notion of perfection. Try to be a bit easier on yourself and others. Don't always act the censor! You love to be the teacher and are drawn to situations where you can change others for the better. But sometimes you must learn to accept others for what they are and enjoy what you have.

Moon in Libra

This is a partnership-oriented placement, and you may find it difficult to be alone or to do things alone. But you must learn to lean on yourself first. When you have learned emotional balance, you can have excellent relationships. It is best for you to avoid extremes or your love life can be precarious. You thrive in a rather conservative, traditional, romantic relationship, where you receive attention and flattery—but not possessiveness—from your partner. You'll be your most charming in an elegant, harmonious atmosphere.

Moon in Scorpio

This is a moon that enjoys and responds to intense, passionate feelings. You may go to extremes and have a very dramatic emotional life, full of ardor, suspicion, jealousy, and obsession. It would be much healthier to channel your need for power and control into meaningful work. This is a good position for anyone in the fields of medicine, police work, research, the occult, psychoanalysis, or intuitive work, because life-and-death situations don't faze you. However, you do take personal disappointments very hard.

Moon in Sagittarius

You take life's ups and downs with good humor and a grain of salt. You'll love 'em and leave 'em, and take off on a great adventure at a moment's notice. "Born free" could be your slogan. You can't stand to be possessed emotionally by anyone. Attracted by the exotic, you have wanderlust mentally and physically. You may be too much in search of new mental and spiritual stimulation to ever settle down.

Moon in Capricorn

Are you ever accused of being too cool and calculating? You have an earthy side, but you take prestige and position very seriously. Your strong drive to succeed extends to your romantic life, where you will be devoted to improving your lifestyle and rising to the top. A structured situation, where you can advance methodically, makes you feel wonderfully secure. You may be attracted to someone older or very much younger or from a different social world. It may be difficult to look at the lighter side of emotional relationships, but the upside of this moon in its detriment is that you tend to be very dutiful and responsible to those you care for.

Moon in Aquarius

You are a people collector with many friends of all backgrounds. You are happiest surrounded by people and are uneasy when left alone. You usually stay friends with those with whom you get involved, but intense emotions could turn you off. Though tolerant and understanding, you can be emotionally unpredictable. You don't like anything to be too rigid—you may resist working on schedule or you may have a very unconventional love life. With plenty of space, you will be able to sustain relationships, but you'll blow away from possessive types.

Moon in Pisces

You are very responsive and empathetic to others, especially if they have problems. (You may have to be on guard against attracting too many people with sob stories.) You'll be happiest if you can find ways to express your creative imagination in the arts or in the spiritual or healing professions. You may tend to escape to a fantasy world or be attracted to exotic places or people. You need an emotional anchor, as you are very sensitive to the moods of others. You are happiest near water, working in a field that gives you emotional variety. But steer clear of too much escapism, especially in alcohol, or reclusiveness. Keep a firm foothold in reality.

Close and Personal—Mercury, Venus, and Mars

These are the planets that work in your immediate personal life. Mercury affects how you communicate and how your mental processes work. Are you a quick study who grasps information rapidly, or do you learn more slowly and thoroughly? How is your concentration? Can you express yourself easily? Are you a good writer? All these questions can be answered by your Mercury placement.

Venus shows what you react to. What turns you on? What appeals to you aesthetically? Are you charming to others? Are you attractive to look at? Your taste, your refinement, your sense of balance and proportion are all Venus ruled.

Mars is your outgoing energy, your drive and ambition. Do you reach out for new adventures? Are you assertive? Are you motivated? Self-confident? Hot-tempered? How you channel your energy and drive is revealed by your Mars placement.

Mercury—The Great Communicator

Mercury shows how you think and speak and how logically your mind works. It stays close to the sun, never more than a sign away, and very often shares the same sign, reinforcing the sun's communicative talents. Mercury functions easily in Gemini and Virgo, the natural analytical signs it rules. Yet Mercury in Sagittarius and Pisces, signs where logic often takes second place to visionary ideas and where Mercury is debilitated, can provide great visionary thinking and poetic expression when the planet is properly used.

Since Mercury never travels far from the sun, read Mercury in your sun sign, the sign preceding and following it. Then decide which most reflects the way your mind works.

Mercury in Aries

Your mind is very active and assertive. You never hesitate to say exactly what you think or shy away from a battle. In fact, you may relish a verbal confrontation.

Mercury in Taurus

You may be a slow learner, but you have good concentration and mental stamina. You want to make your ideas really happen. You'll attack a problem methodically and consider every angle thoroughly, never jumping to conclusions. You'll stick with a subject until you master it.

Mercury in Gemini

You are a wonderful communicator, with a great facility for expressing yourself verbally and in writing. Though you learn fast, you may lack focus and discipline. Watch a tendency to jump from subject to subject.

Mercury in Cancer

You are very intuitive, rather than logical. Your mental processes are usually colored by your emotions. This gives you the advantage of great imagination and empathy for others.

Mercury in Leo

You are enthusiastic and very dramatic in the way you express yourself. You like to hold the attention of groups and could be a great public speaker. Your mind thinks big and likes to deal with the overall picture rather than with details.

Mercury in Virgo

This is one of the best places for Mercury. It should give you critical ability, attention to details, and thorough analysis. Your mind focuses on the practical side of things. You are an excellent teacher and editor.

Mercury in Libra

You are a born diplomat who smoothes over ruffled feathers; you may be a talented debater or lawyer. However, you might vacillate when it comes to taking a stand or making decisions; you're forever weighing the pros and cons.

Mercury in Scorpio

This is the investigative mind, which stops at nothing to get the answer. You may have a sarcastic, stinging wit— a gift for the cutting remark. There's always a grain of truth to your verbal sallies, thanks to your penetrating insight.

Mercury in Sagittarius

You are a super salesman with a tendency to expound. You are very broad minded, but you could be dogmatic when it comes to telling others what's good for them. You won't hesitate to tell the truth as you see it, so watch a tendency toward tactlessness. On the plus side, you have a great sense of humor.

Mercury in Capricorn

This placement endows good mental discipline. You have a love of learning and a very orderly approach to your subjects. You will patiently plod through facts and figures until you master your tasks. You grasp structured situations easily, but may be short on creativity.

Mercury in Aquarius

You are an independent thinker who won't hesitate to break the rules to find the most original, innovative approach to problems. But once your mind is made up, it is difficult to change.

Mercury in Pisces

You have the psychic, intuitive mind of a natural poet.
You should learn to make use of your creative imagination. You also think in terms of helping others, but check
a tendency to be vague and forgetful of details.

Venus—Your Love Planet

Venus is the planet of romantic love, pleasure, and industry. It shows what you react to, your tastes, and what
(or who) turns you on. It is naturally at home in the
planets it rules—Libra, the sign of partnerships, or Taurus, the sign of physical pleasure. Yet in Aries, its detriment, Venus is daring, full of energy, and negatively self-serving. In Pisces, where Venus is exalted, this planet
can go overboard, loving to the point of self-sacrifice.
While Venus in Virgo, its fall, can be the perfectionist
in love, it can also offer affectionate service and true
support.

Venus in Aries

Oh, do you love excitement! You can't stand to be
bored, confined, or ordered around. But a good challenge, maybe even a rousing row turns you on. Confess—don't you pick a fight now and then just to get
everyone stirred up? You're attracted by the chase, not
the catch, which could create problems in your love life
if the object of your affection becomes too attainable.
You like to wear red and to be first with the very latest
fashion. You'll spot a trend before anyone else.

Venus in Taurus

All your senses work in high gear. You love to be surrounded by glorious tastes, smells, textures, sounds, and
visuals—austerity is not for you. Neither is being rushed.
You like time to enjoy your pleasures. Soothing surroundings with plenty of creature comforts are your cup

of tea. You like to feel secure in your nest, with no sudden jolts or surprises. You like familiar objects—in fact, you may hate to let anything or anyone go.

Venus in Gemini

You are a lively, sparkling personality who thrives in a situation that affords a constant variety and a frequent change of scenery. A varied social life is important to you, with plenty of stimulation and a chance to engage in some light flirtation. Commitment may be difficult, when playing the field is so much more fun.

Venus in Cancer

An atmosphere where you feel protected, coddled, and mothered is best for you. You love to be surrounded by children in a cozy, homelike situation. You are attracted to those who are tender and nurturing, who make you feel secure and well provided for. You may be quite secretive about your emotional life or attracted to clandestine relationships.

Venus in Leo

First-class attention in large doses turns you on, and so does the glitter of real gold and the flash of mirrors. You like to feel like a star at all times, surrounded by your admiring audience. The side effect is that you may be attracted to flatterers and tinsel, while the real gold requires some digging.

Venus in Virgo

Everything neatly in its place? On the surface, you are attracted to an atmosphere where everything is in perfect order, but underneath are some basic, earthy urges. You are attracted to those who appeal to your need to teach, be of service, or play out a Pygmalion fantasy.

You're at your best when you are busy doing something useful.

Venus in Libra

Elegance and harmony are your key words. You can't abide an atmosphere of contention. Your taste tends toward the classic, with light harmonies of color—nothing clashing, trendy, or outrageous. You love doing things with a partner and should be careful to pick one who is decisive but patient enough to let you weigh the pros and cons. And steer clear of argumentative types.

Venus in Scorpio

Hidden mysteries intrigue you—in fact, anything that is too open and aboveboard is a bit of a bore. You surely have a stack of whodunits by the bed, along with an erotic magazine or two. You may also be fascinated with the occult, crime, or scientific research. Intense, all-or-nothing situations add spice to your life, but you could get burned by your flair for living dangerously. The color black, spicy food, dark wood furniture, and heady perfume all get you in the right mood.

Venus in Sagittarius

If you are not actually a world traveler, your surroundings are sure to reflect your love of faraway places. You like a casual outdoor atmosphere and a dog or two to pet. There should be plenty of room for athletic equipment and suitcases. You're attracted to kindred souls who love to travel and who share your freedom-loving philosophy of life. Athletics, spiritual, or New-Age pursuits could be other interests.

Venus in Capricorn

No fly-by-night relationships for you! You want substance in life and you are attracted to whatever will help you get where you are going. Status objects turn you on. So do those who have a serious responsible, businesslike approach, or who remind you of a beloved parent. It is characteristic of this placement to be attracted to someone of a different generation. Antiques, traditional clothing, and dignified behavior favor you.

Venus in Aquarius

This Venus wants to make friends more than to make love. You like to be in a group, particularly one pushing a worthy cause. You feel quite at home surrounded by people, remaining detached from any intense commitment. Original ideas and unpredictable people fascinate you. You don't like everything to be planned out in advance, preferring spontaneity and delightful surprises.

Venus in Pisces

This Venus is attracted to being of service. You love to give of yourself and you find plenty of takers. Stray animals and people appeal to your heart and your pocketbook, but be careful to look at their motives realistically once in a while. Fantasy, theater, and psychic or spiritual activities also speak to you.

Mars—How You Go for it

Mars is the mover and shaker in your life. It shows how you pursue your goals and whether you have energy to burn or proceed in a slow, steady pace. Or are you nervous, restless, and unable to sit still? It will also show how you get angry: Do you explode, or do a slow burn, or hold everything inside—then get revenge later?

In Aries, which it rules, and Scorpio, which it corules, Mars is at its most powerful. Yet this drive can be self-serving and impetuous. In Libra, the sign of its detriment, Mars demands cooperation in a relationship. In Capricorn, where it is exalted, Mars becomes an ambitious achiever, headed for the top. But in Cancer, the sign of its fall, Mars aggression becomes tempered by feelings, especially those involving self-protection and security, which are always considered first. The end can never justify the means for Mars in Cancer.

To find your Mars, refer to the Mars chart in this book. If the following description of your Mars sign doesn't ring true, you may have been born on a day when Mars was changing signs, so check the adjacent sign descriptions.

Mars in Aries

In the sign it rules, Mars shows its brilliant fiery nature. You have an explosive temper and can be quite impatient, but on the other hand, you have tremendous courage, energy, and drive. You'll let nothing stand in your way as you race to be first! Obstacles are met head-on and broken through by force. However, those that require patience and persistence can have you exploding in rage. You're a great starter, but not necessarily around for the finish.

Mars in Taurus

Slow, steady, concentrated energy gives you the power. You have great stamina and you never give up. Your tactic is to wear away obstacles with your persistence. Often you come out a winner because you've had the patience to hang in there. When angered, you do a slow burn.

Mars in Gemini

You can't sit still for long. This Mars craves variety. You often have two or more things going on at once—it's all an amusing game to you. Your life can get very complicated, but that only adds spice and stimulation. What drives you into a nervous, hyper state? Boredom, sameness, routine, and confinement. You can do wonderful things with your hands and you have a way with words.

Mars in Cancer

Your rarely attack head-on—instead, you'll keep things to yourself, make plans in secret, and always cover your actions. This might be interpreted by some as manipulative, but you are only being self-protective. You get furious when anyone knows too much about you. But you do like to know all about others. Your mothering and feeding instincts can be put to good use in your work in food, hotel, or child-care related businesses. You may have to overcome your fragile sense of security, which prompts you not to take risks and to get physically upset when criticized. Don't take things so personally!

Mars in Leo

You have a very dominant personality that takes center stage—modesty is not one of your traits, nor is taking a backseat. You prefer giving the orders and have been known to make a dramatic scene if they are not obeyed. Properly used, this Mars confers leadership ability, endurance, and courage.

Mars in Virgo

You are the fault-finder of the zodiac, who notices every detail. Mistakes of any kind make you very nervous. You may worry even if everything is going smoothly. You may not express your anger directly, but you sure can nag. You have definite likes and dislikes and you are sure you can do the job better than anyone else. You are certainly more industrious than most other signs. Why don't you express your Mars energy by teaching instead of by criticizing?

Mars in Libra

This Mars will have a passion for beauty, justice, and art. Generally, you will avoid confrontations at all costs. You prefer to spend your energy finding a diplomatic solution or weighing pros and cons. Your other techniques are passive aggression, or exercising your well-known charm to get people to do what you want.

Mars in Scorpio

This is a powerful placement, so intense that it demands careful channeling into worthwhile activities. Otherwise, you could become obsessed with your sexuality or might use your need for power and control to manipulate others. You are strong-willed, shrewd, and very private about your affairs, and you'll usually have a secret agenda behind your actions. Your great stamina, focus, and discipline would be excellent assets for careers in the military or medical fields, especially research or surgery. When angry, you don't get mad—you get even!

Mars in Sagittarius

This expansive Mars often propels people into sales, travel, athletics, or philosophy. Your energies function well when you are on the move. You have a hot temper and are inclined to say what you think before you consider the consequences. You shoot for high goals—and talk endlessly about them—but you may be weak on groundwork. This Mars needs a solid foundation. Watch a tendency to take unnecessary risks.

Mars in Capricorn

This is an ambitious Mars with an excellent sense of timing. You have an eye for those who can be of use to you, and you may dismiss people ruthlessly when you're angry. But you drive yourself hard and deliver full value. This is a good placement for an executive. You'll aim for status and a high material position in life, and keep climbing despite the odds.

Mars in Aquarius

This is the most rebellious Mars. You seem to have a drive to assert yourself against the status quo. You may enjoy provoking people, shocking them out of traditional views. Or this placement could express itself in an off-beat sex life. Others could find you a bit eccentric—somehow, you often find yourself in unconventional situations. You enjoy being a leader of an active group, which pursues forward-looking studies or goals.

Mars in Pisces

This Mars is a good actor who knows just how to appeal to the sympathies of others. You create and project wonderful fantasies or use your sensitive antennae to crusade for those less fortunate. You get what you want through creating a veil of illusion and glamour. This is a good Mars for a dancer, performer, or photographer, or for someone in motion pictures. Many famous film stars have this placement. Watch a tendency to manipulate by making others feel sorry for you.

Jupiter—Expansion, Luck, Optimism

Jupiter is the planet in your horoscope that makes you want more. This big, bright, swirling mass of gases is associated with abundance, prosperity, and the kind of windfall you get without too much hard work. You're optimistic under Jupiter's influence—anything seems possible. You'll travel, expand your mind with higher education, and publish to share your knowledge widely. But a strong Jupiter has its downside, too. Jupiter's influence is neither discriminating nor disciplined, representing the principle of growth without judgement and resulting in extravagance, weight gain, laziness, and carelessness.

Jupiter also embodies the functions of the higher

mind, where you do complex, expansive thinking and deal with the big overall picture, rather than the specifics (the province of Mercury). Jupiter functions naturally in Sagittarius, the sign of the philosopher, or Pisces, which it corules with Neptune. In Gemini, its detriment, Jupiter can be scattered, a jack-of-all-trades. On the other hand, it can also be a lighthearted, effective communicator. In Cancer, where it is exalted, Jupiter becomes the protective big brother. In Capricorn, its fall, Jupiter is brought down to earth, its vision harnessed to practical goals.

Be sure to look up your Jupiter in the tables in this book. When the current position of Jupiter is favorable, you may get that lucky break. At any rate, it's a great time to try new things, take risks, travel, or get more education. Opportunities seem to open up at this time, so take advantage of them. Once a year, Jupiter changes signs. That means you are due for an expansive time every twelve years, when Jupiter travels through your sun sign. You'll also have "up" periods every four years, when Jupiter is in the same element as your sun sign.

Jupiter in Aries

You are the soul of enthusiasm and optimism. Your luckiest times are when you are getting started on an exciting project or selling an idea that you really believe in. You may have to watch a tendency to be arrogant with those who do not share your enthusiasm. You follow your impulse, often ignoring budget or other commonsense limitations. To produce real, solid benefits, you'll need patience and follow-through wherever this Jupiter falls in your horoscope.

Jupiter in Taurus

You'll spend on beautiful material things, especially those that come from nature—items made of rare woods, natural fabrics, or precious gems, for instance. You can't have too much comfort or too many sensual pleasures. Watch a tendency to overindulge in good food, or to overpamper yourself with nothing but the best. Spartan

66

living is not for you! You may be especially lucky in matters of real estate.

Jupiter in Gemini

You are the great talker of the zodiac, and you may be a great writer, too. But restlessness could be your weak point. You jump around, talk too much, and could be a jack-of-all-trades. Keeping a secret is especially difficult, so you'll also have to watch a tendency to spill the beans. Since you love to be at the center of a beehive of activity, you'll have a vibrant social life. Your best opportunities will come through your talent for language—speaking, writing, communicating, and selling.

Jupiter in Cancer

You are luckiest in situations where you can find emotional closeness or deal with basic security needs, such as food, nurturing, or shelter. You may be a great collector and you may simply love to accumulate things—you are the one who stashed things away for a rainy day. You probably have a very good memory and love children—in fact, you may have many children to care for. The food, hotel, child-care, or shipping businesses hold good opportunities for you.

Jupiter in Leo

You are a natural showman who loves to live in a larger-than-life way. Yours is a personality full of color that always finds its way into the limelight. You can't have too much attention or applause. Show biz is a natural place for you, and any area where you can exercise your flair for drama, your natural playfulness, and your romantic nature brings you good fortune. But watch a tendency to be overly extravagant or to monopolize center stage.

Jupiter in Virgo

You actually love those minute details others find boring. To you, they make all the difference between the perfect and the ordinary. You are the fine craftsman who spots every flaw. You expand your awareness by finding the most practical methods and by being of service to others. Many will be drawn to medical or teaching fields. You'll also have luck in publishing, crafts, nutrition, and service professions. Watch a tendency to overwork.

Jupiter in Libra

This is an other-directed Jupiter that develops best with a partner, for the stimulation of others helps you grow. You are also most comfortable in harmonious, beautiful situations, and you work well with artistic people. You have a great sense of fair play and an ability to evaluate the pros and cons of a situation. You usually prefer to play the role of diplomat rather than adversary.

Jupiter in Scorpio

You love the feeling of power and control, of taking things to their limit. You can't resist a mystery, and your shrewd, penetrating mind sees right through to the heart of most situations and people. You have luck in work that probes for solutions to matters of life and death. You may be drawn to undercover work, behind-the-scenes intrigue, psychotherapy, the occult, and sex-related ventures. Your challenge will be to develop a sense of moderation and tolerance for others' beliefs. This Jupiter can be fanatical. You may have luck in handling others' money—insurance, taxes, and inheritance can bring you a windfall.

Jupiter in Sagittarius

Independent, outgoing, and idealistic, you'll shoot for the stars. This Jupiter compels you to travel far and wide, both physically and mentally, via higher education.

You may have luck while traveling in an exotic place. You also have luck with outdoor ventures, exercise, and animals, particularly horses. Since you tend to be very open about your opinions, watch a tendency to be tactless and to exaggerate. Instead, use your wonderful sense of humor to make your point.

Jupiter in Capricorn

Jupiter is much more restrained in Capricorn. Here, Jupiter can make you overwork, and heighten any ambition or sense of duty you may have. You'll expand in areas that advance your position, putting you farther up the social or corporate ladder. You are lucky working within the establishment in a very structured situation, where you can show off your ability to organize and reap rewards for your hard work.

Jupiter in Aquarius

This is another freedom-loving Jupiter, with great tolerance and originality. You are at your best when you are working for a humanitarian cause and in the company of many supporters. This is a good Jupiter for a political career. You'll relate to all kinds of people on all social levels. You have an abundance of original ideas, but you are best off away from routine and any situation that imposes rigid rules. You need mental stimulation!

Jupiter in Pisces

You are a giver whose feeling and pocketbook are easily touched by others, so choose your companions with care. You could be the original sucker for a hard-luck story. Better find a worthy hospital or charity to appreciate your selfless support. You have a great creative imagination and may attract good fortune in fields related to oil, perfume, pharmaceuticals, petroleum, dance, footwear, and alcohol. But beware of overindulgence in alcohol—focus on a creative outlet instead.

Saturn—The Taskmaster

Saturn has suffered from a bad reputation, always cast as the heavy in the chart. However, the flip side of Saturn is that teacher whose class is the toughest in school, but whose lessons you never forget. And the tests of Saturn, which come at regular seven-year exam periods, are the ones you need to pass to survive as a conscious, independent adult. Saturn gives us the grade we've earned, so if we have studied and prepared for our tests we needn't be afraid of the big, bad wolf. Saturn in Capricorn, its ruler, is comfortable with this sign's emphasis on structure and respect for authority. Cancer, Saturn's detriment, suggests both that feeling must become responsible and that authority cannot operate effectively without concern for the chart.

Your Saturn position can illuminate your fears, your hangups, and your important lessons in life. Remember that Saturn is concerned with your maturity, and with what you need to know to survive in the world.

When Saturn returns to its location at the time of your birth, at approximately age 28, you'll have your first Saturn return. At this time, a person usually takes stock or settles down to find a mission in life and assume full adult duties and responsibilities.

Another way Saturn helps us is to reveal the karmic lessons from previous lives and give us the chance to overcome them. So look at Saturn's challenges as much-needed opportunities for self-improvement. Under a Jupiter influence, you'll have more fun, but Saturn gives you solid, long-lasting results.

Look up your natal Saturn in the tables in this book for clues on where you need work.

Saturn in Aries

Saturn here gives you great ambition and independence—you don't let anyone push you around and you know what's best for you. Following orders is not your strong point, and neither is diplomacy. Because no one quite lives up to your standards, you often wind up doing everything yourself. You are best off running your own business, though you may be quite lonely at times.

Saturn in Taurus

A big issue is getting control of the cash flow. There will be lean periods that can be frightening, but you have the patience and endurance to stick them out and the methodical drive to prosper in the end. Learn to take a philosophical attitude like Ben Franklin, who also had this placement and who said, "A penny saved is a penny earned."

Saturn in Gemini

You are a rather cold, detached, serious student, uninclined to communicate or share your knowledge. You dwell in the realms of science, theory, or abstract analysis, even when you are dealing with the emotions, like Sigmund Freud, who had this placement.

Saturn in Cancer

Your tests come with establishing a secure emotional base. In doing so, you may have to deal with some very basic fears centering on your early home environment. Most of your Saturn tests will have emotional roots in those early childhood experiences. You may have difficulty remaining objective in terms of what you try to achieve, so it will be especially important for you to deal with negative feelings such as guilt, paranoia, jealousy, resentment, and suspicion. Galileo and Michelangelo also navigated these murky waters.

Saturn in Leo

This is an authoritarian Saturn, a strict, demanding parent who may deny the pleasure principle in your zeal to see that rules are followed. Though you may feel guilty about taking the spotlight, you are very ambitious and loyal. You have to watch a tendency toward rigidity, also toward overwork and holding back affection. Joseph Kennedy and Billy Graham share this placement.

Saturn in Virgo

This is a cautious, exacting Saturn, intensely hard on yourself, most of all. You give yourself the roughest time with your constant worries about every little detail, often making yourself sick. Your tests will come in learning tolerance and understanding of others. Charles de Gaulle and Nathaniel Hawthorne had this meticulous Saturn.

Saturn in Libra

Saturn is exalted here, which makes this planet an ally. You may choose very serious, older partners in life, perhaps stemming from a fear of dependency. You need to learn to stand solidly on your own before you commit to another. You are extremely cautious as you deliberate every involvement—with good reason. It is best that you find an occupation that makes good use of your sense of duty and honor. Steer clear of fly-by-night situations. Khrushchev and Mao Tse-tung had this placement, too.

Saturn in Scorpio

You have great staying power. This Saturn tests you in matters of control and transformation. You may feel drawn to some kind of intrigue or undercover work, like J. Edgar Hoover. Or there may be an air of mystery surrounding your life and death, like Marilyn Monroe and Robert Kennedy, who had this placement. There are lessons to be learned from your sexual involvements—often sex is used for manipulation or is somehow out of the ordinary. The Roman emperor Caligula and the transvestite Christine Jorgensen are extreme cases.

Saturn in Sagittarius

Your challenges and lessons will come from tests of your spiritual and philosophical values, as happened to Martin Luther King and Gandhi. You are high minded and sincere with this reflective, moral placement. Uncompromising in your ethical standards, you could be a benevolent despot.

Saturn in Capricorn

With the help of Saturn at maximum strength, your judgment will improve with age. And, like Spencer Tracy's screen image, you'll be the gray-haired hero with a strong sense of responsibility. You advance in life slowly but steadily, always with a strong hand at the helm and an eye for the advantageous situation. Negatively, you may be a loner, prone to periods of melancholy.

Saturn in Aquarius

Your tests come from your relationships with groups. Do you care too much about what others think? You may fear being different from others and therefore slight your own unique, forward-looking gifts or, like Lord Byron and Howard Hughes, take the opposite tack and rebel in the extreme. You can apply discipline to accomplish great humanitarian goals, as Albert Schweitzer did.

Saturn in Pisces

Your fear of the unknown and the irrational may lead you to a secluded, solitary lifestyle. You may go on the run like Jesse James, who had this placement, to avoid looking too deeply inside. Or you might go in the opposite, more positive direction and develop a disciplined psychoanalytic approach, which puts you more in control of your feelings. Some of you will take refuge in work with hospitals, charities, or religious institutions. Queen Victoria, who had this placement, symbolized an era when institutions of all kinds were sustained. Discipline

73

applied to artistic work, especially poetry and dance, or spiritual work, such as yoga or meditation, might be helpful.

Uranus, Neptune, and Pluto Affect Your Whole Generation

These three planets remain in signs such a long time that a whole generation bears the imprint of the sign. Mass movements, great sweeping changes, fads that characterize a generation, even the issues of the conflicts and wars of the time are influenced by the "outer three." When one of these distant planets changes signs, there is a definite shift in the atmosphere, the feeling of the end of an era.

Since these planets are so far away from the sun—too distant to be seen by the naked eye—they pick up signals from the universe at large. These planetary receivers literally link the sun with distant energies, and then perform a similar function in your horoscope by linking your central character with intuitive, spiritual, transformative forces from the cosmos. Each planet has a special domain and will reflect this in the area of your life where it falls.

Uranus—The Planet of Surprises

There is nothing ordinary about this quirky green planet that seems to be traveling on its side, surrounded by a swarm of at least fifteen moons. Is it any wonder that astrologers assigned it to Aquarius, the most eccentric and gregarious sign? Uranus seems to wend its way around the sun, marching to its own tune.

Uranus energy is electrical, happening in sudden flashes. It is not influenced by karma or past events, nor does it regard tradition, sex, or sentiment. The Uranian key words are surprise and awakening. Uranus wakes you up, jolting you out of your comfortable rut. Suddenly, there's that flash of inspiration, that bright idea or totally new approach to revolutionize whatever scheme you were undertaking. The Uranus place in your life is where you awaken and become your own person. And it is probably the most unconventional place in your chart.

Look up the sign of Uranus at the time of your birth and see where you follow your own tune.

Uranus in Aries—A Fiery Shocker

Birth dates: March 31–November 4, 1927; January 13, 1928–June 6, 1934; October 10, 1934–March 28, 1935. Your generation is original, creative, pioneering; it developed the computer, the airplane, and the cyclotron. You let nothing hold you back from exploring the unknown and have a powerful mixture of fire and electricity behind you. Women of your generation were among the first to be liberated. You were the unforgettable style setters. You have a surprise in store for everyone. Like Yoko Ono, Grace Kelly, and Jacqueline Onassis, your life may be jolted by sudden and violent changes.

Uranus in Taurus—Sudden Shakeups

Birth dates: June 6, 1934–October 10, 1934; March 28, 1935–August 7, 1941; October 5, 1941–May 15, 1942. You are probably self-employed or would like to be. You have original ideas about making money, and you brace yourself for sudden changes of fortune. This Uranus can cause shakeups, particularly in finances, but it can also make you a born entrepreneur.

Uranus in Gemini—The Walking Talk Show

Birth date: August 7–October 5, 1941; May 15, 1942–August 30, 1948; November 12, 1948–June 10, 1949. You were the first children to be influenced by television, and in your adult years, your generation stocks up on answering machines, cordless phones, car phones, computers, and fax machines—any new way you can communicate. You have an inquiring mind, but your interests are rather short lived. This Uranus can be easily fragmented if there is no structure and focus.

Uranus in Cancer—Domestic Disturbances

Birth date: August 30–November 12, 1948; June 10, 1949–August 24, 1955; January 28–June 10, 1956. This generation came at a time when divorce was becoming commonplace, so your home image is unconventional. You may have an unusual relationship with your parents; you may have come from a broken home or an unconventional one. You'll have unorthodox ideas about parenting, intimacy, food, and shelter. You may also be interested in dreams, psychic phenomena, and memory work.

Uranus in Leo—A Flashy Performer

Birth date: August 24, 1955–January 28, 1956; June 10, 1956–November 1, 1961; January 10–August 10, 1962. This generation understood how to use electronic media. Many of your group are now leaders in the high-tech industries, and you also understand how to use the new media to promote yourself. Like Isadora Duncan, you may have a very eccentric kind of charisma and a life that is sparked by unusual love affairs. Your children, too, may have traits that are out of the ordinary. Where this planet falls in your chart, you'll have a love of freedom, be a bit of an egomaniac, and show the full force of your personality in a unique way, like tennis great Martina Navratilova.

Uranus in Virgo—Eccentric Genius

Birth date: November 1, 1961–January 10, 1962; August 10, 1962–September 28, 1968; May 20, 1969–June 24, 1969.

You'll have highly individual work methods, and many will be finding newer, more practical ways to use computers. Like Einstein, who had this placement, you'll break the rules brilliantly. Your generation came at a time of student rebellions, the civil rights movement, and the general acceptance of health foods. Chances are, you are concerned abut pollution and cleaning up the environment. You may also be involved with nontraditional healing methods. Heavyweight champ Mike Tyson has this placement.

Uranus in Libra—On Again, Off Again Partners

Birth date: September 28, 1968–May 20, 1969; June 24, 1969–November 21, 1974; May 1–September 8, 1975. Your generation will be always changing partners. Born during the time of women's liberation, you may have come from a broken home and have no clear image of what a marriage entails. There will be many sudden splits and experiments before you settle down. Your generation will be much involved in legal and political reforms and in changing artistic and fashion looks.

Uranus in Scorpio—The New Age

Birth date: November 21, 1974–May 1, 1975; September 8, 1975–February 17, 1981; March 20–November 16, 1981. Interest in transformation, meditation, and life after death signaled the beginning of New-Age consciousness. Your generation recognizes no boundaries, no limits, and no external controls. You'll have new attitudes toward death and dying, psychic phenomena, and the occult. Like Mae West and Casanova, you'll shock 'em sexually, too.

Uranus in Sagittarius—Space Trippers

Birth date: February 17–March 20, 1981; November 16, 1981–February 15, 1988; May 27, 1988–December 2, 1988. Could this generation be the first to travel in outer space? The last generation with this placement included

Charles Lindbergh—at that time, the first Zeppelins and the Wright Brothers were conquering the skies. Uranus here forecasts great discoveries, mind expansion, and long-distance travel. Like Galileo and Martin Luther, those born in these years will generate new theories about the cosmos and man's relation to it.

Uranus in Capricorn—Movers and Shakers

Birth date: December 20, 1904–January 30, 1912; September 4–November 12, 1912; February 15–May 27, 1988; December 2, 1988–April 1, 1995; June 9, 1995–January 12, 1996. This generation will challenge traditions with the help of electronic gadgets. In these years, we got organized with the help of technology put to practical use. Great leaders, who were movers and shakers of history, like Julius Caesar and Henry VIII, were born under this placement.

Uranus in Aquarius—The Innovators

Birth date: January 30–September 4, 1912; November 12, 1912–April 1, 1919; August 16, 1919–January 22, 1920; April 1,–June 9, 1995; January 12, 1996 through the end of this century. The last generation with this placement produced great innovative minds such as Leonard Bernstein and Orson Welles. The next will become another radical breakthrough generation, much concerned with global issues that involve all humanity. Intuition, innovation, and sudden changes will surprise everyone when Uranus is in its home sign. This will be a time of experimentation on every level.

Uranus in Pisces—That's Entertainment

Birth date: April 1–August 16, 1919; January 22, 1920–March 31, 1927; November 4, 1927–January 12, 1928. In this century, Uranus in Pisces focused attention on the rise of electrical entertainment—radio and the cinema, and the secretiveness of Prohibition. This produced a generation of idealists exemplified by Judy Garland's theme, "Somewhere Over the Rainbow."

What You See Is Not What You Get With Neptune, Planet of Dreams, Imagination, Illusions

Under Neptune's influence, you see what you want to see. But Neptune also encourages you to create, letting your fantasies and daydreams run free. Neptune is often maligned as the planet of illusions, drugs, and alcohol, where you can't bear to face reality. But it also embodies the energy of glamour, subtlety, mystery, and mysticism, and governs anything that takes you out of the mundane world, including out-of-body experiences.

Neptune acts to break through your ordinary perceptions and take you to another level of reality, where you can experience either confusion or ecstasy. Neptune's force can pull you off course in the way this planet affects its neighbor, Uranus, but only if you allow this to happen. Those who use Neptune wisely can translate their daydreams into poetry, theater, design, or inspired moves in the business world, avoiding the tricky con-artist side of this planet.

Find your Neptune listed below:

Neptune in Cancer

Birth Date: July 19–December 25, 1901; May 21, 1902–September 23, 1914; December 14, 1914–July 19, 1915; March 19–May 2, 1916. Dreams of the homeland, idealistic patriotism, and glamorization of the nurturing assets of women are characterized this time. You who were born here have unusual psychic ability and deep insights into basic needs of others.

Neptune in Leo

Birth Date: September 23–December 14, 1914; July 19, 1915–March 19, 1916; May 2, 1916–September 21, 1928; February 19, 1929–July 24, 1929. This sign brought us the glamour of the 1920s and the big spenders, where gambling, seduction, theater, and lavish entertaining distracted from the realities of the age. Those born now have been part of a generation that made great advances in the arts.

Neptune in Virgo

Birth Date: September 21, 1928–February 19, 1929; July 24, 1929–October 3, 1942; April 17–August 2, 1943. Neptune in Virgo encompassed the Great Depression and World War II, while those born at this time later spread the gospel of health and fitness. This generation's devotion to spending hours at the office inspired the term "workaholic."

Neptune in Libra

Birth Date: October 3, 1942–April 17, 1943; August 2, 1943–December 24, 1955; March 12–October 19, 1956; June 15–August 6, 1957. Neptune in Libra was the romantic generation who would later be concerned with relating. As this generation matured, there was a new trend toward marriage and commitment. Racial and sexual equality became important issues, as they redesigned traditional roles to suit modern times.

Neptune in Scorpio

Birth Date: December 24, 1955–March 12, 1956; October 19, 1956–June 15, 1957; August 6, 1957–January 4, 1970; May 3–November 6, 1970. Neptune in Scorpio brought in a generation that would become interested in transformative power. Born in an era that glamorized sex, drugs, rock and roll, and Eastern religion, they matured in a more sobering time of AIDS, cocaine abuse, and New-Age spirituality. As they mature, they will become active in healing the planet from the results of the abuse of power.

Neptune in Sagittarius

Birth Date: January 4–May 3, 1970; November 6, 1970–January 19, 1984; June 23–November 21, 1984. Neptune in Sagittarius was the time when space and astronaut travel became a reality. The Neptune influence glamorized new approaches to mysticism, religion, and mind expansion. This generation will take a new approach to spiritual life, with emphasis on visions, mysticism, and clairvoyance.

Neptune in Capricorn

Birth Date: January 19, 1984–June 23, 1984; November 21, 1984–January 29, 1998. Neptune in Capricorn, which began in 1984 and will stay until 1998, brought a time when delusions about material power were first glamorized, then dashed on the rocks of reality. It was also a time when the psychic and occult worlds spawned a new category of business enterprise, and sold services on television.

Neptune in Aquarius

Birth Date: starting January 29, 1998 through the end of this century.

This should be a time of breakthroughs, when the creative influence of Neptune reaches a universal audience. This is a time of dissolving barriers, when we truly become one world.

Your Pluto Place Is the Power Spot!

To find out how someone handles power, look for the sign and house of Pluto. Because Pluto moves so slowly—only seven signs in this century—it reveals general trends for your whole generation. But if you know which house Pluto inhabits in a chart, you'll then know which area of life this little planet will pack a wallop in an individual's chart. Pluto tells you what makes your gang seem "cool" to each other, but uncool to the next generation. For example, the hedonistic rock-and-roll generation of Pluto in Leo *vs.* the workaholic Pluto in Virgo yuppies who came next.

Pluto brings our deep subconscious feelings to life

through painful probing. Nothing escapes—or is sacred—with Pluto. Because Pluto was discovered only recently, the signs of its exaltation and fall are debated. But in Scorpio, which Pluto rules, we have been able to witness this planet's fullest effect as it traveled through this sign from 1984 to 1995. Pluto symbolizes death and rebirth, the process of elimination, violence, and renewal.

Much of the strength of Pluto will depend on its position in your chart and the aspects it makes to other planets. The Pluto place in your horoscope is where you have invisible power (Mars governs the visible power), where you can transform, heal, and affect the unconscious needs of the masses. Though it is a tiny planet, its influence is great. When Pluto zaps a strategic point in your horoscope, you'll know it—your life is sure to change dramatically.

Pluto in Gemini (Late 1800s–May 28, 1914)

This is a time of mass suggestion and breakthroughs in communications, when many brilliant writers, such as Ernest Hemingway and F. Scott Fitzgerald, were born. Henry Miller, D. H. Lawrence, and James Joyce scandalized society by using explicit sexual images in their literature. "Muckraking" journalists exposed corruption. Pluto-ruled Scorpio President Theodore Roosevelt said, "Speak softly, but carry a big stick." This generation had an intense need to communicate and made major breakthroughs in knowledge. A compulsive restlessness and a thirst for a variety of experiences characterizes many of this generation.

Pluto in Cancer (May 28, 1914– June 14, 1939)

Dictators and mass media arose to wield emotional power over the masses. Women's rights was a popular issue. Deep sentimental feelings, acquisitiveness, and possessiveness characterized these times and people.

Pluto in Leo (June 14, 1939–August 19, 1957)

The performing arts played on the emotions of the masses. Mick Jagger, John Lennon, and rock and roll were born at this time. Those born here tend to be self-centered, powerful, and boisterous. This generation does its own thing, for better or for worse.

Pluto in Virgo (August 19, 1957–October 5, 1971; April 17, 1972–July 30, 1972)

This is the "yuppie" generation that sparked a mass movement toward fitness, health, and career. During this time, machines were invented to process detail work perfectly. Inventions took on a practical turn, as answering machines, fax machines, car phones, and home office equipment all contributed to transform the workplace.

Pluto in Libra (October 5, 1971–April 17, 1972; July 30, 1972–August 28, 1984)

People born at this time will be concerned with partnerships, working together, and finding diplomatic solutions to problems. Marriage is becoming redefined for these couples along more traditional, but equal-partnership lines. This was a time of women's liberation, gay rights, ERA, and legal battles over abortion, all of which transformed our ideas about relationships.

Pluto in Scorpio (August 28, 1984–January 17, 1995)

Pluto was in its ruling sign for a comparatively short period of time. In 1989, it was at its perihelion, or closest point to the sun and Earth. We have all felt the transforming power somewhere in our lives. This was a time of record achievements, destructive sexually transmitted diseases, nuclear power controversies, and explosive political issues. Pluto destroys in order to create new understanding—the phoenix rising from the ashes, which should be some consolation for those of you who have felt Pluto's force before 1995. Sexual shockers were par for the course during these intense years, when black clothing, transvestites, body piercing, tattoos, and sexually explicit advertising pushed the boundaries of good taste.

Pluto in Sagittarius (January 17, 1995 through the end of the century)

During our current Pluto transit, we'll be pushed to expand our horizons. For many of us, this will mean rolling down the information superhighway into the future. It signals a time of spiritual emphasis, when religion will exert much power in our political life as well. Since this is the sign that rules travel, there's a good possibility that Pluto, the planet of extremes, will make space travel a reality for some of us. Discovery of life on Mars, traveling here in meteors, could transform our ideas about where we came from. New dimensions in electronic publishing, concern with animal rights and the environment, and an increasing emphasis on extreme forms of religion could signal this period. We'll be developing far-reaching philosophies designed to elevate our lives with a new sense of purpose.

Look Up Your Planets

The following tables are provided so that you can look up the signs of seven major planets—Venus, Mars, Saturn, Jupiter, Uranus, Neptune, and Pluto. We do not have room for tables for the moon and Mercury, which change signs often.

How to Use the Venus Table

Find the year of your birth in the vertical column on the left, then follow across the page until you find the correct date. Your Venus sign is at the top of that column.

VENUS SIGNS 1901–2000

	Aries	Taurus	Gemini	Cancer	Leo	Virgo
1901	3/29–4/22	4/22–5/17	5/17–6/10	6/10–7/5	7/5–7/29	7/29–8/23
1902	5/7–6/3	6/3–6/30	6/30–7/25	7/25–8/19	8/19–9/13	9/13–10/7
1903	2/28–3/24	3/24–4/18	4/18–5/13	5/13–6/9	6/9–7/7	7/7–8/17
						9/6–11/8
1904	3/13–5/7	5/7–6/1	6/1–6/25	6/25–7/19	7/19–8/13	8/13–9/6
1905	2/3–3/6	3/6–4/9	7/8–8/6	8/6–9/1	9/1–9/27	9/27–10/21
	4/9–5/28	5/28–7/8				
1906	3/1–4/7	4/7–5/2	5/2–5/26	5/26–6/20	6/20–7/16	7/16–8/11
1907	4/27–5/22	5/22–6/16	6/16–7/11	7/11–8/4	8/4–8/29	8/29–9/22
1908	2/14–3/10	3/10–4/5	4/5–5/5	5/5–9/8	9/8–10/8	10/8–11/3
1909	3/29–4/22	4/22–5/16	5/16–6/10	6/10–7/4	7/4–7/29	7/29–8/23
1910	5/7–6/3	6/4–6/29	6/30–7/24	7/25–8/18	8/19–9/12	9/13–10/6
1911	2/28–3/23	3/24–4/17	4/18–5/12	5/13–6/8	6/9–7/7	7/8–11/8
1912	4/13–5/6	5/7–5/31	6/1–6/24	6/24–7/18	7/19–8/12	8/13–9/5
1913	2/3–3/6	3/7–5/1	7/8–8/5	8/6–8/31	9/1–9/26	9/27–10/20
	5/2–5/30	5/31–7/7				
1914	3/14–4/6	4/7–5/1	5/2–5/25	5/26–6/19	6/20–7/15	7/16–8/10
1915	4/27–5/21	5/22–6/15	6/16–7/10	7/11–8/3	8/4–8/28	8/29–9/21
1916	2/14–3/9	3/10–4/5	4/6–5/5	5/6–9/8	9/9–10/7	10/8–11/2
1917	3/29–4/21	4/22–5/15	5/16–6/9	6/10–7/3	7/4–7/28	7/29–8/21
1918	5/7–6/2	6/3–6/28	6/29–7/24	7/25–8/18	8/19–9/11	9/12–10/5
1919	2/27–3/22	3/23–4/16	4/17–5/12	5/13–6/7	6/8–7/7	7/8–11/8
1920	4/12–5/6	5/7–5/30	5/31–6/23	6/24–7/18	7/19–8/11	8/12–9/4
1921	2/3–3/6	3/7–4/25	7/8–8/5	8/6–8/31	9/1–9/25	9/26–10/20
	4/26–6/1	6/2–7/7				
1922	3/13–4/6	4/7–4/30	5/1–5/25	5/26–6/19	6/20–7/14	7/15–8/9
1923	4/27–5/21	5/22–6/14	6/15–7/9	7/10–8/3	8/4–8/27	8/28–9/20
1924	2/13–3/8	3/9–4/4	4/5–5/5	5/6–9/8	9/9–10/7	10/8–11/12
1925	3/28–4/20	4/21–5/15	5/16–6/8	6/9–7/3	7/4–7/27	7/28–8/21

85

Libra	Scorpio	Sagittarius	Capricorn	Aquarius	Pisces
8/23–9/17	9/17–10/12	10/12–1/16	1/16–2/9	2/9	3/5–3/29
			11/7–12/5	12/5–1/11	
10/7–10/31	10/31–11/24	11/24–12/18	12/18–1/11	2/6–4/4	1/11–2/6
					4/4–5/7
8/17–9/6	12/9–1/5			1/11–2/4	2/4–2/28
11/8–12/9					
9/6–9/30	9/30–10/25	1/5–1/30	1/30–2/24	2/24–3/19	3/19–4/13
		10/25–11/18	11/18–12/13	12/13–1/7	
10/21–11/14	11/14–12/8	12/8–1/1/06			1/7–2/3
8/11–9/7	9/7–10/9	10/9–12/15	1/1–1/25	1/25–2/18	2/18–3/14
	12/15–12/25	12/25–2/6			
9/22–10/16	10/16–11/9	11/9–12/3	2/6–3/6	3/6–4/2	4/2–4/27
			12/3–12/27	12/27–1/20	
11/3–11/28	11/28–12/22	12/22–1/15			1/20–2/4
8/23–9/17	9/17–10/12	10/12–11/17	1/15–2/9	2/9–3/5	3/5–3/29
			11/17–12/5	12/5–1/15	
10/7–10/30	10/31–11/23	11/24–12/17	12/18–12/31	1/1–1/15	1/16–1/28
				1/29–4/4	4/5–5/6
11/19–12/8	12/9–12/31		1/1–1/10	1/11–2/2	2/3–2/27
9/6–9/30	1/1–1/4	1/5–1/29	1/30–2/23	2/24–3/18	3/19–4/12
	10/1–10/24	10/25–11/17	11/18–12/12	12/13–12/31	
10/21–11/13	11/14–12/7	12/8–12/31		1/1–1/6	1/7–2/2
8/11–9/6	9/7–10/9	10/10–12/5	1/1–1/24	1/25–2/17	2/18–3/13
	12/6–12/30	12/31			
9/22–10/15	10/16–11/8	1/1–2/6	2/7–3/6	3/7–4/1	4/2–4/26
		11/9–12/2	12/3–12/26	12/27–12/31	
11/3–11/27	11/28–12/21	12/22–12/31		1/1–1/19	1/20–2/13
8/22–9/16	9/17–10/11	1/1–1/14	1/15–2/7	2/8–3/4	3/5–3/28
		10/12–11/6	11/7–12/5	12/6–12/31	
10/6–10/29	10/30–11/22	11/23–12/16	12/17–12/31	1/1–4/5	4/6–5/6
11/9–12/8	12/9–12/31		1/1–1/9	1/10–2/2	2/3–2/26
9/5–9/30	1/1–1/3	1/4–1/28	1/29–2/22	2/23–3/18	3/19–4/11
	9/31–10/23	10/24–11/17	11/18–12/11	12/12–12/31	
10/21–11/13	11/14–12/7	12/8–12/31		1/1–1/6	1/7–2/2
8/10–9/6	9/7–10/10	10/11–11/28	1/1–1/24	1/25–2/16	2/17–3/12
	11/29–12/31				
9/21–10/14	1/1	1/2–2/6	2/7–3/5	3/6–3/31	4/1–4/26
	10/15–11/7	11/8–12/1	12/2–12/25	12/26–12/31	
11/13–11/26	11/27–12/21	12/22–12/31		1/1–1/19	1/20–2/12
8/22–9/15	9/16–10/11	1/1–1/14	1/15–2/7	2/8–3/3	3/4–3/27
		10/12–11/6	11/7–12/5	12/6–12/31	

VENUS SIGNS 1901–2000

	Aries	Taurus	Gemini	Cancer	Leo	Virgo
1926	5/7–6/2	6/3–6/28	6/29–7/23	7/24–8/17	8/18–9/11	9/12–10/5
1927	2/27–3/22	3/23–4/16	4/17–5/11	5/12–6/7	6/8–7/7	7/8–11/9
1928	4/12–5/5	5/6–5/29	5/30–6/23	6/24–7/17	7/18–8/11	8/12–9/4
1929	2/3–3/7 4/20–6/2	3/8–4/19 6/3–7/7	7/8–8/4	8/5–8/30	8/31–9/25	9/26–10/19
1930	3/13–4/5	4/6–4/30	5/1–5/24	5/25–6/18	6/19–7/14	7/15–8/9
1931	4/26–5/20	5/21–6/13	6/14–7/8	7/9–8/2	8/3–8/26	8/27–9/19
1932	2/12–3/8	3/9–4/3	4/4–5/5 7/13–7/27	5/6–7/12 7/28–9/8	9/9–10/6	10/7–11/1
1933	3/27–4/19	4/20–5/28	5/29–6/8	6/9–7/2	7/3–7/26	7/27–8/20
1934	5/6–6/1	6/2–6/27	6/28–7/22	7/23–8/16	8/17–9/10	9/11–10/4
1935	2/26–3/21	3/22–4/15	4/16–5/10	5/11–6/6	6/7–7/6	7/7–11/8
1936	4/11–5/4	5/5–5/28	5/29–6/22	6/23–7/16	7/17–8/10	8/11–9/4
1937	2/2–3/8 4/14–6/3	3/9–4/17 6/4–7/6	7/7–8/3	8/4–8/29	8/30–9/24	9/25–10/18
1938	3/12–4/4	4/5–4/28	4/29–5/23	5/24–6/18	6/19–7/13	7/14–8/8
1939	4/25–5/19	5/20–6/13	6/14–7/8	7/9–8/1	8/2–8/25	8/26–9/19
1940	2/12–3/7	3/8–4/3	4/4–5/5 7/5–7/31	5/6–7/4 8/1–9/8	9/9–10/5	10/6–10/31
1941	3/27–4/19	4/20–5/13	5/14–6/6	6/7–7/1	7/2–7/26	7/27–8/20
1942	5/6–6/1	6/2–6/26	6/27–7/22	7/23–8/16	8/17–9/9	9/10–10/3
1943	2/25–3/20	3/21–4/14	4/15–5/10	5/11–6/6	6/7–7/6	7/7–11/8
1944	4/10–5/3	5/4–5/28	5/29–6/21	6/22–7/16	7/17–8/9	8/10–9/2
1945	2/2–3/10 4/7–6/3	3/11–4/6 6/4–7/6	7/7–8/3	8/4–8/29	8/30–9/23	9/24–10/18
1946	3/11–4/4	4/5–4/28	4/29–5/23	5/24–6/17	6/18–7/12	7/13–8/8
1947	4/25–5/19	5/20–6/12	6/13–7/7	7/8–8/1	8/2–8/25	8/26–9/18
1948	2/11–3/7	3/8–4/3	4/4–5/6 6/29–8/2	5/7–6/28 8/3–9/7	9/8–10/5	10/6–10/31
1949	3/26–4/19	4/20–5/13	5/14–6/6	6/7–6/30	7/1–7/25	7/26–8/19
1950	5/5–5/31	6/1–6/26	6/27–7/21	7/22–8/15	8/16–9/9	9/10–10/3
1951	2/25–3/21	3/22–4/15	4/16–5/10	5/11–6/6	6/7–7/7	7/8–11/9

Libra	Scorpio	Sagittarius	Capricorn	Aquarius	Pisces
10/6–10/29	10/30–11/22	11/23–12/16	12/17–12/31	1/1–4/5	4/6–5/6
11/10–12/8	12/9–12/31	1/1–1/7	1/8	1/9–2/1	2/2–2/26
9/5–9/28	1/1–1/3	1/4–1/28	1/29–2/22	2/23–3/17	3/18–4/11
	9/29–10/23	10/24–11/16	11/17–12/11	12/12–12/31	
10/20–11/12	11/13–12/6	12/7–12/30	12/31	1/1–1/5	1/6–2/2
8/10–9/6	9/7–10/11	10/12–11/21	1/1–1/23	1/24–2/16	2/17–3/12
	11/22–12/19				
9/20–10/13	1/1–1/3	1/4–2/6	2/7–3/4	3/5–3/31	4/1–4/25
	10/14–11/6	11/7–11/30	12/1–12/24	12/25–12/31	
11/2–11/25	11/26–12/20	12/21–12/31		1/1–1/18	1/19–2/11
8/21–9/14	9/15–10/10	1/1–1/13	1/14–2/6	2/7–3/2	3/3–3/26
		10/11–11/5	11/6–12/4	12/5–12/31	
10/5–10/28	10/29–11/21	11/22–12/15	12/16–12/31	1/1–4/5	4/6–5/5
11/9–12/7	12/8–12/31		1/1–1/7	1/8–1/31	2/1–2/25
9/5–9/27	1/1–1/2	1/3–1/27	1/28–2/21	2/22–3/16	3/17–4/10
	9/28–10/22	10/23–11/15	11/16–12/10	12/11–12/31	
10/19–11/11	11/12–12/5	12/6–12/29	12/30–12/31	1/1–1/5	1/6–2/1
8/9–9/6	9/7–10/13	10/14–11/14	1/1–1/22	1/23–2/15	2/16–3/11
	11/15–12/31				
9/20–10/13	1/1–1/3	1/4–2/5	2/6–3/4	3/5–3/30	3/31–4/24
	10/14–11/6	11/7–11/30	12/1–12/24	12/25–12/31	
11/1–11/25	11/26–12/19	12/20–12/31		1/1–1/18	1/19–2/11
8/21–9/14	9/15–10/9	1/1–1/12	1/13–2/5	2/6–3/1	3/2–3/26
		10/10–11/5	11/6–12/4	12/5–12/31	
10/4–10/27	10/28–11/20	11/21–12/14	12/15–12/31	1/1–4/4	4/6–5/5
11/9–12/7	12/8–12/31		1/1–1/7	1/8–1/31	2/1–2/24
9/3–9/27	1/1–1/2	1/3–1/27	1/28–2/20	2/21–3/16	3/17–4/9
	9/28–10/21	10/22–11/15	11/16–12/10	12/11–12/31	
10/19–11/11	11/12–12/5	12/6–12/29	12/30–12/31	1/1–1/4	1/5–2/1
8/9–9/6	9/7–10/15	10/16–11/7	1/1–1/21	1/22–2/14	2/15–3/10
	11/8–12/31				
9/19–10/12	1/1–1/4	1/5–2/5	2/6–3/4	3/5–3/29	3/30–4/24
	10/13–11/5	11/6–11/29	11/30–12/23	12/24–12/31	
11/1–11/25	11/26–12/19	12/20–12/31		1/1–1/17	1/18–2/10
8/20–9/14	9/15–10/9	1/1–1/12	1/13–2/5	2/6–3/1	3/2–3/25
		10/10–11/5	11/6–12/5	12/6–12/31	
10/4–10/27	10/28–11/20	11/21–12/13	12/14–12/31	1/1–4/5	4/6–5/4
11/10–12/7	12/8–12/31		1/1–1/7	1/8–1/31	2/1–2/24

VENUS SIGNS 1901–2000

	Aries	Taurus	Gemini	Cancer	Leo	Virgo
1952	4/10–5/4	5/5–5/28	5/29–6/21	6/22–7/16	7/17–8/9	8/10–9/3
1953	2/2–3/13	3/4–3/31	7/8–8/3	8/4–8/29	8/30–9/24	9/25–10/18
	4/1–6/5	6/6–7/7				
1954	3/12–4/4	4/5–4/28	4/29–5/23	5/24–6/17	6/18–7/13	7/14–8/8
1955	4/25–5/19	5/20–6/13	6/14–7/7	7/8–8/1	8/2–8/25	8/26–9/18
1956	2/12–3/7	3/8–4/4	4/5–5/7	5/8–6/23	9/9–10/5	10/6–10/31
				6/24–8/4	8/5–9/8	
1957	3/26–4/19	4/20–5/13	5/14–6/6	6/7–7/1	7/2–7/26	7/7–8/19
1958	5/6–5/31	6/1–6/26	6/27–7/22	7/23–8/15	8/16–9/9	9/10–10/3
1959	2/25–3/20	3/21–4/14	4/15–5/10	5/11–6/6	6/7–7/8	7/9–9/20
					9/21–9/24	9/25–11/9
1960	4/10–5/3	5/4–5/28	5/29–6/21	6/22–7/15	7/16–8/9	8/10–9/2
1961	2/3–6/5	6/6–7/7	7/8–8/3	8/4–8/29	8/30–9/23	9/24–10/17
1962	3/11–4/3	4/4–4/28	4/29–5/22	5/23–6/17	6/18–7/12	7/13–8/8
1963	4/24–5/18	5/19–6/12	6/13–7/7	7/8–7/31	8/1–8/25	8/26–9/18
1964	2/11–3/7	3/8–4/4	4/5–5/9	5/10–6/17	9/9–10/5	10/6–10/31
				6/18–8/5	8/6–9/8	
1965	3/26–4/18	4/19–5/12	5/13–6/6	6/7–6/30	7/1–7/25	7/26–8/19
1966	5/6–6/31	6/1–6/26	6/27–7/21	7/22–8/15	8/16–9/8	9/9–10/2
1967	2/24–3/20	3/21–4/14	4/15–5/10	5/11–6/6	6/7–7/8	7/9–9/9
					9/10–10/1	10/2–11/9
1968	4/9–5/3	5/4–5/27	5/28–6/20	6/21–7/15	7/16–8/8	8/9–9/2
1969	2/3–6/6	6/7–7/6	7/7–8/3	8/4–8/28	8/29–9/22	9/23–10/17
1970	3/11–4/3	4/4–4/27	4/28–5/22	5/23–6/16	6/17–7/12	7/13–8/8
1971	4/24–5/18	5/19–6/12	6/13–7/6	7/7–7/31	8/1–8/24	8/25–9/17
1972	2/11–3/7	3/8–4/3	4/4–5/10	5/11–6/11		
			6/12–8/6	8/7–9/8	9/9–10/5	10/6–10/30
1973	3/25–4/18	4/18–5/12	5/13–6/5	6/6–6/29	7/1–7/25	7/26–8/19
1974						
	5/5–5/31	6/1–6/25	6/26–7/21	7/22–8/14	8/15–9/8	9/9–10/2
1975	2/24–3/20	3/21–4/13	4/14–5/9	5/10–6/6	6/7–7/9	7/10–9/2
					9/3–10/4	10/5–11/9

Libra	Scorpio	Sagittarius	Capricorn	Aquarius	Pisces
9/4–9/27	1/1–1/2	1/3–1/27	1/28–2/20	2/21–3/16	3/17–4/9
	9/28–10/21	10/22–11/15	11/16–12/10	12/11–12/31	
10/19–11/11	11/12–12/5	12/6–12/29	12/30–12/31	1/1–1/5	1/6–2/1
8/9–9/6	9/7–10/22	10/23–10/27	1/1–1/22	1/23–2/15	2/16–3/11
	10/28–12/31				
9/19–10/13	1/1–1/6	1/7–2/5	2/6–3/4	3/5–3/30	3/31–4/24
	10/14–11/5	11/6–11/30	12/1–12/24	12/25–12/31	
11/1–11/25	11/26–12/19	12/20–12/31		1/1–1/17	1/18–2/11
8/20–9/14	9/15–10/9	1/1–1/12	1/13–2/5	2/6–3/1	3/2–3/25
		10/10–11/5	11/6–12/16	12/7–12/31	
10/4–10/27	10/28–11/20	11/21–12/14	12/15–12/31	1/1–4/6	4/7–5/5
11/10–12/7	12/8–12/31		1/1–1/7	1/8–1/31	2/1–2/24
9/3–9/26	1/1–1/2	1/3–1/27	1/28–2/20	2/21–3/15	3/16–4/9
	9/27–10/21	10/22–11/15	11/16–12/10	12/11–12/31	
10/18–11/11	11/12–12/4	12/5–12/28	12/29–12/31	1/1–1/5	1/6–2/2
8/9–9/6	9/7–12/31		1/1–1/21	1/22–2/14	2/15–3/10
9/19–10/12	1/1–1/6	1/7–2/5	2/6–3/4	3/5–3/29	3/30–4/23
	10/13–11/5	11/6–11/29	11/30–12/23	12/24–12/31	
11/1–11/24	11/25–12/19	12/20–12/31		1/1–1/16	1/17–2/10
8/20–9/13	9/14–10/9	1/1–1/12	1/13–2/5	2/6–3/1	3/2–3/25
		10/10–11/5	11/6–12/7	12/8–12/31	
10/3–10/26	10/27–11/19	11/20–12/13	2/7–2/25	1/1–2/6	4/7–5/5
			12/14–12/31	2/26–4/6	
11/10–12/7	12/8–12/23		1/1–1/6	1/7–1/30	1/31–2/23
9/3–9/26	1/1	1/2–1/26	1/27–2/20	2/21–3/15	3/16–4/8
	9/27–10/21	10/22–11/14	11/15–12/9	12/10–12/31	
10/18–11/10	11/11–12/4	12/5–12/28	12/29–12/31	1/1–1/4	1/5–2/2
8/9–9/7	9/8–12/31		1/1–1/21	1/22–2/14	2/15–3/10
9/18–10/11	1/1–1/7	1/8–2/5	2/6–3/4	3/5–3/29	3/30–4/23
	10/12–11/5	11/6–11/29	11/30–12/23	12/24–12/31	
	11/25–12/18	12/19–12/31		1/1–1/16	1/17–2/10
10/31–11/24					
8/20–9/13		1/1–1/12	1/13–2/4	2/5–2/28	3/1–3/24
		10/9–11/5	11/6–12/7	12/8–12/31	
			1/30–2/28	1/1–1/29	
10/3–10/26	10/27–11/19	11/20–12/13	12/14–12/31	3/1–4/6	4/7–5/4
			1/1–1/6	1/7–1/30	1/31–2/23
11/10–12/7	12/8–12/31				

VENUS SIGNS 1901–2000

	Aries	Taurus	Gemini	Cancer	Leo	Virgo
1976	4/8–5/2	5/2–5/27	5/27–6/20	6/20–7/14	7/14–8/8	8/8–9/1
1977	2/2–6/6	6/6–7/6	7/6–8/2	8/2–8/28	8/28–9/22	9/22–10/17
1978	3/9–4/2	4/2–4/27	4/27–5/22	5/22–6/16	6/16–7/12	7/12–8/6
1979	4/23–5/18	5/18–6/11	6/11–7/6	7/6–7/30	7/30–8/24	8/24–9/17
1980	2/9–3/6	3/6–4/3	4/3–5/12 6/5–8/6	5/12–6/5 8/6–9/7	9/7–10/4	10/4–10/30
1981	3/24–4/17	4/17–5/11	5/11–6/5	6/5–6/29	6/29–7/24	7/24–8/18
1982	5/4–5/30	5/30–6/25	6/25–7/20	7/20–8/14	8/14–9/7	9/7–10/2
1983	2/22–3/19	3/19–4/13	4/13–5/9	5/9–6/6	6/6–7/10 8/27–10/5	7/10–8/27 10/5–11/9
1984	4/7–5/2	5/2–5/26	5/26–6/20	6/20–7/14	7/14–8/7	8/7–9/1
1985	2/2–6/6	6/8–7/6	7/6–8/2	8/2–8/28	8/28–9/22	9/22–10/16
1986	3/9–4/2	4/2–4/26	4/26–5/21	5/21–6/15	6/15–7/11	7/11–8/7
1987	4/22–5/17	5/17–6/11	6/11–7/5	7/5–7/30	7/30–8/23	8/23–9/16
1988	2/9–3/6	3/6–4/3	4/3–5/17 5/27–8/6	5/17–5/27 8/28–9/22	9/7–10/4 9/22–10/16	10/4–10/29
1989	3/23–4/16	4/16–5/11	5/11–6/4	6/4–6/29	6/29–7/24	7/24–8/18
1990	5/4–5/30	5/30–6/25	6/25–7/20	7/20–8/13	8/13–9/7	9/7–10/1
1991	2/22–3/18	3/18–4/13	4/13–5/9	5/9–6/6	6/6–7/11 8/21–10/6	7/11–8/21 10/6–11/9
1992	4/7–5/1	5/1–5/26	5/26–6/19	6/19–7/13	7/13–8/7	8/7–8/31
1993	2/2–6/6	6/6–7/6	7/6–8/1	8/1–8/27	8/27–9/21	9/21–10/16
1994	3/8–4/1	4/1–4/26	4/26–5/21	5/21–6/15	6/15–7/11	7/11–8/7
1995	4/22–5/16	5/16–6/10	6/10–7/5	7/5–7/29	7/29–8/23	8/23–9/16
1996	2/9–3/6	3/6–4/3	4/3–8/7	8/7–9/7	9/7–10/4	10/4–10/29
1997	3/23–4/16	4/16–5/10	5/10–6/4	6/4–6/28	6/28–7/23	7/23–8/17
1998	5/3–5/29	5/29–6/24	6/24–7/19	7/19–8/13	8/13–9/6	9/6–9/30
1999	2/21–3/18	3/18–4/12	4/12–5/8	5/8–6/5	6/5–7/12 8/15–10/7	7/12–8/15 10/7–11/9
2000	4/6–5/1	5/1–5/25	5/25–6/13	6/13–7/13	7/13–8/6	8/6–8/31

Libra	Scorpio	Sagittarius	Capricorn	Aquarius	Pisces
9/1–9/26	9/26–10/20	1/1–1/26	1/26–2/19	2/19–3/15	3/15–4/8
		10/20–11/14	11/14–12/6	12/9–1/4	
10/17–11/10	11/10–12/4	12/4–12/27	12/27–1/20		1/4–2/2
8/6–9/7	9/7–1/7			1/20–2/13	2/13–3/9
9/17–10/11	10/11–11/4	1/7–2/5	2/5–3/3	3/3–3/29	3/29–4/23
		11/4–11/28	11/28–12/22	12/22–1/16	
10/30–11/24	11/24–12/18	12/18–1/11			1/16–2/9
8/18–9/12	9/12–10/9	10/9–11/5	1/11–2/4	2/4–2/28	2/28–3/24
			11/5–12/8	12/8–1/23	
10/2–10/26	10/26–11/18	11/18–12/12	1/23–3/2	3/2–4/6	4/6–5/4
			12/12–1/5		
11/9–12/6	12/6–1/1			1/5–1/29	1/29–2/22
9/1–9/25	9/25–10/20	1/1–1/25	1/25–2/19	2/19–3/14	3/14–4/7
		10/20–11/13	11/13–12/9		
10/16–11/9	11/9–12/3	12/3–12/27			1/4–2/2
8/7–9/7	9/7–1/7			1/20–3/13	2/13–3/9
9/16–10/10	10/10–11/3	1/7–2/5	2/5–3/3	3/3–3/28	3/28–4/22
		11/3–11/28	11/28–12/22	12/22–1/15	
10/29–11/23	11/23–12/17	12/17–1/10			1/15–2/9
8/18–9/12	9/12–10/8	10/8–11/5	1/10–2/3	2/3–2/27	2/27–3/23
			11/5–12/10	12/10–1/16	
10/1–10/25	10/25–11/18	11/18–12/12	1/16–3/3	3/3–4/6	4/6–5/4
			12/12–1/5		
8/21–12/6	12/6–12/31	12/21–1/25/92		1/5–1/29	1/29–2/22
8/31–9/25	9/25–10/19	10/19–11/13	1/25–2/18	2/18–3/13	3/13–4/7
			11/13–12/8	12/8–1/3	
10/16–11/9	11/9–12/2	12/2–12/26	12/26–1/19		1/3–2/2
8/7–9/7	9/7–1/7			1/19–2/12	2/12–3/8
9/16–10/10	10/10–11/13	1/7–2/4	2/4–3/2	3/2–3/28	3/28–4/22
		11/3–11/27	11/27–12/21	12/21–1/15	
10/29–11/23	11/23–12/17	12/17–1/10/97			1/15–2/9
8/17–9/12	9/12–10/8	10/8–11/5	1/10–2/3	2/3–2/27	2/27–3/23
			11/5–12/12	12/12–1/9	
9/30–10/24	10/24–11/17	11/17–12/11	1/9–3/4	3/4–4/6	4/6–5/3
11/9–12/5	12/5–12/31	12/31–1/24		1/4–1/28	1/28–2/21
8/31–9/24	9/24–10/19	10/19–11/13	1/24–2/18	2/18–3/12	3/13–4/6
			11/13–12/8	12/8	

How to Use the Mars, Jupiter, and Saturn Tables

Find the year of your birth on the left side of each column. The dates when the planet entered each sign are listed on the right side of each column. (Signs are abbreviated to the first three letters.) Your birthday should fall on or between each date listed, and your planetary placement should correspond to the earlier sign of that period.

MARS SIGN 1901–2000

1901	MAR	1	Leo	1905	JAN	13	Scp
	MAY	11	Vir		AUG	21	Sag
	JUL	13	Lib		OCT	8	Cap
	AUG	31	Scp		NOV	18	Aqu
	OCT	14	Sag		DEC	27	Pic
	NOV	24	Cap	1906	FEB	4	Ari
1902	JAN	1	Aqu		MAR	17	Tau
	FEB	8	Pic		APR	28	Gem
	MAR	19	Ari		JUN	11	Can
	APR	27	Tau		JUL	27	Leo
	JUN	7	Gem		SEP	12	Vir
	JUL	20	Can		OCT	30	Lib
	SEP	4	Leo		DEC	17	Scp
	OCT	23	Vir	1907	FEB	5	Sag
	DEC	20	Lib		APR	1	Cap
1903	APR	19	Vir		OCT	13	Aqu
	MAY	30	Lib		NOV	29	Pic
	AUG	6	Scp	1908	JAN	11	Ari
	SEP	22	Sag		FEB	23	Tau
	NOV	3	Cap		APR	7	Gem
	DEC	12	Aqu		MAY	22	Can
1904	JAN	19	Pic		JUL	8	Leo
	FEB	27	Ari		AUG	24	Vir
	APR	6	Tau		OCT	10	Lib
	MAY	18	Gem		NOV	25	Scp
	JUN	30	Can	1909	JAN	10	Sag
	AUG	15	Leo		FEB	24	Cap
	OCT	1	Vir		APR	9	Aqu
	NOV	20	Lib		MAY	25	Pic

	JUL	21	Ari
	SEP	26	Pic
	NOV	20	Ari
1910	JAN	23	Tau
	MAR	14	Gem
	MAY	1	Can
	JUN	19	Leo
	AUG	6	Vir
	SEP	22	Lib
	NOV	6	Scp
	DEC	20	Sag
1911	JAN	31	Cap
	MAR	14	Aqu
	APR	23	Pic
	JUN	2	Ari
	JUL	15	Tau
	SEP	5	Gem
	NOV	30	Tau
1912	JAN	30	Gem
	APR	5	Can
	MAY	28	Leo
	JUL	17	Vir
	SEP	2	Lib
	OCT	18	Scp
	NOV	30	Sag
1913	JAN	10	Cap
	FEB	19	Aqu
	MAR	30	Pic
	MAY	8	Ari
	JUN	17	Tau
	JUL	29	Gem
	SEP	15	Can
1914	MAY	1	Leo
	JUN	26	Vir
	AUG	14	Lib
	SEP	29	Scp
	NOV	11	Sag
	DEC	22	Cap
1915	JAN	30	Aqu
	MAR	9	Pic
	APR	16	Ari
	MAY	26	Tau
	JUL	6	Gem
	AUG	19	Can
	OCT	7	Leo
1916	MAY	28	Vir
	JUL	23	Lib
	SEP	8	Scp
	OCT	22	Sag
	DEC	1	Cap
1917	JAN	9	Aqu
	FEB	16	Pic
	MAR	26	Ari
	MAY	4	Tau
	JUN	14	Gem
	JUL	28	Can
	SEP	12	Leo
	NOV	2	Vir
1918	JAN	11	Lib
	FEB	25	Vir
	JUN	23	Lib
	AUG	17	Scp
	OCT	1	Sag
	NOV	11	Cap
	DEC	20	Aqu
1919	JAN	27	Pic
	MAR	6	Ari
	APR	15	Tau
	MAY	26	Gem
	JUL	8	Can
	AUG	23	Leo
	OCT	10	Vir
	NOV	30	Lib
1920	JAN	31	Scp
	APR	23	Lib
	JUL	10	Scp
	SEP	4	Sag
	OCT	18	Cap
	NOV	27	Aqu
1921	JAN	5	Pic
	FEB	13	Ari
	MAR	25	Tau
	MAY	6	Gem
	JUN	18	Can
	AUG	3	Leo
	SEP	19	Vir

	NOV	6	Lib		APR	7	Pic
	DEC	26	Scp		MAY	16	Ari
1922	FEB	18	Sag		JUN	26	Tau
	SEP	13	Cap		AUG	9	Gem
	OCT	30	Aqu		OCT	3	Can
	DEC	11	Pic		DEC	20	Gem
1923	JAN	21	Ari	1929	MAR	10	Can
	MAR	4	Tau		MAY	13	Leo
	APR	16	Gem		JUL	4	Vir
	MAY	30	Can		AUG	21	Lib
	JUL	16	Leo		OCT	6	Scp
	SEP	1	Vir		NOV	18	Sag
	OCT	18	Lib		DEC	29	Cap
	DEC	4	Scp	1930	FEB	6	Aqu
1924	JAN	19	Sag		MAR	17	Pic
	MAR	6	Cap		APR	24	Ari
	APR	24	Aqu		JUN	3	Tau
	JUN	24	Pic		JUL	14	Gem
	AUG	24	Aqu		AUG	28	Can
	OCT	19	Pic		OCT	20	Leo
	DEC	19	Ari	1931	FEB	16	Can
1925	FEB	5	Tau		MAR	30	Leo
	MAR	24	Gem		JUN	10	Vir
	MAY	9	Can		AUG	1	Lib
	JUN	26	Leo		SEP	17	Scp
	AUG	12	Vir		OCT	30	Sag
	SEP	28	Lib		DEC	10	Cap
	NOV	13	Scp	1932	JAN	18	Aqu
	DEC	28	Sag		FEB	25	Pic
1926	FEB	9	Cap		APR	3	Ari
	MAR	23	Aqu		MAY	12	Tau
	MAY	3	Pic		JUN	22	Gem
	JUN	15	Ari		AUG	4	Can
	AUG	1	Tau		SEP	20	Leo
1927	FEB	22	Gem		NOV	13	Vir
	APR	17	Can	1933	JUL	6	Lib
	JUN	6	Leo		AUG	26	Scp
	JUL	25	Vir		OCT	9	Sag
	SEP	10	Lib		NOV	19	Cap
	OCT	26	Scp		DEC	28	Aqu
	DEC	8	Sag	1934	FEB	4	Pic
1928	JAN	19	Cap		MAR	14	Ari
	FEB	28	Aqu		APR	22	Tau

	JUN	2	Gem		AUG	19	Vir
	JUL	15	Can		OCT	5	Lib
	AUG	30	Leo		NOV	20	Scp
	OCT	18	Vir	1941	JAN	4	Sag
	DEC	11	Lib		FEB	17	Cap
1935	JUL	29	Scp		APR	2	Aqu
	SEP	16	Sag		MAY	16	Pic
	OCT	28	Cap		JUL	2	Ari
	DEC	7	Aqu	1942	JAN	11	Tau
1936	JAN	14	Pic		MAR	7	Gem
	FEB	22	Ari		APR	26	Can
	APR	1	Tau		JUN	14	Leo
	MAY	13	Gem		AUG	1	Vir
	JUN	25	Can		SEP	17	Lib
	AUG	10	Leo		NOV	1	Scp
	SEP	26	Vir		DEC	15	Sag
	NOV	14	Lib	1943	JAN	26	Cap
1937	JAN	5	Scp		MAR	8	Aqu
	MAR	13	Sag		APR	17	Pic
	MAY	14	Scp		MAY	27	Ari
	AUG	8	Sag		JUL	7	Tau
	SEP	30	Cap		AUG	23	Gem
	NOV	11	Aqu	1944	MAR	28	Can
	DEC	21	Pic		MAY	22	Leo
1938	JAN	30	Ari		JUL	12	Vir
	MAR	12	Tau		AUG	29	Lib
	APR	23	Gem		OCT	13	Scp
	JUN	7	Can		NOV	25	Sag
	JUL	22	Leo	1945	JAN	5	Cap
	SEP	7	Vir		FEB	14	Aqu
	OCT	25	Lib		MAR	25	Pic
	DEC	11	Scp		MAY	2	Ari
1939	JAN	29	Sag		JUN	11	Tau
	MAR	21	Cap		JUL	23	Gem
	MAY	25	Aqu		SEP	7	Can
	JUL	21	Cap		NOV	11	Leo
	SEP	24	Aqu		DEC	26	Can
	NOV	19	Pic	1946	APR	22	Leo
1940	JAN	4	Ari		JUN	20	Vir
	FEB	17	Tau		AUG	9	Lib
	APR	1	Gem		SEP	24	Scp
	MAY	17	Can		NOV	6	Sag
	JUL	3	Leo		DEC	17	Cap

Year	Mon	Day	Sign		Year	Mon	Day	Sign
1947	JAN	25	Aqu			MAR	20	Tau
	MAR	4	Pic			MAY	1	Gem
	APR	11	Ari			JUN	14	Can
	MAY	21	Tau			JUL	29	Leo
	JUL	1	Gem			SEP	14	Vir
	AUG	13	Can			NOV	1	Lib
	OCT	1	Leo			DEC	20	Scp
	DEC	1	Vir		1954	FEB	9	Sag
1948	FEB	12	Leo			APR	12	Cap
	MAY	18	Vir			JUL	3	Sag
	JUL	17	Lib			AUG	24	Cap
	SEP	3	Scp			OCT	21	Aqu
	OCT	17	Sag			DEC	4	Pic
	NOV	26	Cap		1955	JAN	15	Ari
1949	JAN	4	Aqu			FEB	26	Tau
	FEB	11	Pic			APR	10	Gem
	MAR	21	Ari			MAY	26	Can
	APR	30	Tau			JUL	11	Leo
	JUN	10	Gem			AUG	27	Vir
	JUL	23	Can			OCT	13	Lib
	SEP	7	Leo			NOV	29	Scp
	OCT	27	Vir		1956	JAN	14	Sag
	DEC	26	Lib			FEB	28	Cap
1950	MAR	28	Vir			APR	14	Aqu
	JUN	11	Lib			JUN	3	Pic
	AUG	10	Scp			DEC	6	Ari
	SEP	25	Sag		1957	JAN	28	Tau
	NOV	6	Cap			MAR	17	Gem
	DEC	15	Aqu			MAY	4	Can
1951	JAN	22	Pic			JUN	21	Leo
	MAR	1	Ari			AUG	8	Vir
	APR	10	Tau			SEP	24	Lib
	MAY	21	Gem			NOV	8	Scp
	JUL	3	Can			DEC	23	Sag
	AUG	18	Leo		1958	FEB	3	Cap
	OCT	5	Vir			MAR	17	Aqu
	NOV	24	Lib			APR	27	Pic
1952	JAN	20	Scp			JUN	7	Ari
	AUG	27	Sag			JUL	21	Tau
	OCT	12	Cap			SEP	21	Gem
	NOV	21	Aqu			OCT	29	Tau
	DEC	30	Pic		1959	FEB	10	Gem
1953	FEB	8	Ari			APR	10	Can

	JUN	1	Leo
	JUL	20	Vir
	SEP	5	Lib
	OCT	21	Scp
	DEC	3	Sag
1960	JAN	14	Cap
	FEB	23	Aqu
	APR	2	Pic
	MAY	11	Ari
	JUN	20	Tau
	AUG	2	Gem
	SEP	21	Can
1961	FEB	5	Gem
	FEB	7	Can
	MAY	6	Leo
	JUN	28	Vir
	AUG	17	Lib
	OCT	1	Scp
	NOV	13	Sag
	DEC	24	Cap
1962	FEB	1	Aqu
	MAR	12	Pic
	APR	19	Ari
	MAY	28	Tau
	JUL	9	Gem
	AUG	22	Can
	OCT	11	Leo
1963	JUN	3	Vir
	JUL	27	Lib
	SEP	12	Scp
	OCT	25	Sag
	DEC	5	Cap
1964	JAN	13	Aqu
	FEB	20	Pic
	MAR	29	Ari
	MAY	7	Tau
	JUN	17	Gem
	JUL	30	Can
	SEP	15	Leo
	NOV	6	Vir
1965	JUN	29	Lib
	AUG	20	Scp
	OCT	4	Sag
	NOV	14	Cap
	DEC	23	Aqu
1966	JAN	30	Pic
	MAR	9	Ari
	APR	17	Tau
	MAY	28	Gem
	JUL	11	Can
	AUG	25	Leo
	OCT	12	Vir
	DEC	4	Lib
1967	FEB	12	Scp
	MAR	31	Lib
	JUL	19	Scp
	SEP	10	Sag
	OCT	23	Cap
	DEC	1	Aqu
1968	JAN	9	Pic
	FEB	17	Ari
	MAR	27	Tau
	MAY	8	Gem
	JUN	21	Can
	AUG	5	Leo
	SEP	21	Vir
	NOV	9	Lib
	DEC	29	Scp
1969	FEB	25	Sag
	SEP	21	Cap
	NOV	4	Aqu
	DEC	15	Pic
1970	JAN	24	Ari
	MAR	7	Tau
	APR	18	Gem
	JUN	2	Can
	JUL	18	Leo
	SEP	3	Vir
	OCT	20	Lib
	DEC	6	Scp
1971	JAN	23	Sag
	MAR	12	Cap
	MAY	3	Aqu
	NOV	6	Pic
	DEC	26	Ari
1972	FEB	10	Tau

	MAR	27	Gem	1978	JAN	26	Can
	MAY	12	Can		APR	10	Leo
	JUN	28	Leo		JUN	14	Vir
	AUG	15	Vir		AUG	4	Lib
	SEP	30	Lib		SEP	19	Scp
	NOV	15	Scp		NOV	2	Sag
	DEC	30	Sag		DEC	12	Cap
1973	FEB	12	Cap	1979	JAN	20	Aqu
	MAR	26	Aqu		FEB	27	Pic
	MAY	8	Pic		APR	7	Ari
	JUN	20	Ari		MAY	16	Tau
	AUG	12	Tau		JUN	26	Gem
	OCT	29	Ari		AUG	8	Can
	DEC	24	Tau		SEP	24	Leo
1974	FEB	27	Gem		NOV	19	Vir
	APR	20	Can	1980	MAR	11	Leo
	JUN	9	Leo		MAY	4	Vir
	JUL	27	Vir		JUL	10	Lib
	SEP	12	Lib		AUG	29	Scp
	OCT	28	Scp		OCT	12	Sag
	DEC	10	Sag		NOV	22	Cap
1975	JAN	21	Cap		DEC	30	Aqu
	MAR	3	Aqu	1981	FEB	6	Pic
	APR	11	Pic		MAR	17	Ari
	MAY	21	Ari		APR	25	Tau
	JUL	1	Tau		JUN	5	Gem
	AUG	14	Gem		JUL	18	Can
	OCT	17	Can		SEP	2	Leo
	NOV	25	Gem		OCT	21	Vir
1976	MAR	18	Can		DEC	16	Lib
	MAY	16	Leo	1982	AUG	3	Scp
	JUL	6	Vir		SEP	20	Sag
	AUG	24	Lib		OCT	31	Cap
	OCT	8	Scp		DEC	10	Aqu
	NOV	20	Sag	1983	JAN	17	Pic
1977	JAN	1	Cap		FEB	25	Ari
	FEB	9	Aqu		APR	5	Tau
	MAR	20	Pic		MAY	16	Gem
	APR	27	Ari		JUN	29	Can
	JUN	6	Tau		AUG	13	Leo
	JUL	17	Gem		SEP	30	Vir
	SEP	1	Can		NOV	18	Lib
	OCT	26	Leo	1984	JAN	11	Scp

	AUG	17	Sag		JUL	12	Tau
	OCT	5	Cap		AUG	31	Gem
	NOV	15	Aqu		DEC	14	Tau
	DEC	25	Pic	1991	JAN	21	Gem
1985	FEB	2	Ari		APR	3	Can
	MAR	15	Tau		MAY	26	Leo
	APR	26	Gem		JUL	15	Vir
	JUN	9	Can		SEP	1	Lib
	JUL	25	Leo		OCT	16	Scp
	SEP	10	Vir		NOV	29	Sag
	OCT	27	Lib	1992	JAN	9	Cap
	DEC	14	Scp		FEB	18	Aqu
1986	FEB	2	Sag		MAR	28	Pic
	MAR	28	Cap		MAY	5	Ari
	OCT	9	Aqu		JUN	14	Tau
	NOV	26	Pic		JUL	26	Gem
1987	JAN	8	Ari		SEP	12	Can
	FEB	20	Tau	1993	APR	27	Leo
	APR	5	Gem		JUN	23	Vir
	MAY	21	Can		AUG	12	Lib
	JUL	6	Leo		SEP	27	Scp
	AUG	22	Vir		NOV	9	Sag
	OCT	8	Lib		DEC	20	Cap
	NOV	24	Scp	1994	JAN	28	Aqu
1988	JAN	8	Sag		MAR	7	Pic
	FEB	22	Cap		APR	14	Ari
	APR	6	Aqu		MAY	23	Tau
	MAY	22	Pic		JUL	3	Gem
	JUL	13	Ari		AUG	16	Can
	OCT	23	Pic		OCT	4	Leo
	NOV	1	Ari		DEC	12	Vir
1989	JAN	19	Tau	1995	JAN	22	Leo
	MAR	11	Gem		MAY	25	Vir
	APR	29	Can		JUL	21	Lib
	JUN	16	Leo		SEP	7	Scp
	AUG	3	Vir		OCT	20	Sag
	SEP	19	Lib		NOV	30	Cap
	NOV	4	Scp	1996	JAN	8	Aqu
	DEC	18	Sag		FEB	15	Pic
1990	JAN	29	Cap		MAR	24	Ari
	MAR	11	Aqu		MAY	2	Tau
	APR	20	Pic		JUN	12	Gem
	MAY	31	Ari		JUL	25	Can

	SEP	9	Leo		NOV	27	Lib
	OCT	30	Vir	1999	JAN	26	Scp
1997	JAN	3	Lib		MAY	5	Lib
	MAR	8	Vir		JUL	5	Scp
	JUN	19	Lib		SEP	2	Sag
	AUG	14	Scp		OCT	17	Cap
	SEP	28	Sag		NOV	26	Aqu
	NOV	9	Cap	2000	JAN	4	Pic
	DEC	18	Aqu		FEB	12	Ari
1998	JAN	25	Pic		MAR	23	Tau
	MAR	4	Ari		MAY	3	Gem
	APR	13	Tau		JUN	16	Can
	MAY	24	Gem		AUG	1	Leo
	JUL	6	Can		SEP	17	Vir
	AUG	20	Leo		NOV	4	Lib
	OCT	7	Vir		DEC	23	Scp

JUPITER SIGN 1901–2000

1901	JAN	19	Cap		OCT	26	Ari
1902	FEB	6	Aqu	1917	FEB	12	Tau
1903	FEB	20	Pic		JUN	29	Gem
1904	MAR	1	Ari	1918	JUL	13	Can
	AUG	8	Tau	1919	AUG	2	Leo
	AUG	31	Ari	1920	AUG	27	Vir
1905	MAR	7	Tau	1921	SEP	25	Lib
	JUL	21	Gem	1922	OCT	26	Scp
	DEC	4	Tau	1923	NOV	24	Sag
1906	MAR	9	Gem	1924	DEC	18	Cap
	JUL	30	Can	1926	JAN	6	Aqu
1907	AUG	18	Leo	1927	JAN	18	Pic
1908	SEP	12	Vir		JUN	6	Ari
1909	OCT	11	Lib		SEP	11	Pic
1910	NOV	11	Scp	1928	JAN	23	Ari
1911	DEC	10	Sag		JUN	4	Tau
1913	JAN	2	Cap	1929	JUN	12	Gem
1914	JAN	21	Aqu	1930	JUN	26	Can
1915	FEB	4	Pic	1931	JUL	17	Leo
1916	FEB	12	Ari	1932	AUG	11	Vir
	JUN	26	Tau	1933	SEP	10	Lib

1934	OCT	11	Scp	1960	MAR	1	Cap
1935	NOV	9	Sag		JUN	10	Sag
1936	DEC	2	Cap		OCT	26	Cap
1937	DEC	20	Aqu	1961	MAR	15	Aqu
1938	MAY	14	Pic		AUG	12	Cap
	JUL	30	Aqu		NOV	4	Aqu
	DEC	29	Pic	1962	MAR	25	Pic
1939	MAY	11	Ari	1963	APR	4	Ari
	OCT	30	Pic	1964	APR	12	Tau
	DEC	20	Ari	1965	APR	22	Gem
1940	MAY	16	Tau		SEP	21	Can
1941	MAY	26	Gem		NOV	17	Gem
1942	JUN	10	Can	1966	MAY	5	Can
1943	JUN	30	Leo		SEP	27	Leo
1944	JUL	26	Vir	1967	JAN	16	Can
1945	AUG	25	Lib		MAY	23	Leo
1946	SEP	25	Scp		OCT	19	Vir
1947	OCT	24	Sag	1968	FEB	27	Leo
1948	NOV	15	Cap		JUN	15	Vir
1949	APR	12	Aqu		NOV	15	Lib
	JUN	27	Cap	1969	MAR	30	Vir
	NOV	30	Aqu		JUL	15	Lib
1950	APR	15	Pic		DEC	16	Scp
	SEP	15	Aqu	1970	APR	30	Lib
	DEC	1	Pic		AUG	15	Scp
1951	APR	21	Ari	1971	JAN	14	Sag
1952	APR	28	Tau		JUN	5	Sc
1953	MAY	9	Gem		SEP	11	Sag
1954	MAY	24	Can	1972	FEB	6	Cap
1955	JUN	13	Leo		JUL	24	Sag
	NOV	17	Vir		SEP	25	Cap
1956	JAN	18	Leo	1973	FEB	23	Aqu
	JUL	7	Vir	1974	MAR	8	Pic
	DEC	13	Lib	1975	MAR	18	Ari
1957	FEB	19	Vir	1976	MAR	26	Tau
	AUG	7	Lib		AUG	23	Gem
1958	JAN	13	Scp		OCT	16	Tau
	MAR	20	Lib	1977	APR	3	Gem
	SEP	7	Scp		AUG	20	Can
1959	FEB	10	Sag		DEC	30	Gem
	APR	24	Scp	1978	APR	12	Can
	OCT	5	Sag		SEP	5	Leo

1979	FEB	28	Can				
					JUL	30	Can
	APR	20	Leo	1990	AUG	18	Leo
	SEP	29	Vir	1991	SEP	12	Vir
1980	OCT	27	Lib	1992	OCT	10	Lib
1981	NOV	27	Scp	1993	NOV	10	Scp
1982	DEC	26	Sag	1994	DEC	9	Sag
1984	JAN	19	Cap	1996	JAN	3	Cap
1985	FEB	6	Aqu	1997	JAN	21	Aqu
1986	FEB	20	Pic	1998	FEB	4	Pic
1987	MAR	2	Ari	1999	FEB	13	Ari
1988	MAR	8	Tau		JUN	28	Tau
	JUL	22	Gem		OCT	23	Ari
	NOV	30	Tau	2000	FEB	14	Tau
1989	MAR	11	Gem		JUN	30	Gem

SATURN SIGN 1903–2000

1903	JAN	19	Aqu	1929	MAR	15	Cap
1905	APR	13	Pic		MAY	5	Sag
	AUG	17	Aqu		NOV	30	Cap
1906	JAN	8	Pic	1932	FEB	24	Aqu
1908	MAR	19	Ari		AUG	13	Cap
1910	MAY	17	Tau		NOV	20	Aqu
	DEC	14	Ari	1935	FEB	14	Pic
1911	JAN	20	Tau	1937	APR	25	Ari
1912	JUL	7	Gem		OCT	18	Pic
	NOV	30	Tau	1938	JAN	14	Ari
1913	MAR	26	Gem	1939	JUL	6	Tau
1914	AUG	24	Can		SEP	22	Ari
	DEC	7	Gem	1940	MAR	20	Tau
1915	MAY	11	Can	1942	MAY	8	Gem
1916	OCT	17	Leo	1944	JUN	20	Can
	DEC	7	Can	1946	AUG	2	Leo
1917	JUN	24	Leo	1948	SEP	19	Vir
1919	AUG	12	Vir	1949	APR	3	Leo
1921	OCT	7	Lib		MAY	29	Vir
1923	DEC	20	Scp	1950	NOV	20	Lib
1924	APR	6	Lib	1951	MAR	7	Vir
	SEP	13	Scp		AUG	13	Lib
1926	DEC	2	Sag	1953	OCT	22	Scp

1956	JAN	12	Sag	1978	JAN	5	Leo
	MAY	14	Scp		JUL	26	Vir
	OCT	10	Sag	1980	SEP	21	Lib
1959	JAN	5	Cap	1982	NOV	29	Scp
1962	JAN	3	Aqu	1983	MAY	6	Lib
1964	MAR	24	Pic		AUG	24	Scp
	SEP	16	Aqu	1985	NOV	17	Sag
	DEC	16	Pic	1988	FEB	13	Cap
1967	MAR	3	Ari		JUN	10	Sag
1969	APR	29	Tau		NOV	12	Cap
1971	JUN	18	Gem	1991	FEB	6	Aqu
1972	JAN	10	Tau	1993	MAY	21	Pic
	FEB	21	Gem		JUN	30	Aqu
1973	AUG	1	Can	1994	JAN	28	Pic
1974	JAN	7	Gem	1996	APR	7	Ari
	APR	18	Can	1998	JUN	9	Tau
1975	SEP	17	Leo		OCT	25	Ari
1976	JAN	14	Can	1999	MAR	1	Tau
	JUN	5	Leo	2000	AUG	10	Gem
1977	NOV	17	Vir		OCT	16	Tau

How to Use the Uranus, Neptune, and Pluto Tables

Find your birthday in the list following each sign.

Look up your Uranus placement by finding your birthday on the following lists.

URANUS IN ARIES BIRTH DATES

March 31–November 4, 1927
January 13, 1928–June 6, 1934
October 10, 1934–March 28, 1935

URANUS IN TAURUS BIRTH DATES

June 6, 1934–October 10, 1934
March 28, 1935–August 7, 1941
October 5, 1941–May 15, 1942

URANUS IN GEMINI BIRTH DATES

August 7–October 5, 1941
May 15, 1942–August 30, 1948
November 12, 1948–June 10, 1949

URANUS IN CANCER BIRTH DATES

August 30–November 12, 1948
June 10, 1949–August 24, 1955
January 28–June 10, 1956

URANUS IN LEO BIRTH DATES

August 24, 1955–January 28, 1956
June 10, 1956–November 1, 1961
January 10–August 10, 1962

URANUS IN VIRGO BIRTH DATES

November 1, 1961–January 10, 1962
August 10, 1962–September 28, 1968
May 20, 1969–June 24, 1969

URANUS IN LIBRA BIRTH DATES

September 28, 1968–May 20, 1969
June 24, 1969–November 21, 1974
May 1–September 8, 1975

URANUS IN SCORPIO BIRTH DATES

November 21, 1974–May 1, 1975
September 8, 1975–February 17, 1981
March 20–November 16, 1981

URANUS IN SAGITTARIUS BIRTH DATES

February 17–March 20, 1981
November 16, 1981–February 15, 1988
May 27, 1988–December 2, 1988

URANUS IN CAPRICORN BIRTH DATES

December 20, 1904–January 30, 1912
September 4–November 12, 1912
February 15–May 27, 1988
December 2, 1988–April 1, 1995
June 9, 1995–January 12, 1996

URANUS IN AQUARIUS BIRTH DATES

January 30–September 4, 1912
November 12, 1912–April 1, 1919
August 16, 1919–January 22, 1920
April 1–June 9, 1995
January 12, 1996 through end of the century

URANUS IN PISCES BIRTH DATES

April 1–August 16, 1919
January 22, 1920–March 31, 1927
November 4, 1927–January 13, 1928

Look up your Neptune placement by finding your birthday on the following lists.

NEPTUNE IN CANCER BIRTH DATES

July 19–December 25, 1901
May 21, 1902–September 23, 1914
December 14, 1914–July 19, 1915
March 19–May 2, 1916

NEPTUNE IN LEO BIRTH DATES

September 23–December 14, 1914
July 19, 1915–March 19, 1916
May 2, 1916–September 21, 1928
February 19, 1929–July 24, 1929

NEPTUNE IN VIRGO BIRTH DATES

September 21, 1928–February 19, 1929
July 24, 1929–October 3, 1942
April 17–August 2, 1943

NEPTUNE IN LIBRA BIRTH DATES

October 3, 1942–April 17, 1943
August 2, 1943–December 24, 1955
March 12–October 19, 1956
June 15–August 6, 1957

NEPTUNE IN SCORPIO BIRTH DATES

December 24, 1955–March 12, 1956
October 19, 1956–June 15, 1957
August 6, 1957–January 4, 1970
May 3–November 6, 1970

NEPTUNE IN SAGITTARIUS BIRTH DATES

January 4–May 3, 1970
November 6, 1970–January 19, 1984
June 23–November 21, 1984

NEPTUNE IN CAPRICORN BIRTH DATES

January 19, 1984–June 23, 1984
November 21, 1984–January 29, 1998

Find your Pluto placement in the following list:
Pluto in Gemini—Late 1800s until May 28, 1914
Pluto in Cancer—May 26, 1914–June 14, 1939
Pluto in Leo—June 14, 1939–August 19, 1957
Pluto in Virgo—August 19, 1957–October 5, 1971
           April 17, 1972–July 30, 1972
Pluto in Libra—October 5, 1971—April 17, 1972
           July 30, 1972–August 28, 1984
Pluto in Scorpio—August 28, 1984–January 17, 1995
Pluto in Sagittarius—starting January 17, 1995

CHAPTER 7

The Sign Language of Astrology
Your Glyph Guide and How to Use It

The first time you see an astrology chart, you might as well be looking at a Chinese manuscript for all the sense it makes! What do those odd-looking symbols mean? Are they a code? You're right to ask. Astrology has a symbolic language, a kind of universal shorthand, which is used by astrologers all over the world, so any astrology-savvy reader, regardless of nationality, could read your chart. These symbols or *glyphs* are also used in all the new astrology programs available for your computer, so, if you want to progress in astrology enough to read a printout of a horoscope, you've got to know the meaning of the glyphs.

Learning to decipher the glyphs can not only help you read a computer chart, but can help you understand the meaning of the signs and planets, because each symbol contains clues to what it represents. And, since there are only 12 signs and 10 planets (not counting a few asteroids and other space creatures some astrologers use), it's a lot easier to read than, say, Chinese!

Here's a code-cracker for the glyphs, beginning with the glyphs for the planets. If you already know their glyphs, don't just skim over the chapter! There are hidden meanings to discover, so test your glyph-ese.

The Glyphs for the Planets

The glyphs for the planets are simply combinations of the circle, the semicircle or arc, and the cross. Each component of a glyph has a special meaning in relation to the others, which combines to create the total meaning of the symbol.

The circle, which has no beginning or end, is one of the oldest symbols of spirit or spiritual forces. All of the early diagrams of the heavens—spiritual territory—are shown in circular form. The semicircle or arc symbolizes the receptive, finite soul, which contains spiritual potential in the curving line. The vertical line of the cross symbolizes movement from heaven to earth. The horizontal line describes temporal movement, here and now, in time and space. Superimposed together, the vertical and horizontal planes symbolize manifestation in the material world.

The Sun Glyph ☉

The sun is always shown by this powerful solar symbol, a circle with a point in the center. The point is you, your spiritual center, and the symbol represents your infinite personality incarnating (the point) into the finite cycles of birth and death.

This symbol was brought into common use in the sixteenth century, after a German occultist and scholar, Cornelius Agrippa (1486–1535), wrote a book called *Die Occulta Philosophia*, which became accepted as the standard work in its field. Agrippa collected many medieval astrological and magical symbols in this book, which were copied by astrologers thereafter.

The Moon Glyph ☽

This is surely the easiest symbol to spot on a chart. The Moon glyph is a left-facing arc stylized into the crescent moon, which perfectly captures the reactive, receptive, emotional nature of the moon.

As part of a circle, the arc symbolizes the potential fulfillment of the entire circle. It is the life force that is still incomplete.

The Mercury Glyph ☿

Mercury contains all three elements—the crescent, the circle, and the cross, in vertical order. This is the "Venus with a hat" glyph (compare it with the symbol of Venus). With another stretch of the imagination, can't you see the winged cap of Mercury the messenger? Think of the upturned crescent as antennae that tune in and transmit messages from the sun, reminding you that Mercury is the way you communicate and the way your mind works. The upturned arc is receiving energy into the spirit or solar circle, which will later be translated into action on the material plane, symbolized by the cross. All the elements are equally sized because Mercury is neutral—it doesn't play favorites! This planet symbolizes objective, detached, unemotional thinking.

The Venus Glyph ♀

Here the relationship is between two elements, the circle or spirit above the cross of matter. Spirit is elevated over matter, pulling it upward. Venus asks, "What is beautiful? What do you like best? What do you love to have done to you?" Venus determines both your ideal of beauty and what feels good sensually. It governs your own allure and power to attract, as well as what attracts and pleases you.

The Mars Glyph ♂

In this glyph, the cross of matter is stylized into an arrowhead pointed up and outward, propelled by the circle of spirit. You can deduce that Mars embodies your spiritual energy projected into the outer world. It's your assertiveness, your initiative, your aggressive drive, what you like to do to others, your temper. If you know someone's Mars, you know whether they'll blow up when angry or do a slow burn. Your task is to use your outgoing Mars energy wisely and well.

The Jupiter Glyph ♃

Jupiter is the basic cross of matter, with a large stylized crescent perched on the left side of the horizontal, temporal plane. You might think of the crescent as an open hand—one meaning of Jupiter is "luck," what's handed to you. You don't work for what you get from Jupiter—it comes to you if you're open to it.

The Jupiter glyph might also remind you of a jumbo jet plane with a huge tail fin, about to take off. Jupiter is the planet of travel, both mental and spiritual, and the planet of expanding your horizons via new ideas, new spiritual dimensions, and new places. Jupiter embodies the optimism and enthusiasm of the traveler about to embark on an exciting adventure.

The Saturn Glyph ♄

Flip Jupiter over and you've got Saturn. (This might not be immediately apparent, because Saturn is usually stylized into an "h" form like the one shown here.) But the principle it expresses is the opposite of Jupiter's expansive tendencies. Saturn pulls you back to earth—the receptive arc is pushed down underneath the cross of matter. Before there are any rewards or expansion, the duties and obligations of the material world must be considered. Saturn says, "Stop, wait, finish your chores before you take off!"

Saturn's glyph also resembles the sickle of old Father Time. Saturn was first known as Chronos, the Greek god of time, for time brings all matter to an end. When it was thought to be the most distant planet, before the discovery of Uranus, Saturn was believed to be the place where time stopped. After the soul, having departed from earth, journeyed back to the outer reaches of the universe, it finally stopped at Saturn, the end of time.

The Uranus Glyph ♅

The glyph for Uranus is often stylized to form a capital "H" after Sir William Herschel, the name of the planet's discoverer. But the more esoteric version curves the two pillars of the H into crescent antennae, or ears, or satellite discs receiving signals from space. These are perched on the horizontal material line of the cross (matter) and pushed from below by the circle of the spirit. To many sci-fi fans, Uranus looks like an orbiting satellite.

Uranus channels the highest energy of all, the white electrical light of the universal spiritual sun, the force that holds the cosmos together. This pure electrical energy is gathered from all over the universe. Because Uranian energy doesn't follow an ordinary celestial drumbeat, it can't be controlled or predicted—which is also true of those who are strongly influenced by this eccentric planet. In the symbol, this energy is manifested through the balance of polarities (the two opposite arms of the glyph) like the two polarized wires of a light bulb.

The Neptune Glyph Ψ

Neptune's glyph is usually stylized to look like a trident, the weapon of the Roman god Neptune. However, on a more esoteric level, it shows the large, upturned crescent of the soul pierced through by the cross of matter. Neptune nails down, or materializes, soul energy, bringing impulses from the soul level into manifestation. That is why Neptune is associated with imagination or "imagining in," making an image of the soul. Neptune works through feeling, sensitivity, and mystical capacity to bring the divine into the earthly realm.

The Pluto Glyph ♀

Pluto is written two ways. One is a composite of the letters "PL," the first two letters of the wold Pluto and coincidentally in the initial of Percival Lowell, one of the planet's discoverers. The other, more esoteric, symbol is a small circle above a large open crescent which surmounts the cross of matter. This depicts Pluto's power to regenerate—imagine a new little spirit emerging from the sheltering cup of the soul. Pluto rules the forces of life and death—after this planet has passed a sensitive point in your chart, you are transformed or reborn in some way.

Sci-fi fans might visualize this glyph as a small satellite (the circle) being launched. It was shortly after Pluto's discovery that we learned how to harness the nuclear forces that made space exploration possible. Pluto rules the transformative power of atomic energy, which totally changed our lives and from which there was no turning back.

The Glyphs for the Signs

On an astrological chart, the glyph for the sign will appear after that of the planet. For example, when you see the moon glyph followed by first a number and then another glyph representing the sign, this means that the moon was passing over a certain degree of that astrological sign when the chart was cast. On the dividing lines between the segments or houses on your chart, you'll find the symbol for the sign that was passing over the house cusp (or spoke of the wheel) at the time.

Because sun-sign symbols do not contain the same geometric components as the glyphs for the planets, we must look elsewhere for clues to their meanings. Many have been passed down from ancient Egyptian and Chaldean civilizations with few modifications. Others have been adapted over the centuries. In deciphering many of the glyphs, you'll often find that the symbols reveal a dual nature of the sign, which is not always apparent in the usual sun-sign descriptions. For instance, the Gemini glyph is similar to the Roman numeral for two, and reveals this sign's longing to discover a twin soul. The Cancer glyph may be interpreted as either resembling the nurturing breasts, or the self-protective claws of the crab, both symbols associated with the contrasting qualities of this sign. Libra's glyph embodies the duality of the spirit balanced with material reality. The Sagittarius glyph shows that the aspirant must also carry along the earthly animal nature in his quest. The Capricorn sea goat is another symbol with dual emphasis. The goat climbs high, yet is always pulled back by the deep waters of the unconscious. Aquarius embodies the double waves of mental detachment, balanced by the desire for connection with others in a friendly way. And finally, the two fishes of Pisces, which are forever tied together, show the duality of the soul and the spirit that must be reconciled.

The Aries Glyph ♈

Since the symbol for Aries is the ram, this glyph's most obvious association is with a ram's horns, which characterizes one aspect of the Aries personality—an aggressive, me-first, leaping-head-first attitude. But the symbol may have other meanings for you, too. Some astrologers liken it to a fountain of energy, which Aries people also embody. The first sign of the zodiac bursts on the scene eagerly and ready to go. Another analogy is to the eyebrows and nose of the human head, which Aries rules, and to the thinking power that is initiated in the brain.

One theory of the origin of this symbol links it to the Egyptian god Amun, represented by a ram. As Amon-Ra, this god was believed to embody the creator of the universe, the leader of all the other gods. This relates easily to the position of Aries as the leader, or first sign, of the zodiac, which begins at the spring equinox, a time of the year when nature is renewed.

The Taurus Glyph ♉

This is another easy glyph to draw and identify. It takes little imagination to decipher the bull's head with long, curving horns. Like the bull, the archetypal Taurus is slow to anger but ferocious when provoked, as well as stubborn, steady, and sensual. Another association is the larynx and thyroid of the throat area (ruled by Taurus) and the Eustachian tubes running up to the ears, which coincides with the relationship of Taurus to the voice, song, and music. Many famous singers, musicians, and composers have prominent Taurus influences.

Many ancient religions involved a bull as the central figure in fertility rites or initiations, usually symbolizing the victory of man over his animal nature. Another possible origin is in the sacred bull of Egypt, who embodied the incarnate form of Osiris, god of death and resurrection. In early Christian imagery, the Taurean bull represented St. Luke.

The Gemini Glyph Ⅱ

The standard glyph immediately calls to mind the Roman numeral for two and the symbol for Gemini, the twins. In almost all images for this sign, the relationship between two persons is emphasized. This is the sign of communication and human contact; it manifests the desire to share.

Many of the figurative images for Gemini show twins with their arms around each other, emphasizing that they are sharing the same ideas and the same ground. In the glyph, the top line indicates mental communication, while the bottom line indicates shared physical space.

The most famous Gemini legend is that of the twin sons, Castor and Pollux, one of whom had a mortal father, while the other was the son of Zeus, king of the gods. When it came time for the mortal twin to die, his grief-stricken brother pleaded with Zeus, who finally agreed to let them spend half the year on earth, in mortal form, and half in immortal life, with the gods on Mt. Olympus. This reflects the basic nature of humankind, which possesses an immortal soul yet is also subject to the limits of mortality.

The Cancer Glyph ♋

Two convenient images relate to the Cancer glyph. The easiest to picture is the curving claws of the Cancer symbol, the crab. Like the crab, Cancer's element is water. This sensitive sign also has a hard protective shell to protect its tender interior. It must be wily to escape predators, scampering sideways and hiding shyly under rocks. The crab also responds to the cycles of the moon, as do all shellfish. The other image is that of two female breasts, which Cancer rules, showing that this is a sign that nurtures and protects others as well as itself.

In ancient Egypt, Cancer was also represented by the scarab beetle, a symbol of regeneration and eternal life.

The Leo Glyph ♌

Notice that the Leo glyph seems to be an extension of Cancer's glyph, with a significant difference. In the Cancer glyph, the lines curve inward protectively, while the Leo glyph expresses energy outwardly and there is no duality in the symbol (or in Leo).

Lions have belonged to the sign of Leo since earliest times and it is not difficult to imagine the king of beasts with his sweeping mane and curling tail from this glyph. The upward sweep of the glyph easily describes the positive energy of Leos; the flourishing tail, their flamboyant qualities. Another analogy, which is a stretch of the imagination, is that of a heart leaping up with joy and enthusiasm, also very typical of Leo, which also rules the heart. In early Christian imagery, the Leo lion represented St. mark.

The Virgo Glyph ♍

You can read much into this mysterious glyph. For instance, it could represent the initials of "Mary Virgin," or a young woman holding a staff of wheat, or stylized female genitalia, all common interpretations. The "M" shape might also remind you that Virgo is ruled by Mercury. The cross beneath the symbol could indicate the grounded, practical nature of this earth sign.

The earliest zodiacs link Virgo with the Egyptian goddess Isis, who gave birth to the god Horus after her husband Osiris had been killed, in the archetype of a miraculous conception. There are many statues of Isis nursing her baby son, which are reminiscent of medieval Virgin and Child motifs. This sign has also been associated with the image of the Holy Grail, when the Virgo symbol was substituted with a chalice.

The Libra Glyph ♎

It is not difficult to read the standard image for Libra, the scales, into this glyph. There is another meaning, however, that is equally relevant—the setting sun as it descends over the horizon. Libra's natural position on the zodiac wheel in the descendant or sunset position (as the Aries natural position is the ascendant, or rising sign). Both images relate to Libra's personality. Libra is always weighing pros and cons for a balanced decision. In the sunset image, the sun (male) hovers over the horizontal Earth (female) before setting. Libra is the space between these lines, harmonizing yin and yang, spiritual and material, male and female, ideal and real worlds. The glyph has also been linked to the kidneys, which are ruled by Libra.

The Scorpio Glyph ♏

With its barbed tail, this glyph is easy to identify with the sign of the Scorpion. It also represents the male sexual parts, over which the sign rules. However, some earlier symbols for Scorpio, such as the Egyptian, represent it as an erect serpent. You can also draw the conclusion that Mars is its ruler by the arrowhead.

Another image for Scorpio, which is not identifiable in this glyph, is the eagle. Scorpios can go to extremes, soaring like the eagle or self-destructing like the scorpion. In early Christian imagery, which often used zodiacal symbols, the Scorpio eagle was chosen to symbolize the intense apostle, St. John the Evangelist.

The Sagittarius Glyph ♐

This glyph is one of the easiest to spot and draw—an upward-pointing arrow lifting up a cross. The arrow is pointing skyward, while the cross represents the four elements of the material world, which the arrow must convey. Elevating materiality into spirituality is an important Sagittarius quality, which explains why this sign is associated with higher learning, religion, philosophy, and travel—the aspiring professions. Sagittarius can also send barbed arrows of frankness in their pursuit of truth. This is also the sign of the super salesman, who can persuade you that an ordinary item is truly extraordinary.

Sagittarius is symbolically represented by the centaur, a mythological creature who is half-man, half-horse, aiming his arrow toward the skies. Though Sagittarius is motivated by spiritual aspiration, it also must balance this with powerful earthbound appetites of the animal nature. The centaur Chiron, a figure in Greek mythology, became a wise teacher after many adventures and world travels.

The Capricorn Glyph ♑

One of the most difficult symbols to draw, this glyph may take some practice. It is a representation of the sea goat—a mythical goat with a curving fish's tail. The goat part of Capricorn wants to leave the waters of the emotions and climb to the elevated areas of life. But the fish part represents the unconscious, chaotic psychic forces that keep drawing the goat back. Capricorns often try to escape the deep, feeling part of life by submerging themselves in work, steadily rising to the top of their professions or social ladders. Another interpretation of this glyph is a seated figure with a bent knee, a reminder that Capricorn governs the knee area of the body.

An interesting aspect of this glyph is how the sharp, pointed horns of the symbol, which represent the penetrating, shrewd, conscious side of Capricorn, contrast with the swishing tail that represents its serpentine, unconscious, emotional force. One Capricorn legend, which dates from Roman times, tells of the earthy fertility god, Pan, who tried to save himself from uncontrollable sexual desires by jumping into the Nile. His upper body then turned into a goat, while the lower part became a fish. Later, Jupiter gave him a safe haven in the skies, as a constellation.

The Aquarius Glyph ♒

This ancient water symbol can be traced back to an Egyptian hieroglyph representing streams of life force.

Symbolized by the water bearer, Aquarius is distributor of the waters of life—the magic liquid of regeneration. The two waves can also be linked to the positive and negative charges of the electrical energy that Aquarius rules, a sort of universal wavelength. Aquarius is tuned in intuitively to higher forces via this electrical force. The duality of the glyph could also refer to the dual nature of Aquarius, a sign that runs hot and cold, is friendly but also detached in the mental world of air signs.

In Greek legends, Aquarius is represented by Ganymede, who was carried to heaven by an eagle in order to become the cup bearer of Zeus, and to supervise the annual flooding of the Nile. the sign became associated with aviation and notions of flight.

The Pisces Glyph ♓

Here is an abstraction of the familiar image of Pisces, two fishes swimming in opposite directions, yet bound together by a cord. The fishes represent spirit, which yearns for the freedom of heaven, while the soul remains attached to the desires of the temporal world. During life on earth, the spirit and the soul are bound together and when they complement each other, instead of pulling in opposite directions, this facilitates the creative expression for which Pisceans are known. The ancient version of this glyph, taken from the Egyptians, had no connecting line; this was added in the fourteenth century.

Another interpretation is that the left fish symbolizes involution or the beginning of the cycle, the right-hand fish the direction of evolution, the completion of a cycle. It's an appropriate meaning for Pisces, the last sign of the zodiac.

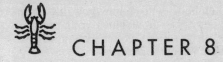

CHAPTER 8

Your Astrological Love-Links
Rating Relationships Sign by Sign

"I've got your number!" is the old saying when you've finally figured out what makes someone tick. But, in astrology, this cliché takes on new meaning—getting someone's astrological number in relation to your sign can give you terrific clues, not only to how you relate to each other, but why.

Use the chart in this chapter to get the "number" of those close to you and then read the following explanation. It's called the "ultimate compatibility chart," because you can use it not only to compare sun signs, but to relate any two planets within your own horoscope chart or to compare your planets with those of another chart.

Use it to help you understand the dynamics between you and the people you interact with. You might find it the key to getting along better with your boss and coworkers. Or discover what the real dynamics are with your difficult relatives and your best friends.

What this chart won't do is tell you that there are signs you *can't* get along with. There are no totally incompatible signs—there are many happy marriages between signs that succeed because of the stimulation and chemistry their differences provide. To understand your astrological connection with another person, you need to identify the spatial relationship between signs. The sign "next door" is something like your next-door neighbor who loans you his lawn-mower or feeds your cats—or disputes your property boundaries. Signs distant from yours also have attitudes based on their "neighborhoods."

Some Sign Basics

A sign by definition is a specific territory, a division of an energy belt called the zodiac, which circles the Earth. Each division is distinguished by an element (earth, air, fire, water), a quality or modality (cardinal, fixed, mutable), and a polarity or charge (positive/negative). No two signs have the same combination. These variables alternate around the zodiac belt in an established order: first fire, followed by earth, air, and water. The qualities alternate first with cardinal (active), then fixed (growth), and last mutable (change) signs. It follows that the positive and negative signs also alternate, like the charge of a battery. As the energy flow progresses around the zodiac, starting with Aries, the signs become more complex and less self-oriented. So the place in line around the belt becomes a factor, too.

Play the Numbers Game

Since the zodiac is a circle, the signs also relate to each other according to the angle of the distance between them. Between signs of the same polarity (masculine/feminine, positive/negative, yin/yang), which are numbers 0, 2, and 4, energy flows most easily (with one exception: the sign opposite yours, number 6). Between signs of different polarity, which are numbered 1, 3, and 5, you'll experience tension or challenge (and possibly a very sexy "charge"!) Here's how it works out:

THE ULTIMATE COMPATIBILITY CHART

	AR	TA	GEM	CAN	LEO	VIR	LIB	SCO	SAG	CAP	AQ	PI
Aries	0	1	2	3	4	5	6	5	4	3	2	1
Taurus	1	0	1	2	3	4	5	6	5	4	3	2
Gemini	2	1	0	1	2	3	4	5	6	5	4	3
Cancer	3	2	1	0	1	2	3	4	5	6	5	4
Leo	4	3	2	1	0	1	2	3	4	5	6	5
Virgo	5	4	3	2	1	0	1	2	3	4	5	6
Libra	6	5	4	3	2	1	0	1	2	3	4	5
Scorpio	5	6	5	4	3	2	1	0	1	2	3	4
Sagittarius	4	5	6	5	4	3	2	1	0	1	2	3
Capricorn	3	4	5	6	5	4	3	2	1	0	1	2
Aquarius	2	3	4	5	6	5	4	3	2	1	0	1
Pisces	1	2	3	4	5	6	5	4	3	2	1	0

Find your sign in the vertical list. Then read across the row until you come to the column under the sign of your parner, mate, lover, boss and so on. Then read the descripton of the number in this chapter.

Your "0" Relationships—Signmates

"0" relationships are with those of your own sign, so naturally you'll have much in common. This could be the soulmate you've been looking for—one who understands and sympathizes with you like no other sign can! Your signmate understands your need for space, yet knows how and when to be there for you. There are many examples of long-term partnerships between sun-sign twins—Roy Rogers and Dale Evans (both Scorpio), Abigail and John Adams (Scorpio), George and Barbara Bush (Gemini), Bob and Dolores Hope (Gemini), Frank and Kathie Lee Gifford (Leo). Working relationships fare especially well with sun signs in common, though you may have to delegate unwanted tasks to others. In a public lifestyle or one where there is much separation or stimulation, your similarities can hold you together— there is the feeling of "you and me against the world."

The problem is when there is too much of a good thing with no stimulation or challenge—or when there is no "chemistry," which can often happen between signs that share so much, including the same element, quality, and polarity. The solution is to bring plenty of outside excitement into your lives.

Your "1" Relationships—Next-Door Neighbors

These signs are your next-door neighbors on the zodiac wheel. Your relationship is based on evolution—you've evolved out of the previous sign carrying energies that have been accumulating and developing through the zodiac cycle. The sign following yours is where your energy is headed, the next step. In a way, it's like sitting at a dinner table and passing the plate from left to right. You receive certain qualities from the previous sign and pass on those, plus your own, to the next.

This is also a sibling relationship where the sign before yours is like a protective older brother or sister, who's been there, and the next sign is your eager younger sibling. Every sign also has a compensating factor for its predecessor—this sign embodies lessons you should have learned (and which could trip you up if you've forgotten them).

But although both are in the same family, sibling signs actually have little in common, because you have different basic values (elements), ways of operating (qualities), and types of energy (polarity). You probably won't feel sparks of chemistry or the deep rapport of a solute unless other planets in your horoscopes provide this bond. Instead, the emphasis is on pals, best friends, working partners, who are enhanced by the sibling sign position.

The sign ahead can inspire you—they're where you are heading, but you may be afraid to take the first brave step. For example, to Pisces, Aries embodies dynamic, forceful, self-oriented will—whereas Pisces is the formless, selfless, imaginative state where Aries originated. So Aries energizes Pisces and gets Pisces moving. This sign behind backs you up and supports you. This relationship often makes one of the most lasting and contented unions—several famous examples are the Duke and Duchess of Windsor (Cancer/Gemini), Paul Newman and Joanne Woodward (Aquarius/Pisces), and Jerry Hall/Mick Jagger (Cancer/Leo).

To reveal how you'll relate to your zodiac sibling, here's how energy evolves through the twelve signs.

Aries, the first sign of the zodiac, is "born" from Pisces, the last. In Pisces, individual energy dissolved into universal energy—to be asserted again in Aries. Aries is the new "baby," while Pisces is the prebirth generation, living in the otherworldly realm of spirit. Pisces reminds self-oriented Aries that there is more to life than "me." Pisces teaches Aries compassion and a consciousness of others, while Aries infuses Pisces with new energy and gets Pisces to assert itself.

Taurus is the baby taking the first steps into the material world, feeling its way with the senses., Taurus stabilizes Aries, giving this sign direction and purpose and directing all that energy and drive. Taurus also imposes boundaries and limits to Aries, pulling it down to earth and stubbornly insisting, "You can't have it your way all the time" or "What are you really getting done?" or "What will it cost?"

Gemini teaches Taurus, who is often stuck on its own turf, to communicate, to socialize, to reach out to others, paving the way for the first emotional water sign, Cancer, where feelings are top priority and the energy becomes nurturing and self-protective. Cancer adds the dimension of caring to Gemini, who would rather not deal with emotions at all.

The nurturing qualities of Cancer burst forth in Leo. Leo's confidence and self-expression come out of the security Cancer provides. Leo, who needs this kind of caring to shine, can be quite insecure and demanding if good mothering has not been received. And that becomes a hallmark of the Cancer–Leo relationship: Ideally, Cancer nurtures Leo (in a not so ideal relationship, Cancer's fearfulness holds Leo back) and Leo in turn brings this vulnerable sign out into public life. Virgo is concerned with making things work, with helping, and says, "Leo, this is all very impressive, but is it useful? Will it work? Here's how to improve it." Virgo edits Leo creativity, which Leo might resent, but which makes for a better end result. Leo's confidence rubs off on shyer Virgo.

Like Virgo, Libra is also concerned with measuring up. While Virgo is interested in whatever is most practical, Libra is in love with beauty. When Virgo asks, "What good is something beautiful if it doesn't if it doesn't work?" Libra answers, "Beauty is its own justification." Virgo stimulates and grounds Libra; Libra takes Virgo further into aesthetics.

Scorpio plunges into deep emotional territory that Libra might prefer not to enter. However, the balance of Libra is required for Scorpio to reach its most positive, decisive expression. In return, Scorpio's intensity challenges Libra to look deeper, not to be content with superficial beauty.

Sagittarius takes Scorpio's deep understanding and then projects this to higher levels. Sagittarius adds optimism, uplifting ideals, and humor, which counteract Scorpio's pessimism. Jupiter-ruled, expansive Sagittarius then gains direction from the following sign, Saturn-ruled Capricorn, who brings the structure, discipline, and order that can help Sagittarius achieve its goals.

Though Capricorn can be inspired by Sagittarius, this bottom-line earth sign is interested in getting concrete results. Aquarius, its neighbor, then brings in higher principles, plus the elements of surprise, inventiveness, and unpredictability. There is always a higher purpose with Aquarius that lifts Capricorn out of the ordinary.

Pisces, the final sign in the cycle, is most sensitive to outside input, and as a result can be self-sacrificing or self-pitying. It shares a universal outlook with Aquarius, who reminds Pisces of detachment, social life, and the need to maintain perspective. The following sign, Aries, which has no patience for self-pity, will dry out this watery sign with its optimism and drive. In return, Pisces, which represents the amorphous prenatal world, often brings the spiritual dimension to the Aries life, which becomes an important part of their relationship.

Your "2" Relationships

With your "2" signs, you share the same electrical charge, so energy flows freely between you, and you also have compatible elements. For example, air signs and fire signs work well together—air makes fire burn brighter. But too much of either element can suffocate or blow out the flame. Earth and water signs can either make flowers, or mud flats, or wastelands.

The "2's" line up as follows:

Combination A. The earth signs (Taurus, Virgo, Capricorn) with water signs (Cancer, Scorpio, Pisces). These are usually very fertile nurturing combinations, each providing the emotional and material security the other sign needs to reach full potential. Problems arise when the earth sign's material orientation and "here-and-nowness" stifles the more cosmic water sign's creativity.

Combination B. The air signs (Gemini, Libra, Aquarius) with fire signs (Aries, Leo, Sagittarius). These are very stimulating, energetic combinations. Both kinds of signs are positive, outgoing, and active, and this usually describes their relationship as well. The problem is that the more objective, detached air sign's preference for reason over enthusiasm could cool the fire sign's ardor. And the fire sign's enthusiastic, but often egocentric and unreasonable, approach could exasperate reasoning, relationship-oriented air signs.

Your "3" Relationships

If you recognize that stress in a relationship often stimulates growth, and sexual tension can be heightened by a challenge, you can succeed with a "3" relationship. Relationships between signs of a similar quality are charged with erotic energy and sparks of passion. Some of these can thrive on difficulty. But, even though you can declare a truce with this sign, the person probably won't be easy to live with. However, these will also be your least boring partners.

"3s" share the same modality; you're both either cardinal, fixed, or mutable signs. So you'll understand how the other operates, though you won't necessarily share the same basic values or type of energy. It often happens with this relationship that you continually confront each other—here is a sign that is just as restless, stubborn, or driven as you are! This person isn't one to provide security, settle down, or back you up. So will you choose to compete or join forces, forging an equal partnership?

Mutable signs (Gemini, Virgo, Sagittarius, Pisces), which are the most changeable, understand each other's restlessness and low tolerance for boredom. This is a couple that can easily fragment, however, going off in different directions. This union often falls apart under stress, but challenges mutables to make order out of chaos. In other words, get your act together.

Cardinal couples (Aries, Cancer, Libra, Capricorn) with equal drive and energy often are characterized by goal-driven intensity—they never sit still. Fixed signs (Taurus, Leo, Scorpio, Aquarius) can be the most stable partners or, negatively, they can wrestle for control, war over territory, or have a stubborn standoff.

Positively, this is one of the sexiest aspects—these two signs challenge each other and bring about growth. Here are some of the issues likely to arise between each "3" pair-up:

Aries–Cancer Aries is forced by Cancer to consider the consequences of actions, particularly those that threaten security and hurt feelings. However, introspection cramps Aries style—this sign wants perfect freedom to act as they please and has no patience for Cancer's self-pity or self-protectiveness. Although Cancer admires Aries courage, the interaction will have to confront the conflict between the Aries outdirected desire to have their own way and Cancer's inward-turning drive to create safety and security.

Cancer–Libra Cancer is most satisfied by symbiotic, intimate, emotionally dependent relationships. So when you meet someone who is very independent, you feel hurt, rejected, and throw up a defensive shell, or you get moody and depressed. Unfortunately, you risk this happening with Libra, a romantic but rather emotionally cool sign. Libras want an equal partner and they tend to judge their partner on a detached, idealistic level, by their looks, style, ideas, and conversation. Libra recognizes that the best partnerships are between equals, but the issue here is what do you have to share? Libra won't be able to escape emotions through social activities or intellectual analysis here.

Libra–Capricorn Both of you love the good life, but you may have conflicting ideas about how to get it. Capricorn is a very disciplined, goal-directed, ordered worker, who requires concrete results. Libra is more about style and abstract principles, and can be quite self-indulgent. Libran indulgence *vs.* Capricorn discipline could be the cruncher here. Another bone to pick would be differing ideas about what's fair and just. Capricorn often believes that the end justifies the means, while Libra upholds fairness over bottom-line concerns.

Capricorn–Aries Earth signs want solidity, fire signs want freedom. Both are survivors who love to win, but Capricorn works for status and material rewards while Aries works for glory, heroism, and the joy of being first. Capricorn wants to stay in control; Aries wants freedom. In a positive way, Aries must grow up with Capricorn, but in return it can give this tradition-oriented sign a new and younger lease on life.

Taurus–Leo Leo has an insatiable appetite for admiration, Taurus for pleasure. Taurus sensuality can make Leo feel like a star, while Leo's romantic gestures appeal to Taurus on a grand scale. Taurus will have to learn courtship and flattery to keep Leo happy, bringing on the champagne and caviar! Leo will have to learn not to tease the bull, especially by withholding affection, and to enjoy simple meat-and-potatoes kinds of pleasures as well. Money can be so important here—Leo likes to spend royally, Taurus to accumulate and hoard.

Scorpio–Leo Scorpio wants adventure in the psychic underworld; Leo wants to stay in the throne room. Scorpio challenges Leo to experience life intensely, which can bring out the best in Leo. Leo burns away Scorpio negativity, with a low tolerance for dark moods. Scorpio is content to work behind the scenes, giving Leo center stage. But Leo must never mistake a quiet Scorpio for a gentle pussycat. There will be plenty of action behind the scenes. Settle issues of control without playing power games.

Scorpio–Aquarius Aquarian love of freedom and Scorpio possessiveness could clash here. Scorpio wants to own you; Aquarius wants to remain friends. This is one unpredictable sign that Scorpio can't figure out, but has fun trying. The Aquarian flair for group dynamics could bring Scorpio out, but too many outside interests could put a damper on this combination.

Taurus–Aquarius Taurus lives in the touchable realm of the earth. Aquarius is in the electric, invisible realm of air, which can't be fenced in. It's anyone's guess if Taurus can ground Aquarius or if Aquarius can uplift Taurus. The Taurean talent as a realist could be the anchor this free sprit needs, while Aquarian originality opens new territory to Taurus.

Gemini–Virgo Nerves can be stimulated or frayed when these Mercury-ruled signs sound off. Both have much to say to each other, from different points of view. Gemini deals in abstractions, Virgo in down-to-earth facts. Common interests could keep this pair focused on each other.

Virgo–Sagittarius Safety versus risk could be the hallmark of this relationship. Virgo plays it safe and cautious, while Sagittarius operates on faith and enthusiasm. You're two natural teachers who have different philosophies and have much to learn from each other. When Virgo picks things apart or gets bogged down in details, Sag urges them to look for the truth—the big picture. Sag's lack of organization or follow-though will either drive Virgo crazy or provide a job. Virgo puts Sagittarius down with facts, deflating overblown promises and sales pitches.

Sagittarius–Pisces There should be many philosophical and spiritual discussions and debates here. When Sagittarius says, "I'm right," Pisces says, "Everything's relative. We're all right and wrong. So what?" Sagittarius is about elevating the self and Pisces is about merging the self, losing the self. On a less cosmic level, these two high-flying signs may never get down to earth. Pisces' super-sensitive feelings are easily wounded by Sagittarius' moments of truth telling. But Sag can help sell those creative Piscean ideas; that is, if you don't wander off in different directions.

Pisces–Gemini Gemini is always trying to understand, abstract, and rationalize. Pisces wants to merge and flow, find a soulmate, go beyond the mind. Piscean moods get on Gemini's nerves. Gemini runs away from emotional mergers, which really matter to Pisces. Yet Piscean glamour can intrigue Gemini and Gemini lightness and wit help Pisces laugh away the blues.

Your "4" Relationships

These are considered the easiest relationship possible, the most compatible partnerships. You share the same element and the same polarity, but sometimes there is too much of a good thing. These tend to lack the dynamism and sexy sparks of the "3" and "5" relationships. They can be too comfortable as you adjust very easily to each other. But what can you teach each other? If it's too easy, you might look for excitement elsewhere.

Relationships between the three earth signs (Taurus, Virgo, Capricorn) are mutually profitable, both professionally and personally. You won't find the other sign tampering with your financial security, frittering away hard-earned funds, or flirting with danger. You could fulfill your dreams of a comfortable life together. Too much comfort could leave you yawning, however—you need someone to shake you up once in a while.

Fire signs (Aries, Leo, Sagittarius) can ignite each other, but watch out for temper and jealousy. You both demand exclusive attention and are happiest when your ego is stroked and you feel like number one, so you may have to curb any tendency to flirt. Because you tend to be big risk takers and free spenders, you may have to delegate the financial caretaking carefully or find an expert adviser.

Water signs (Cancer, Scorpio, Pisces) have found partners who aren't afraid of emotional depths or heights. These are the ones who can understand and sympathize with your moods. This could be your solute who gives you the emotional security you need. When moods collide, however, you could find it difficult to get each other out of deep water.

Air signs (Gemini, Libra, Aquarius) communicate well together. There is no heavy emotionalism or messy ego or possessiveness to deal with. You both respect the need for freedom and personal space and can make your own rules for an open, equal partnership. Staying in touch is the problem here. You could become so involved in your own pursuits that you let romance fly by or are never there for each other. Be sure to cultivate things in common because, unless there are many shared interests, it is easy to float away.

Your "5" Relationships

This is the relationship that challenges your sign the most. You have to stretch yourself to make this work. You are totally different in basic values (element), way of acting (quality), and kind of energy (polarity). And, unlike your next-door signs that also have those differences, you don't have the proximity of being next in line. Instead of being beside you, the other sign is off on the other side of the zodiac. On the other hand, this very separateness can have an exotic quality, the attraction of the unknown and the unattainable. This is someone you'll never quite figure out. And this sign also has many threatening traits—if you get into this relationship, there will be risks and you won't quite know what to expect.

132

The "5" relationship is the proverbial square peg and round hole. Even though the stress of making this relationship work can be great, so can the stimulation and creativity that result from trying to find out what makes each other tick.

When positive and negative signs come together, lights go on, as you discover methods in dealing with situations and different ways of viewing the world, which can move you out of the doldrums. Here is how your sign relates to the "5" partners.

Aries: Scorpio/Virgo Scorpio, who tends to be secretive and manipulative, embodies everything that is foreign to Aries. Aries is clear cut and openly demanding. If an Aries attacks, it will be swift and open. Scorpio will wait for the time when an opponent is most vulnerable—years, if necessary—to deal the lethal blow. Aries burns out much sooner. Yet your very strong differences only make the conquest more exciting.

Virgo thinks the way to solve problems is to get organized and think things through, while steamrollering Aries wants fast action and quick results. Both Scorpio and Virgo will challenge Aries to go against the grain, being careful, organized, and persevering, and delving deeply while looking at the long haul. Aries will have to tone down impulsiveness with these signs.

Taurus: Libra/Sagittarius Libra, also Venus ruled, is involved with the abstract, idealistic side of the planet, whereas Taurus is involved with the sensual, materialistic, self-indulgent side. Libra challenges Taurus to abstract, to get into the mind as well as the body. Taurus will bring Libra down to earth and provide stability for this sign.

Sagittarius challenges Taurus to expend its territory. Taurus is the most rooted of signs, and can be immobile. Sagittarius is the happy wanderer. Taurus moves outside its turf with Sagittarius, who challenges it intellectually, spiritually, and physically.

Gemini: Scorpio/Capricorn Here, playful, verbal, mental Gemini is confronted by the failure to probe, the failure to deal with passion. Gemini gets into deep, real, emotional stuff with Scorpio. Contact with Scorpio often precipitates a crisis in Gemini's life, as this sign realizes there is something powerful that it's been missing. Scorpio challenges Gemini to delve deeply and make commitments rather than deals.

Capricorn makes Gemini develop discipline, set goals, and do practical bottom-line things the signs is not prepared to do. Capricorn has no tolerance for fragmented efforts and forces Gemini to focus and produce.

Cancer: Sagittarius/Aquarius Fearful, frugal Cancer must take risks to make a relationship work with Sagittarius, who loves to gamble and has faith in the universe. Everyone's buddy, Aquarius makes Cancer give love with an open hand, placing less emphasis on personal security and property.

Cancer must give up possessiveness with both these signs, who actually enjoy the kind of freedom and insecurity that Cancer most fears. In these relationships, Cancer's expectations of what a relationship should be have to change. It gets no protection from either sign and its favorite sympathy-winning techniques (playing "poor little me," whining, clinging, or complaining) only alienate these signs further. In the process of coping with these distant signs, however, Cancer can eventually become more independent and truly secure within itself.

Leo: Capricorn/Pisces Capricorn demands that Leo deliver on promises. With this down-to-earth sign, Leo can't coast for long on looks and star power. Capricorn wants results and pushes Leo to produce, casting a cold eye on shows of ego and bluffs. Conversely, both enjoy many of the same things, such as a high-profile lifestyle, but for different reasons.

Pisces is on another planet from solar Leo—the Neptunian embodies all that is not-self. This is a sign that devalues the ego. Pisces teaches Leo to be unselfish, to exercise compassion and empathy, to walk in others' shoes. Leo has to give up arrogance and false pride for a lasting relationship with Pisces.

Virgo: Aquarius/Aries Aquarius sheds light on Virgo's problem with getting bogged down in details. Interaction with Aquarius expands Virgo, preparing this sign for the unpredictable, the sudden, and the unexpected. Aquarius gets Virgo to broaden its scope and to risk experimenting. Aries gives Virgo positive energy and draws Virgo away from self-criticism and out into the world.

Libra: Pisces/Taurus Looking for a decision maker? Libra won't find it in Pisces! Pisces and Libra both share an artistic nature, but executed in a different way. Libra can't project its need for direction onto Pisces. Libra says, "What should I do?" Pisces says, "I know how you feel. It's tough not knowing what to do." Pisces challenges Libra to go within, to understand where others are coming from, rather than expecting them to conform to an abstract ideal.

Taurus brings Libra into the practical material world and gives this sign ground, but Taurus will also insist on material value. Taurus will ask, "How much does it cost?" Libra says, "I don't care, it's so pretty." Libra would rather not worry about function and operations, which become the task of Taurus. Libra will either desperately need Taurean practicality or find it a drag.

Scorpio: Aries/Gemini Listen for the clanking of an iron shield with the Mars-ruled Aries and Scorpio combination. Both of you thrive on challenge and find it in each other. The issue here: Who's the conqueror when neither will give in or give up? You'll have to respect each other's courage and bravery, and enjoy the sparks.

Gemini is the sign you can never pin down or possess, and this is super-fascinating for Scorpio. Their quicksilver wit and ability to juggle many people and things are talents not found in the Scorpio repertoire. Scorpios never stop trying to fathom the power of Gemini—just when they've almost got them pegged, Gemini's onto something or someone else! As long as you don't expect devotion, you won't be disappointed.

Sagittarius: Taurus/Cancer This is a dialogue between the rooted and the rootless. Both Taurus and Cancer are the most home-loving signs of the zodiac, while Sagittarius is the eternal wanderer—mentally, physically, or both. Will they be content to keep the home fires burning for Sagittarius? Another sticky point: Both signs are very careful with money. However, these two financially savvy signs could help Sagittarius achieve miracles instead of talking about them. Sag will have to learn patience with Taurus, who will inevitably try to tie Sag down. Cancer could dampen Sag's spirits with self-pity if they feel neglected in any way; Sag will have to learn sensitivity to feelings. If Sag can give up the position as teacher and become a student, these relationships might last.

Capricorn: Gemini/Leo Both of these signs are social charmers who need organization, which is Capricorn's forte. They can help Capricorn get a desired position with Gemini's deft charm or Leo's warmth and poise. The trade-off is that Capricorn will have to learn to take life less seriously and be as devoted to the partnership as to work. Otherwise, these two signs will look for amusement elsewhere. Gemini should inspire Capricorn to diversify, communicate, and spread wings socially, while Leo adds confidence, authority, and status. They'll appreciate Capricorn's structure in their lives.

Aquarius: Cancer/Virgo Aquarius, the most freedom-loving sign, encounters two different dimensions here, both of which tend to bring this sign back to the realities of operating on a day-to-day level (Virgo) and honoring emotional attachments at the level of feeling (Cancer). Cancer is the home-loving sign who values security, family, and emotional connections, an area often dismissed by Aquarius. Virgo is about organization, critical judgment, and efficiency, which enhance Aquarius accomplishments.

Pisces: Leo/Libra With Leo, Pisces learns to find and project itself. Leo enjoys Pisces talent and often profits by it, and in return, Leo gives this often-insecure sign confidence. With Leo, Pisces can't hide any longer, and must come out from the depths—but Leo will not sympathize or indulge Piscean blue moods or self-pity. Pisces has to give up negativity with Leo.

Libra's instinct is to separate and analyze. Pisces instinct is to merge. The more Pisces gets emotional, the more Libra becomes cool and detached. But Pisces can gain objectivity from this relationship, which insists on seeing both sides of any matter equally. Libra can provide the balance that keeps Pisces out of the depths.

Your "6" Relationships

"6" relationships are with your opposite sign in the zodiac. This sign is your complement, your other half, who manifests qualities that you think you don't have. There are many marriages between opposite numbers, because one sign expresses what the other suppresses.

Because most lasting relationships are between equals, the attraction to your opposite number could backfire. What happens if you're an easygoing Aquarius married to a star-quality Leo and you decide it's time to show off your natural charisma on center stage? Or a disorganized Pisces with an efficient Virgo who goes on a clean-up, shape-up program and out-organizes the Virgo? No longer does the opposite partner have exclusive rights to certain talents or attitudes. If they can make adjustments to the new you, fine. Otherwise, someone could be out of a job.

It's an excellent idea to ask yourself if you are attracting your opposite number in love or other relationships, what the signs are acting out for you. It could be a clue to a side of your character you need to develop. Sometimes, after the initial chemistry dies down, and two opposite signs actually begin living together, you'll be irritated by the same qualities that at first attracted you. That's because they reveal the part you are afraid of within yourself—the part you haven't really claimed for yourself. You may resent this other person taking that part over. Here's how it works out with opposite numbers: The more you learn to express both sides of the same coin, the better chance your relationship with a "6" will have.

Aries–Libra Aries brings out Libra's placating, accommodating talents. And, at first, Libra is happy to play the charmer in exchange for Aries decisiveness. Aries revels in the chance to take charge and to be so openly needed. But in close quarters, Aries seems too pushy, too bossy. And when Libra decides to make its own decisions, Aries had better learn to charm.

Taurus–Scorpio This is one of the most powerful attractions, often found in marriages and long-term relationships. Some of these couples manage to balance out their differences nicely; others are just too stubborn to give up or give in. The uncomplicated, earthy, sensual Taurus likes safety, comfort, and pleasurable physical things. Scorpio, who enjoys the challenge and dangers of intense feelings (and could live in a monk's cell), is often attracted to danger and risk. Scorpio wants a deep powerful merger, while Taurus likes to stay above ground, enjoying innocent pleasures. both are possessive and jealous, with a need to control their own territory. Scorpio marvels at the uncomplicated basic drives of Taurus—couldn't they get into trouble together? Taurus enjoys teasing Scorpio with promises of innocent pleasure, but learns that Scorpios sting when teased. Settle issues of control early on—and never underestimate each other's strength.

Gemini–Sagittarius Gemini is the eager student of the world. Sagittarius is the perfect guide, only too happy to teach, enlighten, and expound. This is a very stimulating combination. Sagittarius enjoys telling others what to believe, however, and Gemini can't be bossed. Gemini also turns off fiery confrontations and absolute declarations of truth, and may deflate Sagittarius with barbs of wit. On a positive note, this could be a wonderful combination both socially and professionally. Romantically, the relationship works best if they can be both student and teacher to each other.

Cancer–Capricorn Both of these signs have strong defense mechanisms—Cancer's is a protective shell, while Capricorn's is a cold and stony wall. In a relationship, both of these defenses play off one another. Cancer shows weakness, complaining and whining, as a means of getting protection, which dovetails nicely with Capricorn's need to play the authoritarian father figure (even when it's a female) who takes responsibility for the vulnerable child (Cancer). But if Capricorn shows vulnerability, such as a fear of not being "right," Cancer panics, becomes insecure, and erects a self-protective shell. On the other hand, if Capricorn takes over Cancer's life, this active cardinal sign gets crabby. Learning to parent each other and reinforcing strong traditional values could be the key to happiness here.

Leo–Aquarius Here we have two stubborn fixed signs with opposite points of view. Leo is "me-oriented" and does not like to share, while Aquarius is "them-oriented" and identifies with others. The Leo charisma comes from projecting the self—others are there for applause. Aquarius shines as the symbol or spokesperson of a group, which reflects self-importance. Aquarius is the talk-show host, working from the audience. Leo is the guest star, on stage. Leo is not about to become one of the Aquarius crowd, especially if the crowd includes Aquarian ex-lovers. Aquarius will not confine interests to Leo and become an exclusive Leo fan. If Leo can learn to share and Aquarius can give one-on-one attention, these opposites could balance out.

Virgo–Pisces In Pisces, Virgo finds someone who apparently needs their services badly. Virgo in turn is attracted to Pisces because this sign can deal with the tricky side of life that can't be organized or made to run on schedule. Sensitive Pisces seems to need Virgo's clarity, orderliness, and practicality to keep together and in line. You can see how easy it is for this to become a bargain between the helper and the apparently helpless. When Pisces gets organized and Virgo gets in touch with their own irrational side, these two could form a more solid relationship.

CHAPTER 9

The Love Detector Chart

Whether you're looking for a romantic playmate, a lifetime companion, or a business partner, or whether you are searching the zodiac to find your twin soul, astrology gives you a powerful tool for discovering why you are attracted to a certain person and how the person might act or react toward you. The *five personal planets* can reveal what attracts you both, what your tastes are, your temperament and sex drive, your mutual emotional needs, and how best to communicate—all the most important clues to compatibility!

Size up the overall relationship using the elements.

Get the big picture of your relationship by comparing the elements of each partner's sun, moon, Mercury, Mars, and Venus. The interaction of elements is probably the easiest way to size up a relationship. Planets of the same element have smooth, easy chemistry; these are your *Minimum Compromise Relationships*.

For easy reference, here are the four elements and the signs of each:

EARTH ELEMENT: Taurus, Virgo, Capricorn
AIR ELEMENT: Gemini, Libra, Aquarius
FIRE ELEMENT: Aries, Leo, Sagittarius
WATER ELEMENT: Cancer, Scorpio, Pisces

When your partner has a planet in the same element as your planet in question, the energy will flow freely between these planets. Venus in Aries and Mars in Leo, for instance, should work well together. Complementary elements (fire signs with air signs and earth signs with water signs) also get along easily, though not as well as the same elements.

Some elemental combinations are more challenging. There is tension and possible combustion between fire and water signs or between earth and air signs. Taking the analogy literally, fire brings water to a boil, earth and air create dust storms. These are your *Maximum Compromise Relationships*. However, challenges can be stimulating as well, adding excitement to a relationship, especially when planets of sexual attraction—Mars and Venus—are involved.

Here's an easy chart to give you the big picture:

First find the sign of each partner's planet. Assuming you know the birthdays, you can find the Mars and Venus placements in this book. You'll have to guess the Mercury (either the same sign as the sun or in the sign before or following the sun) and moon placements, if you don't have a chart available.

Then list the planets and elements as follows, grouping earth with water and fire with air, as in the following diagram.

THE LOVE DETECTOR CHART

	EARTH	WATER	FIRE	AIR
SUN	Jack			Jill
MOON	Jack	Jill		
VENUS	Jill		Jack	
MARS		Jack & Jill		
MERCURY			Jack & Jill	

You can see from the above that Jack and Jill have Mars, Mercury, the moon, and the sun in compatible elements. Therefore, it should be a very harmonious relationship. However, Venus could present a challenge.

Now look at the following list to see what each planet stands for. Find out how each planet relates to the others.

141

The Lunar Link—The One You Need

The planet in your chart that governs your emotions is the moon (although the moon is not technically a planet, it is usually referred to as one by astrologers), so you would naturally take this into consideration when evaluating a potential romantic partnership. If a person's moon is in a good relationship to your sun, moon, Venus, or Mars, preferably in the *same sign or element,* you should relate well on some emotional level. Your needs will be compatible; you'll understand each other's feelings without much effort. If the moon is in a *compatible element,* such as earth with water or fire with air, you may have to make a few adjustments, but you will be able to make them easily. With a water–fire, or earth–air combination, you'll have to make a considerable effort to understand where the other is coming from emotionally.

It's worth having a computer chart done, just to find the position of your moon. Because the moon changes signs every two days, the tables are too long to include in this book.

The Mercury Message

Mercury in the same or complementary element means a meeting of minds. In a challenging element, you'll have to work harder to keep lines of communication open and guard against shutdowns.

The Venus Factor—The One You Want

The Venus position in your chart shows what you respond to, so if you and your partner have a good Venus aspect, you should have much in common. You'll enjoy doing things together; the same type of lovemaking will turn you both on. You'll have no trouble pleasing each other.

Your lover's Venus in the same sign or a sign of the same element as your own Venus, Mars, moon, or sun is best. Second-best is a sign of a compatible element (earth with water, air with fire). If Venus is in an incompatible element (water with air or earth with fire), you may have to make a special effort to understand what appeals to the other person, since your tastes are basically different.

The Mars Connection—The One Who Lights Your Fire

The Mars positions reveal your sexual energy—how often you like to make love, for instance. It also shows your temper—do you explode or do a slow burn? Here you'll find out if your partner is direct, aggressive, and hot blooded, or more likely to take the cool, mental approach. Mutually supportive partners have their Mars working together in the same or complementary elements. But any contacts between Mars and Venus in two charts can strike sexy sparks. Even the difficult aspects—your partner's Mars three or six signs away from your sun, Mars, or Venus—can offer sexual stimulation. Who doesn't get turned on by a challenge, from time to time? Sometimes the easy Mars relationships can drift into dullness.

The Solar Bond

The sun is the focus of our personality and therefore the most powerful component involved. Each pair of sun signs has special lessons to teach and learn from each other. As you'll discover, there is a negative side to the most ideal couple and a positive side to the most unlikely match—each has an up and a down side. Read the section on "Your Sign in Love" in the Sun Sign chapters for an interpretation of the upsides and downsides of each relationship.

Remember that most successful relationships have a balance of harmonious points and challenges, which stimulate you to grow and which sustain lively interest over time. So if the forecast for you and your beloved (or business associate) seems like an uphill struggle, take heart! Such legendary lovers as Juan and Eva Perón, Ronald and Nancy Reagan, Harry and Bess Truman, Julius Caesar and Cleopatra, Billy and Ruth Graham, and George and Martha Washington are among the many who have made successful partnerships between supposedly incompatible sun signs.

CHAPTER 10

Astrology Bashers
A Response to Skeptics

In 1814, the proper Bostonian descendant of two American presidents stood on trial for practicing astrology. Evangeline Adams acquitted herself with style, proving her skills with a penetrating analysis of a mystery chart, which turned out to be that of the judge's son. Reported in national media, this marked the beginning of astrology-consciousness in this country on a mass level. For the first time, astrology was recognized as much more than fortune-telling, and became a legitimate practice in its own right.

Since that time, astrology has grown in popularity, with daily horoscopes now a familiar feature in most newspapers. Where once it was difficult to find an astrologer, practitioners now advertise in newspapers and yellow pages. Some are highly qualified professionals, with years of study and proven expertise. Others simply dispense canned horoscopes from one of the many computer programs available. Still others give readings that depend more on supposed psychic talents than astrological technique.

However, astrology still comes in for its share of bashing, mainly from legal and fundamentalist religious or scientific sources. As recently as 1996, astrologers were required to be fingerprinted and subject to police inquiries in California. There has also emerged a wave of debunkers who haunt computer bulletin boards and astrology conferences looking for any opening to bait astrologers. However, most debunkers have very little knowledge of astrology. It is rare to find an attacker who has ever had his or her horoscope chart done professionally, or one who knows any astrological terminology beyond basic sun-sign information. It very often happens that once a skeptic undertakes a serious exploration of astrology, he or she becomes an ardent advocate. In fact, the profession is full of astrologers who came from scientific disciplines, studied astrology for the purpose of disproving it, and ended up with great respect for this ancient art.

One such would-be debunker was a French statistician, Michel Gauquelin, who set out back in 1953 to disprove astrology by correlating astrological data for thousands of doctors, politicians, athletes, and soldiers, and concluded that, indeed, astrology rested on verifiable premises. Among his findings, he showed that Mars and Saturn contacts held true throughout the horoscopes of military leaders, and Mars propelled the horoscopes of athletes. He also confirmed planetary links between parent and child.

Actually, astrology has never claimed to be a science, a religion, or a psychology—though it has links to all three in their mutual origin in the search for the truth and for human beings' real purpose in life. We might say that astrology is the place where science, spirit, and psyche meet. Astrology has deep roots in all religions and can be found embedded in the spiritual history of every race. However, when religion became linked to doctrine and dogma, astrology, which has been accessible to everyone who wishes to study the planets, parted company with religion. In the Christian tradition, astrology was perceived as a threat to the established church, and astrologers were driven underground or persecuted. But the study of the planets and their relationship to the affairs of humanity continued, though astrology gained an unsavory reputation as fortune-telling, a connection that still lingers in the minds of those who try to discredit it.

Astrology is actually the study of cycles, a linking of forces in our own lives with the forces of the universe at large. But most enlightened astrologers believe that you are in charge of your destiny. You can use the planetary forces at your disposal as you wish. It's not unusual to see similar charts, in which one person has used the aspects in a positive way and another, with similar aspects, has become a criminal.

In its fundamental assumption that a given moment in time embodies the forces going on at that instant in the solar system, astrology does link us to a divine plan. When man first looked toward the heavens, it was in a wish to communicate with God, whether from a Babylonian ziggurat or a Mayan pyramid. The character of each sign of the zodiac was developed in a very systematic way, linking elements, qualities, and polarities. And the influence of the planets was determined after much observation. It is interesting that Mars, in all the various systems of astrology around the world, still embodies the same aggressive force; Venus is still the same kind of benevolent energy; and, from the time of the lunar goddesses of Babylonia, Phrygia, and Greece, to modern psychological interpretations, the moon has represented our instinctive, emotional self.

Many religious people are threatened by astrologers, because they equate all astrology with what has been practiced by many charlatans of the past or because they feel that someone interested in astrology will turn away from religion. However, as anyone who has delved seriously into astrology can attest, the study of astrology tends to bring one closer to a spiritual understanding of the interchange among a universal design, the material world, and man's place in it. Astrology can, in a very practical way, help people keep in balance with the forces of the universe.

Scientists, on the other hand, attack astrology as a "pseudoscience" for its supposed lack of factual evidence. We are forever hearing comparisons between astrology and astronomy, which is really more of a parent–child relationship, since astronomy grew out of astrology. History has conveniently forgotten that five of the most famous astronomers of all time were astrologers: Copernicus, Galileo, Tycho Brahe, and Johannes Kepler.

Most scientists have not studied astrology, nor do they approach it scientifically. They do not respect astrology as a discipline in its own right, thereby missing the point of astrology. It is not concerned with linear facts, but with linking humanity to the cosmos, linking the universe without to the universe within. The rise of quantum physics could bridge the gap between science and astrology, as scientists begin to explore a different reality beyond the mechanistic, materialistic view. Scientists are realizing that their own theories of natural phenomena are creations of the mind itself, depending on the position of the observer and the observed, and by no means the last word. When science begins to look within, perhaps the parent–child respect can be renewed and, once again, science and astrology can be part of the same family.

The great psychologist Carl Jung is responsible for creating quite a different attitude—one of partnership—between astrology and psychology. Jung had great respect for astrology and used it in his practice to clarify points that he said he would otherwise have been unable to understand. "Astrology represents the summation of all the psychological knowledge of antiquity," he explained. Today, there are many psychologists who use astrology to help them penetrate in depth into the authentic personality of their clients. In turn, astrologers have benefited by psychological counseling techniques, using them to guide their clients toward personal growth and find positive ways to handle the trends evident in their birth chart.

In the Nineties, when the Aquarian Age takes root, we've all been looking for ways to expand our lives. Perhaps in this era, a new, positive relationship will be forged between astrology and science and between astrology and religion, as we find these disciplines more complementary than competitive.

Meanwhile, there are still parts of the country where, at this writing, well-organized groups work against the practice of astrology. To assist astrologers in dealing with astrology-bashers of all types, the Association for Astrological Networking (AFAN) was formed. AFAN legal committees keep constant watch over those prejudiced against astrology who try to spread misinformation and prevent astrologers from practicing. The organization also works to educate the public about astrological

147

issues and create a network of astrology supporters who are interested in moving astrology forward and advancing the cause of professional freedom. Membership is open to the general public, as well as the professional astrological community, and it's an excellent way to participate in creating a better climate for astrology, as well as protect our individual rights. If interested, contact AFAN, 8306 Wilshire Boulevard, Suite 537, Beverly Hills, California 90211.

CHAPTER 11

Personal Readings
What They Can and Can't Do for You

Readings are everywhere—phone readings, tapes, charts, even celebrity-sponsored readings. Here's what to look for and some cautionary notes.

Though you can learn much about astrology from books such as this one, nothing compares to a personal consultation with a professional astrologer who has analyzed thousands of charts and can pinpoint the potential in yours. With your astrologer, you can address specific problems in your life that may be holding you back. For instance, if you are not getting along with your mate or coworker, you could leave the reading with some new insights and some constructive ways to handle the situation. If you are going through a crisis in your life, an astrologer who is also a trained counselor might help you examine your options; there are many astrologers who now combine their skills with training in psychology.

If you've been wondering about whether an astrological reading could give you the competitive edge in business, help you break through a personal dilemma, decide on the best day for a key event in your life, or help you make a career change, this may be the time to have a personal consultation. Before your reading, a reputable astrologer will ask for the date, time (as accurately as possible), and place of birth of the subject of the reading. (A horoscope can be cast about anything that has a specific time and place.) Most astrologers will then enter this information into a computer, which will calculate your chart in seconds. From the resulting chart, the astrologer will do an interpretation.

If you don't know your exact birth time, you can usually find it filed at the Bureau of Vital Statistics at the city hall or county seat of the state where you were born. If you still have no success in getting your time of birth, some astrologers can estimate an approximate birth time by using past events in your life to determine the chart.

How to Find a Good Astrologer

Your first priority should be to choose a qualified astrologer. Rather than relying on word of mouth or grandiose advertising claims, do this with the same care you would choose any trusted adviser such as a doctor, lawyer, or banker. Unfortunately, anyone can claim to be an astrologer—to date, there is no licensing of astrologers or established professional criteria. However, there are nationwide organizations of serious, committed astrologers that can help you in your search.

Good places to start your investigation are organizations such as the American Federation of Astrologers or the National Council for Geocosmic Research (NCGR), which offers a program of study and certification. If you live near a major city, there is sure to be an active NCGR chapter or astrology club in your area—many are listed in astrology magazines available at your local newsstand. In response to many requests for referrals, the NCGR has compiled a directory of professional astrologers, which includes a glossary of terms and an explanation of specialties within the astrological field. Contact the NCGR headquarters (see the resource list in this book) for information.

As a potentially lucrative freelance business, astrology has always attracted self-styled experts who may not have the knowledge or the counseling experience to give a helpful reading. These astrologers can range from the well-meaning amateur to the charlatan or street-corner gypsy, who have for many years given astrology a bad name. Be very wary of astrologers who claim to have occult powers or who make pretentious claims of celebrated clients or miraculous achievements. You can often tell from the initial phone conversation if the astrologer is legitimate. He or she should ask for your birthday time and place and conduct the conversation in a professional way. Any astrologer who gives a reading based only on your sun sign is highly suspect.

When you arrive at the reading, the astrologer should be prepared. The consultation should be conducted in a private, quiet place. The astrologer should be interested in your problems of the moment. A good reading involves feedback on your part, so if the reading is not relating to your concerns, you should let the astrologer know. You should feel free to ask questions and get clarifications of technical terms. The reading should be an interaction between two people, rather than a solo performance. The more you actively participate, rather than expecting the astrologer to carry the reading or come forth with oracular predictions, the more meaningful your experience will be. An astrologer should help you validate your current experience and be frank about possible negative happenings, but suggest a positive course of action.

In their approach to a reading, some astrologers may be more literal, others more intuitive. Those who have had counseling training may take a more psychological approach. Though some astrologers may seem to have an almost psychic ability, extrasensory perception or any other parapsychological talent is not essential. A very accurate picture can be drawn from the data in your horoscope chart.

An astrologer may do several charts for each client, including one for the time of birth and a "progressed chart," showing the evolution from birth to the present time. According to your individual needs, there are many other possibilities, such as a chart for a different location if you are contemplating a change of place. Relationships between any two people, things, or events can be interpreted with a chart that compares one partner's horoscope with the other's. A composite chart, which uses the midpoint between planets in two individual charts to describe the relationship, is another commonly used device.

An astrologer will be particularly interested in transits—times when planets will pass over the planets or sensitive points in your chart, which signal important events in your life.

Many astrologers offer tape-recorded readings, another option to consider. In this case, you'll be mailed a tape that contains an individual reading based on your birth chart. This type of reading is more personal than a computer printout and can give you valuable insights, but it is not equivalent to a live reading, when you can have a face-to-face dialogue with the astrologer and discuss your specific interests and issues of the moment.

About Telephone Readings

Telephone readings come in two varieties. One is a dial-in taped reading, usually by a well-known astrologer. The other is a live consultation with an "astrologer" on the other end of the line. The taped readings are general daily or weekly forecasts, applied to all members of your sign and charged by the minute, and the quality depends on the astrologer. One caution: Be aware that these readings can run up quite a telephone bill, especially if you get into the habit of calling every day. Be sure that you are aware of the per-minute cost of each call beforehand. Live telephone readings also vary with the expertise of the astrologer. Ideally, the astrologer enters your birth data into a computer and refers to that chart during the consultation. The advantage of a live telephone reading is that your individual chart is used and you can ask about a specific problem. However, before you invest in any reading, be sure that your astrologer is qualified and that you fully understand in advance how much you will be charged.

About Computer Readings

Most of the companies that offer computer programs (such as ACS, Matrix, ASTROLABE) also offer a wide variety of computer-generated horoscope interpretations. These can be quite comprehensive, offering a beautiful printout of the chart plus many pages of information. A big plus is that you get a copy of your chart and a basic natal chart interpretation, which can be an ideal way to learn about your own chart, since most readings interpret all the details of the chart in a very understandable way. However, the interpretations will be general, since there is no input from you, and therefore may not cover your immediate concerns. This is still a good option for a first reading, however, especially since these printouts are much lower in cost than live consultations. You might consider them as either a supplement or preparation for a live reading—study one before you have a live reading to get familiar with your chart and plan specific questions—and they make a terrific gift for someone interested in astrology. If you are interested in this type of reading, there are several companies on our astrology resource list that offer extensive readings.

CHAPTER 12

Your Cancer Potential

The Cancer Man—Tough Outside, Tender Inside

You sometimes wear a hard outer shell to protect yourself from the harsh realities of life. But inside, you're vulnerable and tender, afraid of being exploited if you show this nurturing side to the world. Usually, it comes forth in a professional way, through your choice of a career where you can express your feelings safely in a creative context. Many Cancer men choose nurturing fields in medicine, child care, psychology, hotel work, family businesses, or restaurants for this reason. Or they'll extend their nurturing to an extended family tribe, like the Cancer writer Ernest Hemingway, who was called "Papa" by all who knew him personally.

The Cancer man operates very much like your symbol, the crab. You're a sidewalker who moves indirectly at a situation, never confronting it face on, but always obliquely, subtly, and cleverly. Some might call you shrewd, others surreptitious. But what you are doing is reacting to your keen intuitive understanding of the hidden motives and agendas of others. You'll tune in to this powerful sixth sense before you listen to objective reason.

You have an uncanny ability to read the feelings of others, which gives you great emotional power and understanding. You know exactly how to nurture people by giving them what they need when they need it. On the other hand, you know where to inflict the most hurt (often by withholding what is needed). But your negative side, which can be cool and cruel, is actually a form of resentment in Cancers who have not been nurtured enough. If you can learn how to release the past and any hurts rendered to you, and discover how to nurture yourself, you have a much better chance to reach your full potential. Many Cancers have found psychotherapy extremely helpful in doing this.

Needless to say, a Cancer man's mother is especially important—even more so than to other men. If this relationship is lacking, you may try to replace it by mothering (or smothering) others or by looking for someone else to mother you.

The Cancer man, though you can be extremely masculine and sensual, rarely embodies the stereotypical masculine attitude. There is always a special communication of tenderness in your treatment of women, which makes you one of the zodiac's great lovers. You can tap into a woman's emotional needs and treat her with great understanding and sensitivity. This subtle vulnerability is evident in male Cancer celebrities such as Robin Williams, Tom Cruise, Harrison Ford, and Geraldo Rivera. Their special sensitivity is far more attractive to women than the muscle-flexing of macho types.

In a Relationship

Like the crab, the Cancer man hangs on—you're extremely possessive of whatever and whomever belongs to you. You'll hang on to old memories, old sweaters, and often your first dollar.

In a committed relationship or marriage, you're at last free to show your tender, caring, protective side. Your home is supremely important to you. It's the place where you feel most secure and can thrive in the supportive atmosphere of a long-term love. You treasure the mother of your children, who probably resembles your own mother strongly in some way. You are usually not attracted to independent women (unless your mother was independent), preferring the more maternal, nurturing type or a romantic, creative partner. You'd like her to be interested in domestic life and be an excellent cook. (If your partner is on the go all the time, she'll come home to a crabby mate.) Since you are usually materially successful, your home can be a private paradise for enjoying the good life together.

The Cancer Woman—
The Creative Capitalist

As an active cardinal sign, you know how to capitalize creatively on your deeply sensitive feelings, by finding ways to satisfy or feed the needs of others. Many Cancer women have become successful in business by providing the right product at the right time, like cosmetics tycoon Estée Lauder. However, you can also be quite acquisitive, and the Cancer woman will hoard money or objects as if to store up for hard times. It has been said that nothing upsets a Cancer woman more than an empty refrigerator or an empty closet.

Because of your deep feelings and uncanny intuition, you easily grasp the inner motivations of others, and this knowledge becomes your shell of protection. Cancer women in high places often extend their shell to become mother figures for their country, such as Princess Diana, Imelda Marcos, and Nancy Reagan. The wisest and wealthiest members of your sign use their intuition for personal and professional benefit.

You are especially affected by the moon's phases, especially during the full moon, when you could become super-sensitive and overreact to imagined slights. Let creative projects come to the rescue, turning your negative energies to positive again. You can find emotional fulfillment by providing food and shelter to others; cooking a delicious family dinner is excellent therapy for the Cancer moody blues.

Family influences are more potent with Cancer than with many other signs, so it is especially important that you try to conquer or reprogram negative relationships, so you can express your creative talents fully. You keep strong family ties throughout life and you are often able to combine your career with your home life, either by working at home or in a family business.

In a Relationship

You need a partner who is devoted and demonstrative, who will give you tangible proof of his love, and who will provide you with a stable home life that you need. Your choice of a mate is especially important, for a good relationship can draw you out of your shell and provide the emotional security you crave.

Cancer wives are famous for creating beautiful homes and family times. Many of you marry someone who is wealthy, powerful, and protective, and then provide an indispensable support system for him. (Imelda Marcos, Nancy Reagan, Camilla Parker-Bowles, and Leona Helmsley have done this). Usually, you are quite possessive of your husband and anxious to fulfill his needs. Sometimes a shy Cancer will transform herself into a public person and perfect hostess if her husband's role demands it, like Nancy Reagan and Princess Diana did. You are perfect wives for chief executives, since you are able to embody the feminine power role, and can be seen as maternal figures by large groups of people, becoming corulers with your mate.

The Cancer Family

The Cancer Parent

As the mother of the zodiac (even if you're the dad), you're in your element as a parent. You're at your best cuddling a tiny vulnerable child. Like Princess Diana, this nurturing quality extends to all children, who arouse your deepest caring, nurturing instincts. You can be fiercely protective of your brood and also possessive, hanging onto the mother role long after your children have left the nest. Often the Cancer parent will have a dynasty and sustain their parental role by bringing the children into a family business. One of your greatest lessons will be to let go when the time comes, and to find constructive outlets for your nurturing energies as you evolve out of the parental role.

The Cancer Stepparent

Since a broken home is probably one of the most traumatic events that can happen to a Cancer, you will be full of compassion for your stepchildren. You will intuitively understand their unspoken feelings and their need for emotional support. Much depends, however, on how secure you yourself feel in the new family situation, and if you are getting the emotional support you require from your mate. If not, you may have difficulty sharing your mate with a previous family. If you can be open with your feelings, this situation can be remedied. Establishing open communications can sidestep power struggles and emotional manipulation. You'll easily win the children over when your caring, protective nature is channeled in the right direction, where you can provide a warm, welcoming, extended family.

The Cancer Grandparent

Grandparenthood is a liberating experience for Cancers. Now you're free to enjoy young children without chores or responsibilities. You can fuss over the babies to your heart's content. You'll actually love babysitting the toddlers, pampering them with presents. Family get-togethers, when your brood gathers around a festive table piled with delicious traditional dishes, will be important seasonal events. You'll keep close ties with everyone in the family. Your grandchildren will always have a home with you, and there will probably always be some young visitor toddling about. Grandpa will be especially concerned that his dynasty's future will be secure and has probably provided a substantial nest egg. As you grow older, you'll pass on your sense of tradition, giving each generation a sense of the lasting pleasures of a close and warm family.

CHAPTER 13

Your Rising Sign: Why You May Not Seem Like a Typical Cancer

Aries Rising—Fiery Emotions

You are the most aggressive version of your sun sign, with boundless energy which can be used productively. Watch a tendency to overreact emotionally and blow your top. You come across an openly competitive, a positive asset in business or sports. But be on guard against impatience, which could lead to head injuries. Your walk and bearing could have the telltale head-forward Aries posture. You may wear more bright colors, especially red, than others of your sign, and you may also have a tendency to drive your car faster.

Taurus Rising—The Earth Mother

You'll exude a protective, nurturing quality, even if you're male, which draws those in need of TLC and support. You're slow moving, with a beautiful (or distinctive) speaking or singing voice that can be especially soothing or melodious. You probably surround yourself with comfort, good food, luxurious surroundings, and sensual pleasures, and you prefer welcoming others into your home to gadding about. You may have a talent for business, especially in trading, appraising, or real estate. This ascendant gives a well-padded physique that gains weight easily.

Gemini Rising—Expressive Talents

You have an airier, lighter, more ethereal look than others of your sign, especially if you're female. You love to be with people and express feelings easily. You may have writing or speaking talent. You need variety, a constantly changing scenario, with many different characters, though you may relate at a deeper level than others suspect and you are more sympathetic and caring than you seem. You will probably travel widely, and change partners and jobs several times—or juggle two at once. Physically, you should try to cultivate tranquility and create a calmer atmosphere, because your nerves are quite sensitive.

Cancer Rising—Sensitive Antenna

You easily pick up others' needs and feelings, a great gift in business, the arts, and personal relationships. But guard against overreacting or taking things too personally, especially during full-moon periods. Find creative outlets for your natural nurturing gifts, such as helping the less fortunate, particularly children. Your insights would be useful in psychology; your desire to feed and care for others would be appropriate in the restaurant, hotel, and child-care industries. You may be especially fond of wearing romantic old clothes, collecting antiques, and, of course, good food. Since your body will retain fluids, you should pay attention to diet. Escape to places near water for relaxation.

Leo Rising—Scene Player

You may come across as more poised than you really feel, but you play your role to the hilt, projecting a commanding and royal presence. This ascendant gives you a natural flair for drama that masks your sensitive interior.

You'll also project a much more outgoing, optimistic, sunny personality than others of your sign. You take care to please your public by always projecting your best star quality, probably with a luxuriant mane of hair or, if you're female, a valuable jewelry collection. Since you may have a strong parental nature, you could well be the regal family matriarch or patriarch.

Virgo Rising—Cool and Calculating

Virgo rising masks your inner nature with a practical, analytical outer image. You seem very neat and orderly, and more particular than others of your sign. Others may feel they must live up to your high standards, for you could be openly critical. But underneath you only desire the best for your loved ones. Your sharp eye for details could be used in the financial world, or your literary skills could draw you to teaching or publishing. Health and nutrition also attract many with a Virgo emphasis in their chart. Physically, you have a very sensitive digestive system.

Libra Rising—The Charmer

Libra rising makes you appear as a charmer, more of a social, public person than others of your sign. Your private life will extend beyond your home and family to the social world. You are more likely to smooth the way to negotiate diplomatically than give in to an emotional reaction. Physically, you'll have good proportions and pleasing symmetry, along with having pleasing, if not beautiful, facial features. You move gracefully and have a winning smile, as well as good taste in your clothes and home decor.

Scorpio Rising—Magnetic Power

You project an intriguing air of mystery when Scorpio's secretiveness and sense of underlying power combines with your sign. You are a master manipulator who can move in the world of power. You come across as more intense and controlled, with a direct and penetrating gaze, but you'll never reveal your private agenda. You tend toward paranoia, and even have secret love affairs. You often wear black and are happiest near water.

Sagittarius Rising—The Wanderer

You travel with this ascendant—you may also be a more outdoor, sportive type, with an athletic, casual, outgoing air. Your moods are camouflaged with cheerful optimism or a philosophical attitude—you'll laugh at your troubles or crack a joke more easily than others of your sign. This ascendant can also draw you to the field of higher education or to a spiritual life. You'll seem to have less attachment to things and people and may travel widely. Your strong, fast legs are a physical bonus.

Capricorn Rising—Serious Business

This rising sign makes you come across as serious, goal oriented, disciplined, and careful with cash. You are not one of the zodiac's big spenders, though you might spend on items with good investment value. You're the traditional, conservative type in dress and environment, and you might come across as quite formal. This ascendant could bring out your business sense. You'll function well in a structured or corporate environment where you can climb to the top, always aware of who's the boss. In your personal life, you could be a loner or a single parent who is both father and mother to your children.

Aquarius Rising—One of a Kind

You come across as less concerned about what others think and could even be a bit eccentric. Usually the rock stars, high-tech fanatics, futuristic scientists, or New-Age psychics are found here. You appear more at ease with groups of people, though you still need that solid home base. Your appearance may be unique, either unconventional or unimportant to you. You may exercise your nurturing qualities with a large group, as an extended family, or a day-care or community center.

Pisces Rising—Romantic Roles

Your creative, nurturing talents are heightened and so is your ability to project emotional drama—your dreamy eyes and poetic air bring out the protective instinct in others. You could be attracted to the arts, especially theater, dance, film, or photography, or to careers in psychology or spiritual or charity work. Since you are vulnerable to up-and-down mood swings, it is especially important for you to find interesting, creative work where you can express your talents and boost your self-esteem. Accentuate the positive and be wary of escapist tendencies, particularly involving alcohol or drugs, to which you are super-sensitive.

How to Find Your Rising Sun

At the moment you were born, your horoscope was set in moment by the sign passing over the eastern horizon: the rising sign or ascendant. Like your personal advertisement, this sign shows how you present yourself to the world.

The ascendant is one of the most important factors in your chart because it shows not only how you appear outwardly, but it sets up the path you are to follow. After the rising sign is determined, then each area of your chart is governed by the signs following in sequence.

The rising sun gives the planets a specific context, an area of life where they will operate. Without a valid rising sign, your collection of planets would have no home. Once the rising sign is known, it becomes possible to analyze a chart accurately—that is why many astrologers insist on an accurate birth time before they analyze a chart.

Rising signs change every two hours with the earth's rotation. If you were born early in the morning, when the sun was on the horizon, you'll most likely project an accurate image of the sun sign, as the sun and ascendant reinforce each other. Look up your rising sign on the following chart. Since rising signs change rapidly, it is important to know your birth time as close to the minute as possible. Even a few minutes difference could change the rising sign and the setup of your chart. If you are unsure about the exact time, but know within a few hours, check the descriptions before and after your estimated rising sign to see which is most like the personality you project.

RISING SIGNS—A.M. BIRTHS

	1 AM	2 AM	3 AM	4 AM	5 AM	6 AM	7 AM	8 AM	9 AM	10 AM	11 AM	12 NOON
Jan 1	Lib	Sc	Sc	Sc	Sag	Sag	Cap	Cap	Aq	Aq	Pis	Ar
Jan 9	Lib	Sc	Sc	Sag	Sag	Sag	Cap	Cap	Aq	Aq	Pis	Ar
Jan 17	Sc	Sc	Sc	Sag	Sag	Cap	Cap	Aq	Aq	Pis	Ar	Tau
Jan 25	Sc	Sc	Sag	Sag	Sag	Cap	Cap	Aq	Pis	Ar	Tau	Tau
Feb 2	Sc	Sc	Sag	Sag	Cap	Cap	Aq	Pis	Pis	Ar	Tau	Gem
Feb 10	Sc	Sag	Sag	Sag	Cap	Cap	Aq	Pis	Ar	Tau	Tau	Gem
Feb 18	Sc	Sag	Sag	Cap	Cap	Aq	Pis	Pis	Ar	Tau	Gem	Gem
Feb 26	Sag	Sag	Sag	Cap	Aq	Aq	Pis	Ar	Tau	Tau	Gem	Gem
Mar 6	Sag	Sag	Cap	Cap	Aq	Aq	Pis	Ar	Tau	Gem	Gem	Cap
Mar 14	Sag	Cap	Cap	Aq	Aq	Pis	Ar	Tau	Tau	Gem	Gem	Can
Mar 22	Sag	Cap	Cap	Aq	Pis	Ar	Ar	Tau	Gem	Gem	Can	Can
Mar 30	Cap	Cap	Aq	Pis	Pis	Ar	Tau	Tau	Gem	Can	Can	Can
Apr 7	Cap	Cap	Aq	Pis	Ar	Ar	Tau	Gem	Gem	Can	Can	Leo
Apr 14	Cap	Aq	Aq	Pis	Ar	Tau	Tau	Gem	Gem	Can	Can	Leo
Apr 22	Cap	Aq	Pis	Ar	Ar	Tau	Gem	Gem	Gem	Can	Leo	Leo
Apr 30	Aq	Aq	Pis	Ar	Tau	Tau	Gem	Can	Can	Can	Leo	Leo
May 8	Aq	Pis	Ar	Ar	Tau	Gem	Gem	Can	Can	Leo	Leo	Leo
May 16	Aq	Pis	Ar	Tau	Gem	Gem	Can	Can	Can	Leo	Leo	Vir
May 24	Pis	Ar	Ar	Tau	Gem	Gem	Can	Can	Leo	Leo	Leo	Vir
June 1	Pis	Ar	Tau	Gem	Gem	Can	Can	Can	Leo	Leo	Vir	Vir
June 9	Ar	Ar	Tau	Gem	Gem	Can	Can	Leo	Leo	Leo	Vir	Vir
June 17	Ar	Tau	Gem	Gem	Can	Can	Can	Leo	Leo	Vir	Vir	Vir
June 25	Tau	Tau	Gem	Gem	Can	Can	Leo	Leo	Leo	Vir	Vir	Lib
July 3	Tau	Gem	Gem	Can	Can	Can	Leo	Leo	Vir	Vir	Vir	Lib
July 11	Tau	Gem	Gem	Can	Can	Leo	Leo	Leo	Vir	Vir	Lib	Lib
July 18	Gem	Gem	Can	Can	Can	Leo	Leo	Vir	Vir	Vir	Lib	Lib
July 26	Gem	Gem	Can	Can	Leo	Leo	Vir	Vir	Vir	Lib	Lib	Lib
Aug 3	Gem	Can	Can	Can	Leo	Leo	Vir	Vir	Vir	Lib	Lib	Sc
Aug 11	Gem	Can	Can	Leo	Leo	Leo	Vir	Vir	Lib	Lib	Lib	Sc
Aug 18	Can	Can	Can	Leo	Leo	Vir	Vir	Vir	Lib	Lib	Sc	Sc
Aug 27	Can	Can	Leo	Leo	Leo	Vir	Vir	Lib	Lib	Lib	Sc	Sc
Sept 4	Can	Can	Leo	Leo	Leo	Vir	Vir	Vir	Lib	Lib	Sc	Sc
Sept 12	Can	Leo	Leo	Leo	Vir	Vir	Lib	Lib	Lib	Sc	Sc	Sag
Sept 20	Leo	Leo	Leo	Vir	Vir	Vir	Lib	Lib	Sc	Sc	Sc	Sag
Sept 28	Leo	Leo	Leo	Vir	Vir	Lib	Lib	Lib	Sc	Sc	Sag	Sag
Oct 6	Leo	Leo	Vir	Vir	Vir	Lib	Lib	Sc	Sc	Sc	Sag	Sag
Oct 14	Leo	Vir	Vir	Vir	Lib	Lib	Lib	Sc	Sc	Sag	Sag	Cap
Oct 22	Leo	Vir	Vir	Lib	Lib	Lib	Sc	Sc	Sc	Sag	Sag	Cap
Oct 30	Vir	Vir	Vir	Lib	Lib	Sc	Sc	Sc	Sag	Sag	Cap	Cap
Nov 7	Vir	Vir	Lib	Lib	Lib	Sc	Sc	Sc	Sag	Sag	Cap	Cap
Nov 15	Vir	Vir	Lib	Lib	Sc	Sc	Sc	Sag	Sag	Cap	Cap	Aq
Nov 23	Vir	Lib	Lib	Lib	Sc	Sc	Sag	Sag	Sag	Cap	Cap	Aq
Dec 1	Vir	Lib	Lib	Sc	Sc	Sc	Sag	Sag	Cap	Cap	Aq	Aq
Dec 9	Lib	Lib	Lib	Sc	Sc	Sag	Sag	Sag	Cap	Cap	Aq	Pis
Dec 18	Lib	Lib	Sc	Sc	Sc	Sag	Sag	Cap	Cap	Aq	Aq	Pis
Dec 28	Lib	Lib	Sc	Sc	Sag	Sag	Sag	Cap	Aq	Aq	Pis	Ar

RISING SIGNS—P.M. BIRTHS

	1 PM	2 PM	3 PM	4 PM	5 PM	6 PM	7 PM	8 PM	9 PM	10 PM	11 PM	12 MIDNIGHT
Jan 1	Tau	Gem	Gem	Can	Can	Can	Leo	Leo	Vir	Vir	Vir	Lib
Jan 9	Tau	Gem	Gem	Can	Can	Leo	Leo	Leo	Vir	Vir	Vir	Lib
Jan 17	Gem	Gem	Gem	Can	Can	Can	Leo	Leo	Vir	Vir	Vir	Lib
Jan 25	Gem	Gem	Can	Can	Can	Leo	Leo	Leo	Vir	Vir	Lib	Lib
Feb 2	Gem	Can	Can	Can	Leo	Leo	Vir	Vir	Vir	Lib	Lib	Sc
Feb 10	Gem	Can	Can	Leo	Leo	Leo	Vir	Vir	Lib	Lib	Lib	Sc
Feb 18	Can	Can	Can	Leo	Leo	Vir	Vir	Vir	Lib	Lib	Sc	Sc
Feb 26	Can	Can	Leo	Leo	Leo	Vir	Vir	Lib	Lib	Lib	Sc	Sc
Mar 6	Can	Leo	Leo	Leo	Vir	Vir	Vir	Lib	Lib	Sc	Sc	Sc
Mar 14	Can	Leo	Leo	Vir	Vir	Vir	Lib	Lib	Lib	Sc	Sc	Sag
Mar 22	Leo	Leo	Leo	Vir	Vir	Lib	Lib	Lib	Sc	Sc	Sc	Sag
Mar 30	Leo	Leo	Vir	Vir	Vir	Lib	Lib	Sc	Sc	Sc	Sag	Sag
Apr 7	Leo	Leo	Vir	Vir	Lib	Lib	Lib	Sc	Sc	Sc	Sag	Sag
Apr 14	Leo	Vir	Vir	Vir	Lib	Lib	Sc	Sc	Sc	Sag	Sag	Cap
Apr 22	Leo	Vir	Vir	Lib	Lib	Lib	Sc	Sc	Sc	Sag	Sag	Cap
Apr 30	Vir	Vir	Vir	Lib	Lib	Sc	Sc	Sc	Sag	Sag	Cap	Cap
May 8	Vir	Vir	Lib	Lib	Lib	Sc	Sc	Sag	Sag	Sag	Cap	Cap
May 16	Vir	Vir	Lib	Lib	Sc	Sc	Sc	Sag	Sag	Cap	Cap	Aq
May 24	Vir	Lib	Lib	Lib	Sc	Sc	Sag	Sag	Sag	Cap	Cap	Aq
June 1	Vir	Lib	Lib	Sc	Sc	Sc	Sag	Sag	Cap	Cap	Aq	Aq
June 9	Lib	Lib	Lib	Sc	Sc	Sc	Sag	Sag	Cap	Cap	Aq	Pis
June 17	Lib	Lib	Sc	Sc	Sc	Sag	Sag	Cap	Cap	Aq	Aq	Pis
June 25	Lib	Lib	Sc	Sc	Sag	Sag	Sag	Cap	Cap	Aq	Pis	Ar
July 3	Lib	Sc	Sc	Sc	Sag	Sag	Cap	Cap	Aq	Aq	Pis	Ar
July 11	Lib	Sc	Sc	Sag	Sag	Cap	Cap	Aq	Aq	Pis	Ar	Tau
July 18	Sc	Sc	Sc	Sag	Sag	Cap	Cap	Aq	Aq	Pis	Ar	Tau
July 26	Sc	Sc	Sag	Sag	Sag	Cap	Cap	Aq	Pis	Ar	Tau	Tau
Aug 3	Sc	Sc	Sag	Sag	Cap	Cap	Aq	Aq	Pis	Ar	Tau	Gem
Aug 11	Sc	Sag	Sag	Sag	Cap	Cap	Aq	Pis	Ar	Tau	Tau	Gem
Aug 18	Sc	Sag	Sag	Cap	Cap	Aq	Pis	Pis	Ar	Tau	Gem	Gem
Aug 27	Sag	Sag	Sag	Cap	Cap	Aq	Pis	Ar	Tau	Tau	Gem	Gem
Sept 4	Sag	Sag	Cap	Cap	Aq	Pis	Pis	Ar	Tau	Gem	Gem	Can
Sept 12	Sag	Sag	Cap	Aq	Aq	Pis	Ar	Tau	Tau	Gem	Gem	Can
Sept 20	Sag	Cap	Cap	Aq	Pis	Pis	Ar	Tau	Gem	Gem	Can	Can
Sept 28	Cap	Cap	Aq	Aq	Pis	Ar	Tau	Tau	Gem	Gem	Can	Can
Oct 6	Cap	Cap	Aq	Pis	Ar	Ar	Tau	Gem	Gem	Can	Can	Leo
Oct 14	Cap	Aq	Aq	Pis	Ar	Tau	Tau	Gem	Gem	Can	Can	Leo
Oct 22	Cap	Aq	Pis	Ar	Ar	Tau	Gem	Gem	Can	Can	Leo	Leo
Oct 30	Aq	Aq	Pis	Ar	Tau	Tau	Gem	Can	Can	Leo	Leo	Leo
Nov 7	Aq	Aq	Pis	Ar	Tau	Tau	Gem	Can	Can	Can	Leo	Leo
Nov 15	Aq	Pis	Ar	Tau	Gem	Gem	Can	Can	Can	Leo	Leo	Vir
Nov 23	Pis	Ar	Ar	Tau	Gem	Gem	Can	Can	Leo	Leo	Leo	Vir
Dec 1	Pis	Ar	Tau	Gem	Gem	Can	Can	Leo	Leo	Leo	Vir	Vir
Dec 9	Ar	Tau	Tau	Gem	Gem	Can	Can	Leo	Leo	Leo	Vir	Vir
Dec 18	Ar	Tau	Gem	Gem	Can	Can	Can	Leo	Leo	Vir	Vir	Vir
Dec 28	Tau	Tau	Gem	Gem	Can	Can	Leo	Leo	Vir	Vir	Vir	Lib

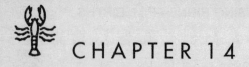

CHAPTER 14

The Cancer Route to Success

Cancer Power

There is no such thing as an emotionally uninvolved Cancer, especially one at the helm. You are extremely possessive of your means of security and hang on to your position despite all odds. As a boss, you operate intuitively rather than openly, which could lead others to suspect a hidden agenda. Your secretiveness can project paranoia, but you usually make up for this with a very protective attitude toward your underlings. Your emotional sensitivity is a plus when negotiating a deal—you know intuitively when to sign and when the competition is about to act. Though your moods may be baffling to associates, chances are they have learned never to underestimate you and to wait out the down times for a few days.

Cancer Teamwork

You are the one who has everyone fooled. Apparently quiet and shy, you are really taking everyone's measure. This is your way of protecting yourself before you reveal your tender, caring side. You work best in a rather traditional, nurturing atmosphere, where you can express your creativity and surprise everyone with your organizational talent and perseverance. Once you care about your work, you really produce. However, it is very important to work with supportive, congenial people, since you are easily upset by criticism and office politics. You'd prefer your office to be a secure home away from home. Your job assets are an excellent sense of marketing and a shrewd eye for quality, plus innate good taste. You do especially well in a business where you are taking care of people and fulfilling their needs. Though you may have up-and-down days, you should avoid bringing personal problems into your job situation.

Cancer Careers

Cancer is emotionally supersensitive, but also gifted with survival skills that can make this quality work for you. From behind your thick protective shell, you psych out just what the job requires, or intuit what the public needs, and then put your creativity to work, finding ways to fulfill those needs. It's no wonder so many millionaires were born under your sign! Your acquisitiveness makes you a shrewd judge of quality, and helps your accumulate a nest egg for yourself and profits for your company. Find a job that nurtures you and gives you a feeling of security—perhaps a family business. Your sensitive stomach rebels at constant nervous tension or stealthy political maneuvers—though you can outmaneuver the experts. Creative fields give you needed self-expression—photography, theater, music, and fashion, especially. The food, shelter, and child-related business are other natural meccas, as well as interior design and architecture. Marine business such as shipping, yacht sales, or marine biology are water-sign havens that would put you in the seaside environment you love.

To get ahead fast, pick a job that combines a supportive atmosphere with creative opportunities. Then play up your finest attributes:

- Creativity
- Intuitive insight
- Perseverance

- Shrewd judgment
- Caring, nurturing qualities
- Organizational talent

Cancer Success Stories

Study the success stories of these colorful Cancers, some of them legends in their own time. Most are featured in biographies, business magazine profiles, or reference books. You might get some useful tips for moving ahead on the fast track.

H. Ross Perot
Leona Helmsley
Stavros Niarchos
L. B. Mayer
Merv Griffin
Richard Branson (Virgin Airlines)
Estée Lauder
Nelson Rockefeller
Daniel Ludwig
Orville Redenbacher
Roone Arledge
P. T. Barnum
Imelda Marcos
Nicky Hilton
Peter de Savery
Michael Miliken

CHAPTER 15

Cancer in Love: How You Get Along with Every Other Sun Sign

Look up your lover, your boss, your potential roommate. But bear in mind that we're all a combination of many different planets, most likely in other signs. So be tolerant of your choices—there could be another planet in the picture that will make a big difference in how well you do—or don't—get along.

Cancer/Aries

Turn-ons: Cancer will give Aries hero-worship and nurturing, plus shrewd business sense and a solid home base to operate from. Aries gives Cancer romance and enthusiasm, along with positive energy and courage to coax out the cautious crab.

Turn-offs: Aries detests complaining or whining, so Cancer will have to suffer in silence. Sulking and possessive behavior are other Aries turn-offs. Cancer may balk when Aries pushes, and finds their behavior too insensitive and self-centered for delicate Cancerian feelings or stomach to bear.

Celebrity couples: Aries Warren Beatty and Cancer Natalie Wood. Aries Marsha Mason and Cancer Neil Simon.

Cancer/Taurus

Turn-ons: In theory, this should be one of the best combinations. Taurus can't get too much affection and TLC, which Cancer provides. And Taurus protects Cancer from the cold world, with solid secure assets. Both are home loving, emotional, and sensual.

Turn-offs: Cancer dark moods plus Taurus stubbornness could create some muddy moments. Both partners should look for constructive ways to let off steam rather than brood and sulk over grievances.

Celebrity couples: Cancer James Brolin and Taurus Barbra Streisand. Cancer Ginger Rogers and Taurus Fred Astaire. Cancer O. J. Simpson and Taurus Nicole Brown Simpson.

Cancer/Gemini

Turn-ons: This is a very public pair with charisma to spare. Gemini charm sets off Cancer's poise with the perfect light touch. Cancer adds warmth and emotional appeal to Gemini. You can go places together.

Turn-offs: It's not easy for Gemini to deliver the emotional intimacy Cancer demands—there are too many other exciting options. Cancer's possessiveness *vs.* Gemini restlessness could sink this one if you don't have strong mutual interests or projects.

Celebrity couples: Cancer John Tesh and Gemini Connie Selleca. Cancer Tom Cruise and Gemini/Cancer cusp Nicole Kidman.

Cancer/Cancer

Turn-ons: Ideally, here is someone who understands your moods, gives you the mothering care you crave, and protects you from the cold, cruel world. Your home can be a loving sanctuary for your extended family and a secure nest for each other.

Turn-offs: You both take slight so personally that disagreements can easily get blown out of proportion. And if you are both in a down mood at the same time, your relationship can self-destruct. You'll need some outside activities for balance and time away from each other to regain perspective. Creative expression can save the day here.

Celebrity couple: Sylvester Stallone and Brigitte Neilson (divorced).

Cancer/Leo

Turn-ons: These neighboring signs come through for each other like good buddies. Cancer gives Leo total attention, backup support, and the VIP treatment the lion craves. Here is someone who won't fight for the spotlight. Leo gives Cancer confidence, and this sign's positive mental outlook is good medicine for Cancer moods.

Turn-offs: Cancer's blue moods and tendency to cling tenaciously can weigh Leo down, while Leo can steamroll sensitive Cancer feelings with high-handed behavior.

Celebrity couples: Cancer Jerry Hall and Leo Mick Jagger. Cancer Sylvester Stallone and Leo Jennifer Flavin.

Cancer/Virgo

Turn-ons: You two vulnerable signs protect and nurture each other. Moody Cancer needs Virgo to refine and focus emotions creatively. Virgo gives Cancer protective care and valuable insight. Cancer's charming romantic tenderness nurtures the shy side of Virgo. You'll have good communication on a practical level, respecting each other's shrewd financial acumen.

Turn-offs: Cancer's extreme self-protection could arouse Virgo suspicion. Why must they be so secretive? Virgo's protectiveness could become smothering, making Cancer overly dependent. Virgo must learn to offer suggestions instead of criticism, to coddle Cancer's feelings at all times.

Celebrity couple: Virgo Anne Bancroft and Cancer Mel Brooks.

Cancer/Libra

Turn-ons: You'll bring out each other's creativity, as Cancer sensitivity merges with Libra's balanced aesthetic sense. Libra's innate sense of harmony could create a serene, elegant atmosphere where Cancer flourishes. You'll create an especially beautiful and welcoming home together.

Turn-offs: Libra's detachment could be mistaken for rejection by Cancer, while Cancer's hypersensitivity could thrown Libra's scales off balance. Emotions—and emotional confrontations—are territories Libra avoids, so Cancer may look elsewhere for sympathy and nurturing.

Celebrity couples: Cancer Richie Sambora and Libra Heather Locklear. Cancer Pamela Anderson ("Baywatch") and Libra Tommy Lee.

Cancer/Scorpio

Turn-ons: Cancer actually enjoys Scorpio's intensity and possessiveness—it shows how much they care! And, like Prince Charles and Diana (or Camilla Parker-Bowles) this pair cares deeply about those they lose. Strong emotions are a great bond that can survive heavy storms.

Turn-offs: Scorpio's mysterious melancholy moods can leave Cancer feeling isolated and insecure. And the more Cancer clings, the more Scorpio withdraws. Outside interests can lighten the mood—or provide a means of escape.

Celebrity couples: Scorpio Prince Charles and either Cancer Princess Diana or Cancer Camilla Parker-Bowles.

Cancer/Sagittarius

Turn-ons: Sagittarius gets a sensual partner who will keep the home fires burning and the coffers full, while Cancer gets a strong dose of optimism that could banish the blues. The Sagittarian carefree, outgoing outdoor lifestyle expands Cancer's sometimes narrow point of view and gets that sign physically fit.

Turn-offs: This joyride could reach a dead end when Sagittarius shows little sympathy for Cancer's need for mothering or runs roughshod over sensitive feelings. Cancer could withdraw into a protective shell or use claws when Sagittarius exercises a free hand with the budget.

Celebrity couple: Sagittarius Liv Ullman and Cancer Ingmar Bergman.

Cancer/Capricorn

Turn-ons: A serious sense of duty, family pride, and a basically traditional outlook bring you together. The zodiac mother (Cancer) and father (Capricorn) establish a strong home base. Cancer's tender devotion could bring out Capricorn's earthly sensual side. This couple gets closer over the years.

Turn-offs: Melancholy moods could muddy this picture. Develop a strategy for coping if depression hits. Capricorn is a lone wolf who may isolate himself emotionally, or withdraw into work, or take on an overload of duties, while Cancer could look elsewhere for comfort and consolation.

Celebrity couple: Capricorn Marlene Dietrich and Cancer Ernest Hemingway.

Cancer/Aquarius

Turn-ons: The clue to this one-of-a-kind couple is basic ideals. If you two share goals and values, there is no limit to how far you can go. Cancer is turned on by the security of a high position and offers Aquarius strong support and caring qualities that touch everyone's heart, the perfect counterpoint to Aquarius charisma. Former President Ronald Reagan and his wife, Nancy, are a case in point.

Turn-offs: Cancers are at their best one-on-one, while Aquarians love a crowd. Cancers have to learn to share their love with many—Aquarians have to learn to show warmth and emotion, rather than turn off Cancer moods.

Celebrity couple: Aquarius Ronald Reagan and Cancer Nancy Reagan.

Cancer/Pisces

Turn-ons: You both love to swim in emotional waters, where your communication flows easily. Cancer's protective attention and support help Pisces gain confidence and direction. Pisces gives Cancer dreamy romance and creative inspiration, and a very meaningful relationship develops over time.

Turn-offs: You two emotionally vulnerable signs know where the soft spots are—and can really hurt each other. Pisces has a way of slipping through clingy Cancer's clutches, possibly to dry out after too much emotion. Learn to give each other space and find creative projects to diffuse negative moods and give you a sense of direction.

Celebrity couple: Pisces James Taylor and Cancer Carly Simon (divorced).

CHAPTER 16

Your Cancer Lifestyle and Fashion Guide

Astrology can help you with all kinds of decisions, from what kind of clothes to wear to what color to paint your room. Here are some of the ways you can use the stars to guide you to the style that suits you best.

How Should I Furnish My Home?

You're the master of creating an atmosphere where everyone feels at home. Some of you have become internationally famous for this talent, such as the late interior designer Sister Parish, the first lady of decorating for the rich and famous. You'll create a mood that is comforting, secure, and relaxing, using crystal, candlelight, silver, and mirrors, so that your home looks especially good at night, when you shine brightest. You'll have many sentimental treasures, and good storage space for belongings you've saved over the years. Since you love to cook, your kitchen and dining room will be especially warm and inviting. You are sure to have one room done in tranquil, restful colors, a place for solitary meditation. A swimming pool nearby or a Jacuzzi tub are special Cancer luxuries. Turn your bathroom into a home spa, a private place where you can relax and rejuvenate.

What Music Will Put Me in a Good Mood?

You love music that stirs your deepest feeling or reminds you of happy times. Some Cancer artists that touch you are Carly Simon, Lena Horne, and Diahann Carroll. Though you gravitate to blues and love songs, you should collect upbeat music that lifts your spirits and cool jazz that soothes your nerves. Why not make special tapes of your favorite songs, themed to evoke moods such as romance, relaxation, and high energy, and put together the perfect background music to complement meals and parties.

Where Should I Go on Vacation?

Water-loving Cancers are in their element on cruises, at seaside resorts, and at tropical-island paradises. Rather than an impersonal resort, you'll prefer a home-away-from-home with a family feeling, or you may bring a relative or intimate friend for company. Investigate renting your own villa or condominium at a resort, rather than staying in a big hotel. This would give you both privacy and a place to entertain new friends. Cancer will actually enjoy shopping at the local food markets and serving regional specialties.

One of the zodiac's great shoppers, you'll probably bring home souvenirs for everyone in the family. Stash an extra collapsible suitcase or ballistic nylon tote bag in your baggage to hold all your finds. Most Cancers love to take photos, so be sure you have a small camera with you at all times. The new disposable cameras are perfect for casual snapshots and eliminate any worry about theft. Some of these cameras can even take photos underwater—attach them to your swimsuit while snorkeling.

Stomach upsets can be your travel foe, so take along

a portable water purifier and all the proper medication. Include a high-SPF sunscreen in all your travel kits.

Cancer likes to be on or under the waves, so ocean liners are the perfect floating vacation homes, or you may rent a sailboat to cruise the Caribbean. Scuba vacations also appeal. Exotic places like Nairobi, Singapore, Istanbul, Venice, and the highlands of Scotland suit Cancer's many travel moods.

What Are My Best Cancer Colors?

You like soft, subtle shades, nothing garish or shouting. All the moonbean shades of pearly white, silver, taupe, moss green, midnight blue, and coral are yours. Cancer decorators are specialists in using color to evoke moods, stimulate appetites, or sooth and comfort.

What Should I Wear?

Your sign is known for elegance and originality. You intuitively understand the right dress for every mood. Like Princess Di, you look best in romantic clothes that play up your intense femininity. Your luminous quality is especially evident at night, when you look your best. Soft, shimmering evening wear brings out the moon maiden in you. Wear silver and pearls, iridescent fabrics, and wavy hair to play up this quality. Accent your expressive eyes with subtle makeup and take care of your sensitive skin, which can react to emotional upsets or overexposure to the sun.

Who Are the Cancer Fashion Designers?

The sign of Cancer has many successful fashion designers who understand the many moods and the perfect styles for your sign—Bill Blass, Oscar de la Renta, Giorgio Armani, Pierre Cardin, Norma Kamali, Claude Montana, and Jacqueline de Ribes. All specialize in the elegant, ultra-feminine look that suits you best.

Where Should I Go for Dinner?

As one of the zodiac's natural gourmets, you'll appreciate the more creative chefs in town. Another possibility is a family-style restaurant, with ethnic food and Mama at the stove cooking her specialties. Many Cancers have delicate digestive systems and fare best on cooking with a light touch. Vegetarian restaurants and seafood specialties are excellent choices for those on a diet. Any restaurant with a romantic view of the water—ocean, stream, or lake—is sure to please. If you live in a city near the ocean or a well-traveled river, look for a floating restaurant, either on a barge, riverboat, or yacht, for a romantic dinner.

CHAPTER 17

Stay Fit and Healthy the Cancer Way

Your Health

Cancer rules digestive difficulties, especially gastric ulcers. When emotionally caused digestive problems—those stomach-knotting insecurities—crop up, baby yourself with some extra pampering, if you're feeling blue. Being with loved ones, old friends, and family could give the support you need. Plan some special family activities that bring everyone close together. The breast area is ruled by Cancer, a reminder to have regular checkups, according to your age and family health history of breast-related illness.

Your Diet

For this sign that loves good food, dieting can be especially difficult and can be laden with problems. Cancer can be conflicted about food: You may want to be fashionably thin to appeal to a loved one, but yours is also a sign that loves to eat and often becomes the family cook. Princess Diana is a good example of a Cancer who has faced and triumphed over an eating disorder. In any diet you choose, it is important not to have a feeling of deprivation. Remember to nurture yourself emotionally by airing problems and finding support to sustain healthier new eating habits, perhaps though a therapy group that is food oriented.

Exercise Tips

Boating and water sports are ideal Cancer-time activities. Sometimes, just a walk by your local pond or sitting for a few moments by a fountain can do wonders to relieve emotional stress and tension that can lead to overeating. Make exercise a family activity by creating a family gym, playing sports together, or going to exercise classes with loved ones.

Celebrity Role Models: Princess Diana, Sylvester Stallone.

CHAPTER 18

Astro-Outlook for Cancer in 1998

For the first five months of 1998, Saturn will be on top of your solar horoscope, in the tenth sector. In June, Saturn enters Taurus, that part of your horoscope representing hopes, wishes, the powers of persuasion, and the ability to win friends and influence people. In October, Saturn retrogrades back to Aries, where it will remain for the rest of the year. This planetary movement represents a kind of challenging, bittersweet period of your life.

Throughout 1998, challenges and restrictions, fearsome at first, ultimately boomerang in your favor. Pay attention to details, be aware of subtle innuendoes, and break down barriers involving distance and language.

Throughout this year, Taurus, Leo, and Scorpio play significant roles. Some of these people are likely to have these letters or initials in their names: D, M, V.

Uranus will be back and forth in Aquarius, your eighth house, representing money belonging to other people but placed in your hands. There is much unorthodoxy in connection with finances—prepare also to fight, if necessary, for your right to an inheritance.

April could be your most memorable, profitable, and romantic month of the year. During April, the spotlight will be on promotion, production, and receiving credit long overdue—your boss gives deserved recognition and cash to bolster compliments.

Study your daily guides. Many will include lucky numbers and valuable information for picking winners at the track. Your life, love, and immediate future unravels for you as you read these daily forecasts, which should be regarded as your diary in advance.

Let us begin; the year ahead awaits you, day by day.

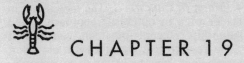

CHAPTER 19

Eighteen Months of Day-by-Day Predictions—July 1997 to December 1998

JULY 1997

Tuesday, July 1 (Moon in Taurus to Gemini 7:35 a.m.) Today, with the moon in Taurus, you'll discover that many of your desires are being fulfilled in an almost magical way. Another Cancer figures prominently. Co-operate in planning holiday festivities. There's an excellent dining experience tonight, with fine wine and food.

Wednesday, July 2 (Moon in Gemini) Lucky lottery: 3, 33, 6, 12, 18, 22. Joy replaces puzzlement and brooding. The financial picture is bright, despite expenses that seem to pile up. Gemini and Sagittarius are involved, and have these letters or initials in their names: C, L, U. Refuse to be distracted by one whose life is in shambles.

Thursday, July 3 (Moon in Gemini to Cancer 2:33 p.m.) Check your holiday schedule, including calls and invitations. Take special care in traffic. Be thorough, verifying historical claims. A talkative Gemini lets the cat out of the bag regarding the secret appearance of someone long absent. Taurus, Leo, and Scorpio are involved, and have these letters or initials in their names: D, M, V.

Friday, July 4 (Moon in Cancer)　　The new moon in your sign coincides with an optimistic approach to the future. A relationship, recently off-track, can be put back in order. The key is to get your thoughts on paper, to express your feelings, and to be open to romance, speculation, and discovery. Celebrate the Fourth with an aspiring writer.

Saturday, July 5 (Moon in Cancer to Leo 11:45 p.m.)　　What a Saturday night! Your cycle is high. Your personality draws to you fascinating individuals who express tremendous admiration. Acknowledge and be thankful, but avoid undue modesty. It's an excellent day for entertainment at home, for beautifying your surroundings, and for making decisions involving your home and your marital status. Your lucky number is 6.

Sunday, July 6 (Moon in Leo)　　Focus on spirituality and on advance knowledge in connection with finance. Don't tell all. Keep an aura of glamour, mystery, and intrigue. Let go of an unnecessary burden—a fresh opportunity presents itself tomorrow. Pisces and Virgo are in the picture, and have these letters in their names: G, P, Y.

Monday, July 7 (Moon in Leo)　　You were promised a fresh opportunity and it arrives now. The moon in Leo means money, payments, collections, and an ability to locate lost articles. The Saturn keynote relates to durable goods, lasting relationships, and a separation of wheat from chaff. Capricorn and another Cancer play major roles.

Tuesday, July 8 (Moon in Leo to Virgo 11:22 a.m.) Concentrate on your ability to see tomorrow. This insight is now honed to razor-sharpness. Emphasize wide appeal, explore overseas markets as distance and language obstacles are removed. An idealistic romance is featured, so continue your search for a soul mate. Aries figures prominently.

Wednesday, July 9 (Moon in Virgo)   A relative shares a plan to corner the market. Today's scenario highlights ideas that can be developed into viable concepts. Highlight independence, originality, and the courage of convictions. Love is revitalized. But avoid heavy lifting! Leo and Aquarius are in the picture, and have these letters or initials in their names: A, S, J.

Thursday, July 10 (Moon in Virgo)   Focus on direction, family, motivation, and the sale or purchase of property. Today's Virgo moon relates to criticism among people close to you, including your brothers or sisters. Don't scatter your forces—finish what you start, giving full play to your intellectual curiosity.

Friday, July 11 (Moon in Virgo to Libra 12:21 a.m.)   Lessons learned 24 hours ago can be put to effective use. What evaded you yesterday will be made available in a sudden, dramatic way. Add to your wardrobe, give attention to your body image, and keep resolutions concerning diet and nutrition. Your lucky number is 3.

Saturday, July 12 (Moon in Libra)   Lucky lottery: 4, 7, 12, 32, 33, 5. Untie the Gordian Knot! What you feared turns out to be a proverbial paper tiger. Know it and proceed accordingly. A Scorpio declares, "When I'm with you I feel as if I could conquer the world!" Taurus is also involved.

Sunday, July 13 (Moon in Libra to Scorpio 12:20 p.m.)   Break tradition if it is repressive. Strive for more freedom of thought and action. Be at home for a visitor who speaks of music and plays an instrument— this person proves inspirational. It's an excellent day for making lists, writing down aspirations, and finding outlets for creative energies.

Monday, July 14 (Moon in Scorpio)   Attention revolves around children, challenge, change, variety, and a major domestic adjustment. Beautify your surroundings, check real estate ads, give serious consideration to your home, your lifestyle, and your marital status. Libra plays a significant role, and could have these letters in a name: F, O, X.

Tuesday, July 15 (Moon in Scorpio to Sagittarius 9:02 p.m.)   A book suggested to you or given as a gift contains a spiritual message and is inspirational. Today's Scorpio moon highlights physical attraction, personality, sensuality, and sex appeal. Pisces and Virgo play outstanding roles, and have these letters or initials in their names: G, P, Y.

Wednesday, July 16 (Moon in Sagittarius)   Say goodbye to financial concerns relating to someone close to you, including a friend, partner, or mate. Within 24 hours, your house will be in order and routine restored. The same approach replaces slap-dash methods. Capricorn and another Cancer play paramount roles. Lucky lottery: 8, 50, 30, 1, 3, 4.

Thursday, July 17 (Moon in Sagittarius)   You no longer need to hold back or pull punches—straight ahead includes taking a chance on love. A bilingual person inspires an interest in language, foreign nations, and ethnic cuisine. An Aries says, "Whenever I feel distraught or that my goal is too far, I think of you and keep going!"

Friday, July 18 (Moon in Sagittarius to Capricorn 1:45 a.m.)   There's a new approach to employment, basic issues, and pets. Romance will be featured. Let go of the status quo and imprint your style. Don't follow others; let them follow you. Special: Avoid heavy lifting. Leo and Aquarius figure in today's exciting scenario, and have these letters in their names: A, S, J. Your lucky number is 1.

Saturday, July 19 (Moon in Capricorn)   The spotlight is on your public image and on special appearances. There could be a clash of ideas with someone associated with the law. The moon in Capricorn relates to your seventh house, which means legal rights, public relations, partnership, and marriage. There's gourmet dining tonight. Dinner is prepared by another Cancer. Lucky lottery: 4, 44, 2, 12, 20, 5.

Sunday, July 20 (Moon in Capricorn to Aquarius 3:29 a.m.)   The full moon relates to how you look to the world and how the world regards you. It could be déjà vu—a missed opportunity. But you'll have a chance to correct errors. Stress universal appeal, look beyond the immediate, and participate in humanitarian project. A Sagittarian plays a role.

Monday, July 21 (Moon in Aquarius)   You'll be dealing with Taurus, Leo, and Scorpio, who are likely to have these letters or initials in their names: D, M, V. Today's lunar position highlights willingness to fight for a cause and to get your fair share in connection with an investment or possible inheritance. A missing key located.

Tuesday, July 22 (Moon in Aquarius to Pisces 4 a.m.) What at first appeared to happen by chance could be something much more than you anticipated. Written material is involved. Close relatives invite you to participate in a unique search or enterprise. Analyze character, trusting your inner feelings. Gemini and Virgo are in the picture.

Wednesday, July 23 (Moon in Pisces)   At the track: post position special—number 2 p.p. in the fourth race. Pick six: 2, 2, 1, 2, 4, 4. The letters F, O, X could appear in the names of winning horses or jockeys. Hot daily doubles: 2 and 2, 3 and 5, 4 and 6. Taurus and Libra help you determine your course of action.

Thursday, July 24 (Moon in Pisces to Aries 5:03 a.m.) A dreamlike quality pervades today's scenario—break through the silence, official and otherwise, by gathering clues and synthesizing information. Let go of a losing proposition. Correct a plumbing problem at home. Pisces and Virgo figure in today's scenario. Look for these letters or initials in their names: G, P, Y.

Friday, July 25 (Moon in Aries) Ride with the tide! Focus on organization, awareness of a time limitation, and a strong love relationship. The Aries moon relates to your career, promotion, production, and standing in the community. A Capricorn decides to become your ally, and might have these letters or initials in a name: H, Q, Z.

Saturday, July 26 (Moon in Aries to Taurus 7:53 a.m.) You'll hear different languages being spoken; you'll be intrigued enough to seriously contemplate a trip overseas. People are drawn to you with their most intimate questions and problems. During a journey or participation in an education group, you might encounter your soul mate.

Sunday, July 27 (Moon in Taurus) A fresh start in a new direction is featured—your wish comes true in connection with finance and romance. You'll have luck in matters of speculation. A Taurus might decide, "You are the person for me!" Be wary, realizing that in actuality there is no free lunch. Your lucky number is 1.

Monday, July 28 (Moon in Taurus to Gemini 1:04 p.m.) You'll be musing, "What goes around, comes around." A family member who recently said, "I shall not return!" does come back. A relationship could resume. Your sense of direction is restored. A goal is in sight. Property value is estimated and a legitimate bargain is available. Capricorn is involved.

Tuesday, July 29 (Moon in Gemini)   Everything moves! What was considered a draw, a tie, is no longer the same—everything moves. Diversify, keep plans flexible, highlight your sense of timing and the ridiculous. Gemini and Sagittarius play memorable roles, and have these letters or initials in their names: C, L, U.

Wednesday, July 30 (Moon in Gemini to Cancer 8:38 p.m.)   A roadblock diminishes—hurdle it. Read between the lines and check signatures. Someone in a hurry decided to use your name for convenience. Let your feelings be known, and don't be too quick to forgive and forget. A secret is revealed, which relates to handwriting, possible plagiarism or forgery. Be careful!

Thursday, July 31 (Moon in Cancer)   The moon will be in your sign within hours. As your cycle moves up, written material becomes important. Publish your findings and advertise. A flirtation or chance meeting lends spice— enjoy the situation, but don't give up something of value for a mere whispered promise. Gemini, Virgo, and Sagittarius play significant roles. Your lucky number is 5.

AUGUST 1997

Friday, August 1 (Moon in Cancer)   Today, with the moon in Cancer and a Jupiter keynote, you might be saying, "This is the way I like to start a month!" Focus on diversity, elements of timing and luck, and social activity getting you in touch with bright, dynamic people. Your lucky number is 3.

Saturday, August 2 (Moon in Cancer to Leo 6:27 a.m.)   Throughout this month, the emphasis is on money, payments, collection, and investments. Today, review budget requirements and check tax and license responsibilities. Taurus, Leo, and Scorpio play significant roles, and have these letters in their names: D, M, V. Lucky lottery: 4, 40, 1, 12, 8, 17.

Sunday, August 3 (Moon in Leo)   The new moon in Leo coincides with earning power, and with an unusual meeting with a representative of a financial institution. Be ready for change, travel, variety, and written material that requires careful proofing. Gemini, Virgo, and Sagittarius are in the picture, and have these letters or initials in their names: E, N, W.

Monday, August 4 (Moon in Leo to Virgo 6:15 p.m.)   The spotlight is on your home and your lifestyle, and on music, gifts, and flowers. A decision is made relating to marriage. A special hint: If you're diplomatic, you win. Conversely, if you attempt to force issues, you lose. The choice is your own! Money comes from a surprise source, which relates to entertainment, commissions, and royalties.

Tuesday, August 5 (Moon in Virgo)   Avoid self-deception. See people and relationships as they are and not merely as you wish they might be. An ultracritical relative needs to be put in place. By so doing, you'll gain respect and ultimate admiration. Pisces and Virgo figure prominently, and have these letters or initials in their names: G, P, Y.

Wednesday, August 6 (Moon in Virgo)   The pressure is on—this relates to time, a unique assignment, added responsibility, or an intense relationship. Attention revolves around a business deal or your marital status. There is news that there might be an addition to your family. Capricorn and another Cancer are in the picture, and could have these letters in their names: H, Q, Z.

Thursday, August 7 (Moon in Virgo to Libra 7:17 a.m.)   The focus is on universal appeal. Reach beyond previous expectations. Communicate with someone familiar with import-export activities. Obtain a wider market or audience for product or talent. A love relationship heats up; it could involve a journey or participation in an educational group.

192

Friday, August 8 (Moon in Libra)   Breakthrough! The darker corners of your life receive the benefit of more light. The sun keynote blends with your moon ruler—you could receive public attention and might appear before the media. Make a fresh start, dealing with Leo and Aquarius who could have these letters in their names: A, S, J.

Saturday, August 9 (Moon in Libra to Scorpio 7:50 p.m.)   Someone who attempts to camouflage the facts will be caught short and exposed. There's gourmet dining tonight. An invitation is extended by another Cancer. A Capricorn individual relates to public relations, credibility, or marital status. The emphasis is on home, security, family, and the conclusion of negotiations involving property. Your lucky number is 2.

Sunday, August 10 (Moon in Scorpio)   On this Sunday, there's a wonderful clash of ideas, which relates to spirituality and the future. The Scorpio moon highlights creativity, style, experimentation, personal magnetism, and a controversy involving a romance. By tonight the controversy will be transformed into passion. Sagittarian is in the picture.

Monday, August 11 (Moon in Scorpio)   Find out where you stand, elevate your self-esteem, and refuse to be bilked. A romantic relationship requires additional clarity—discover where you are going and why. If you're married, a journey is forthcoming, possibly involving your children. Taurus, Leo, and Scorpio are involved, and could have these letters or initials in their names: D, M, V.

Tuesday, August 12 (Moon in Scorpio to Sagittarius 5:45 a.m.)   Within 24 hours, work methods become crystal clear, your fitness report improves, and you'll learn more about employment and how to upgrade your income potential. Get your ideas on paper, submit a format; your suggestions will be taken seriously. Gemini, Virgo and Sagittarius figure prominently.

Wednesday, August 13 (Moon in Sagittarius) Lucky lottery: 6, 51, 30, 3, 4, 9. Attention revolves around beautifying your surroundings, gifts, music, and marital status. You'll be reminded of resolutions concerning exercise, diet, and nutrition. Taurus, Libra, and Scorpio are involved, and have these letters or initials in their names: F, O, X.

Thursday, August 14 (Moon in Sagittarius to Capricorn 11:42 a.m.) At the track: post position special—number 1 p.p. in the sixth race. Pick six: 6, 4, 6, 1, 3, 1. Watch for these letters or initials in the names of potential winning horses or jockeys: G, P, Y. Hot daily doubles: 6 and 4, 1 and 1, 3 and 5. Pisces and Virgo play significant roles.

Friday, August 15 (Moon in Capricorn) Capricorn is especially important today. Activity revolves around legalities, reputation, credibility, and the securing of a lease. Another Cancer is also involved—look for these letters or initials in a name: H, Q, Z. A love relationship is stormy and controversial—but durable. Agreement is reached concerning a career move or a business enterprise.

Saturday, August 16 (Moon in Capricorn to Aquarius 1:58 p.m.) What seemed never-ending will finally be completed—this includes a project that had been moribund. Break free from the prison of inertia—imprint your style, open up the lines of communication, and be vulnerable to love. Special: The search for your soul mate should not be regarded as fruitless. Lucky lottery: 9, 33, 40, 15, 12, 10.

Sunday, August 17 (Moon in Aquarius) Some people will comment, "We never thought you would make it—we regard you as a miracle of survival!" The answer to your question: Affirmative. Make a fresh start, participate in a pioneering project. Love is featured. A current relationship is revitalized. A new romance could be on the horizon. Your lucky number is 1.

Monday, August 18 (Moon in Aquarius to Pisces 2:01 p.m.)   The full moon in Aquarius relates to your eighth house—this equates to mystery, intrigue, and the occult. A love relationship flourishes in a dramatic way. Low lights, dining in an out-of-way place, and discovering hidden resources all are part of a scenario cloaked in a mystery of the spy thriller category.

Tuesday, August 19 (Moon in Pisces)   At the track: post position special—number 5 p.p. in the seventh race. Pick six: 1, 2, 8, 5, 7, 3. Speed horses come in on the money, as Sagittarian jockeys have an excellent ride. These letters or initials could appear in the names of winning horses or jockeys: C, L, U. Hot daily doubles: 3 and 3, 7 and 2, 1 and 2.

Wednesday, August 20 (Moon in Pisces to Aries 1:45 p.m.   Be willing to revise and review; to rebuild, redecorate, and remodel, and to seriously review a current relationship. Someone may not be telling the entire truth—know it and act accordingly. The Pisces moon equates to travel, romance, publishing, and the practice of the healing arts. Your lucky number is 4.

Thursday, August 21 (Moon in Aries)   Be analytical, taking nothing for granted. The money picture is bright, as depicted by the Aries moon. Take the initiative in collecting debts—protect an invention, refuse to give up something of value for a mere whispered promise. Gemini, Virgo, and Sagittarius are involved, and have these letters or initials in their names: E, N, W.

Friday, August 22 (Moon in Aries to Taurus 2:57 p.m.)   Recovery! What was lost is found. Family is involved, and a celebration ensues. But go light on alco hol. With the moon in Aries on this Friday, deal with someone in a position of authority—state your case in a diplomatic way, but don't water down your principles. Libra figures prominently.

Saturday, August 23 (Moon in Taurus)   See people, situations, and places as they exist, not merely as you wish they might be. Today's Taurus moon coincides with your ability to make wishes come true. You'll win friends and influence people. Money comes from an unusual source. You'll have good fortune in connection with both finance and romance. Your lucky number is 7.

Sunday, August 24 (Moon in Taurus to Gemini 6:56 p.m.)   Powerful vibrations! On this Sunday, with a Saturn keynote and the moon in Taurus, you'll get things done. Spiritual values surface, and an intense love is featured. Capricorn and another Cancer play dominant roles. An older person assures you, "You won't be left in the lurch!"

Monday, August 25 (Moon in Gemini)   On this Monday, you'll complete a project. You'll also let go of a burden belonging to someone else. Focus on universal appeal. Make inquiries concerning travel and the expansion of your horizons. Aries and Libra figure prominently, and have these letters or initials in their names: I and R. Your lucky number is 9.

Tuesday, August 26 (Moon in Gemini)   In matters of speculation, stick with the number 1. The Gemini moon relates to secrets, institutions, and galleries—the darker corners of your life will receive benefit of greater light. Answer: Affirmative. Make a fresh start, imprint your style, be vulnerable to love. Leo and Aquarius figure prominently.

Wednesday, August 27 (Moon in Gemini to Cancer 4:11 a.m.)   Focus on your marital status. You can be at the right place at a crucial moment. The moon in your

196

sign relates to an opportunity, personal magnetism, and sex appeal. Another Cancer plays a dominant role, and has these letters or initials in a name: B, K, T. Lucky lottery: 2, 20, 4, 24, 33, 18.

Thursday, August 28 (Moon in Cancer) What a Thursday! Today's scenario highlights popularity, prosperity, personality, and being on the winning side. You'll be wined and dined. A family member who previously took you for granted will confide, "I didn't appreciate you then, but I really do now!" A Sagittarian is in the picture.

Friday, August 29 (Moon in Cancer to Leo 12:19 p.m.) A discussion involves the possibility of a name change. Remembrances concern your family, especially events relating to your mother. On this Friday, grab for the brass ring—money will be made available within 24 hours. Taurus and Scorpio are featured, with these letters or initials in their names: D, M, V.

Saturday, August 30 (Moon in Leo) Focus on added knowledge, wisdom, and ability to learn via the process of teaching others. A clash of ideas with someone of the opposite sex results first in an argument, but later is elevated to fascination. This could be the start of something big! Gemini, Virgo, and Sagittarius are in the picture. Lucky lottery: 5, 50, 7, 17, 30, 31.

Sunday, August 31 (Moon in Leo) On this Sunday, the moon is in Leo, your money sector. A family reunion is featured. Harmony is restored on the domestic front. Focus also on voice, sound, rhythm, and the music of the spheres. Taurus, Libra, and Scorpio are involved, and could have these letters or initials in their names: F, O, X.

SEPTEMBER 1997

Monday, September 1 (Moon in Leo to Virgo 12:27 a.m.) The new moon, solar eclipse in Virgo is fea-

197

tured today. The Pluto keynote relates to the need to handle details, check accounts, bring to light source material previously obscure. Taurus, Leo, and Scorpio are involved, and have these letters or initials in their names: D. M. V.

Tuesday, September 2 (Moon in Virgo)   A harmonious moon aspect coincides with physical attraction, creativity, change, variety, and a surprise presented by a young person who says, "I wish I could do something for you every day!" The focus is on reading and writing, teaching and learning, and getting notices in the press. Your lucky number is 5.

Wednesday, September 3 (Moon in Virgo to Libra 1:30 p.m.)   The money picture brightens within 24 hours. Don't feel guilty about celebrating tonight—dine out, being with friends who appreciate and love you. The emphasis is on music, harmony, luxury items, and fabulous desserts. A gift received tonight adds to your wardrobe. Wear shades of blue. Lucky lottery: 6, 51, 2, 12, 13, 22.

Thursday, September 4 (Moon in Libra)   Those who thought you were counted out will be in for a rude awakening. They'll suffer indigestion as a result of dining on crow. The Libra moon relates to home, security, familiar ground, and an ability to rebuild on a more solid structure. Pisces will play an outstanding role.

Friday, September 5 (Moon in Libra)   At the track: post position special—number 9 p.p. in the eighth race. Pick six: 8, 5, 3, 3, 1, 7. Older horses and favorites are likely to be in the money. Watch for these letters or initials in names of potential winning horses or jockeys: H, Q, Z. Hot daily doubles: 8 and 5, 4 and 7, 1 and 8.

Saturday, September 6 (Moon in Libra to Scorpio 2:10 a.m.)   On this Saturday, with the moon in the last degrees of Libra, you'll be relieved that a mortgage is paid up to date. Release yourself from a prison of pre-conceived notions—stress universal appeal, bringing to light a project that lay dormant. Your lucky number is 9.

Sunday, September 7 (Moon in Scorpio)   Just 24 hours ago, you promised yourself, "If I ever get the chance for a fresh start, I will make the most of it!" Today, this is it—highlight independence, courage, and the initiative to make a new start in a different direction. Leo figures prominently.

Monday, September 8 (Moon in Scorpio to Sagittarius 12:54 p.m.)   Attention revolves around children, challenge, change, and variety. You have the discipline necessary to meet and beat a deadline. The Scorpio moon relates to speculation and stirring of creative juices. You could be physically attracted to someone who "has been waiting for this moment." Capricorn is involved.

Tuesday, September 9 (Moon in Sagittarius)   Focus on joy, fashion, style, and the ability to blend humor with profundity. Get the job done, keeping promises made concerning the care of pets and wardrobe. A decision is made in connection with diet or nutrition. Gemini and Sagittarius persons figure in this scenario, and have these letters or initials in their names: C, L, U.

Wednesday, September 10 (Moon in Sagittarius to Capricorn 8:23 p.m.)   You'll be dealing with a vibrant, stubborn, talented Taurus or Scorpio. Have facts, figures, and research at hand. Read between the lines, study the fine print. Correct mechanical defects in your automobile and home. Check electrical outlets—a visitor should be discouraged from tampering with lights.

Thursday, September 11 (Moon in Capricorn)   On this Thursday, get your papers in order. You'll win a legal dispute if you're prepared—a test comes within 24 hours. The moon moves into Capricorn tomorrow, which coincides with cooperative efforts, a partnership proposal, or your marital status. The key is character analysis—your ability to spot a phony a mile away.

Friday, September 12 (Moon in Capricorn)   Attention revolves around efforts to beautify your surroundings, to bring harmony to the domestic scene. Focus on glamour, intrigue, mystery, and coming to terms with a loved one. You'll be saying, "I'd rather put up with you than to be alone!" A Libra figures prominently.

Saturday, September 13 (Moon in Capricorn to Aquarius 12:10 a.m.)   In some ways you'll feel that this is your day. Conversely, perhaps because of restrictions contained in a written agreement, you might be rebellious. The key is to strike a balance between pleasure and resentment. Pisces and Virgo figure prominently, and are likely to have these initials in their names: G, P, Y. Your lucky number is 7.

Sunday, September 14 (Moon in Aquarius)   A motion picture attracts attention and is the subject of discussion among associates and family members. You'll have extra responsibility and more opportunity to hit the financial jackpot. A Capricorn helps clarify contractual obligations. Partnership and marriage proposals are emphasized.

Monday, September 15 (Moon in Aquarius to Pisces 12:59 a.m.)   On this Monday, you might be fantasizing, "I'm a bird and can fly to any land or climate I choose." Focus on travel, publishing, and an ability to gain a wider audience locally and overseas. An Aries puts forth a promotional concept—it's worth taking seriously.

Tuesday, September 16 (Moon in Pisces)   The full moon, lunar eclipse falls in Pisces—this emphasizes the possible disruption of communication. Proofread written material, checking your meanings to be sure they're crystal clear. Someone attempts to black out previous good deeds. Be on the alert and ready to begin the project in the original manner.

Wednesday, September 17 (Moon in Pisces to Aries 12:25 a.m.)   At the track: post position special—number 6 p.p. in the fifth race. Pick six: 4, 1, 6, 8, 6, 1. Be alert for these letters or initials in the names of potential winning horses or jockeys: F, O, X. Hot daily doubles: 4 and 1, 2 and 2, 5 and 6. Another Cancer invites you to dinner—accept with pleasure!

Thursday, September 18 (Moon in Aries)   Diversify, giving full play to your intellectual curiosity. Get your clothes and passport in order—you could be rubbing elbows with big shots. The emphasis is on information, distribution, publishing, and advertising. You have a valuable gift today—the ability to make people laugh, even through their tears.

Friday, September 19 (Moon in Aries to Taurus 12:21 a.m.)   An obstacle is removed. You have the choice of fighting the odds or sidestepping an avalanche. Use lessons learned recently involving Taurus or Scorpio. Don't be intimidated by someone who attempts to boss you. What you own is valuable; don't give it away! Your lucky number is 4.

Saturday, September 20 (Moon in Aquarius)   Saturday night special! Focus on personality, charm, persuasiveness, popularity, and the ability to win friends and have your way despite envious people who desire otherwise. All stops are out! A chance meeting could result in a serious relationship—written words prove meaningful. Lucky lottery: 5, 50, 6, 12, 1, 10.

Sunday, September 21 (Moon in Taurus to Gemini 2:38 a.m.)   Today is ideal for a family gathering, music, a concert, or for viewing art objects or luxury items. A discussion of your property value and home is featured—ultimately you'll be musing, "I really do have everything, more than most persons." A young relative talks about a possible career involving music. Libra is involved.

Monday, September 22 (Moon in Gemini)   The focus is on mystery, intrigue, and glamour—be alert to a possible deception by someone who talks big, but knows the price of everything and the value of nothing. A project is completed. Check costs and expenses. It is likely you have a refund coming—don't hesitate to speak up, to let people know you are not without allies.

Tuesday, September 23 (Moon in Gemini to Cancer 8:33 a.m.)   A remarkable comeback! What was hidden is revealed to your advantage. Some persons proclaim, "You came back when most of us thought you were down and out!" Focus on intense love, responsibility, challenge, and your ability to bring order out of chaos. Capricorn and another Cancer figure in today's scenario.

Wednesday, September 24 (Moon in Cancer)   Look beyond the immediate. Your cycle is high as opportunities abound and circumstances take dramatic turn in your favor. Travel overseas should not be ruled out— you could encounter your soul mate during a journey or participation in an educational project. Focus on romantic love, style, panache, and foreign language. The lucky number is 9.

Thursday, September 25 (Moon in Cancer to Leo 6:12 p.m.)   The moon in your sign emphasizes independence, creativity, originality, and the ability to persuade others to join your camp. Make a fresh start; stress your vulnerability to love, to peer into the future. Focus on the adventure of discovery and the realization that life can be beautiful if enriched with love.

Friday, September 26 (Moon in Leo)   At the track: post position special—number 6 p.p. in the fifth race.

Pick six: 2, 1, 4, 3, 3, 8. Watch for these letters or initials in names of potential winning horses or jockeys: B, K, T. Older horses and favorites come in the money. Hot daily doubles: 2 and 1, 2 and 6, 4 and 4.

Saturday, September 27 (Moon in Leo)   The Leo moon relates to cash flow and to your ability to retrieve a lost article. Your cycle is high; take a chance on your capabilities. Others are impressed. You could win money and love. Diversify, trying different modes of transportation. You'll be complimented on your appearance or wardrobe. Lucky lottery: 3, 33, 1, 18, 22, 5.

Sunday, September 28 (Moon in Leo to Virgo 6:27 a.m.)   By tonight, you'll be saying, "I'm glad the money pressure is off!" Check facts and figures; be sure of research and references. A roadblock can be transformed into a stepping-stone toward your goal. Taurus, Leo, and Scorpio play meaningful roles. Look for these letters or initials in their names: D, M, V.

Monday, September 29 (Moon in Virgo)   A discussion revolves around a possible change of name involving you or your business—emphasize the unorthodox. Do things your way, despite objections from a family member. If a relationship ends, don't fear or brood—new love is on the horizon. A short trip is featured in connection with Gemini, Virgo, or Sagittarius.

Tuesday, September 30 (Moon in Virgo to Libra 7:32 p.m.)   Today, with a Venus keynote and the moon in Virgo, you'll hear sweet music. A close relative, a brother or a sister, makes a concession relating to past experience, finally saying, "Thank you!" A domestic adjustment occurs, much to your relief. Taurus figures in this scenario.

Wednesday, October 1 (Moon in Libra)   Today, with the new moon in Libra and a Mercury keynote, your words pack a wallop. Dine out if possible, being part of a lively group. This means exchange your views, welcome a clash of ideas, and don't be surprised if a usually shy individual says, "I always want to be close to you!" Your lucky number is 5.

Thursday, October 2 (Moon in Libra)   You'll be invited to view an automobile assembly-plant operation. Attention also revolves around home, security, income potential, and marital status. A gift received adds to the beauty of your home. Music is involved. Taurus and Libra are represented, and have these letters or initials in their names: F, O, X.

Friday, October 3 (Moon in Libra to Scorpio 7:57 a.m.) Within 24 hours, you might be madly in love. For tonight, make your intentions crystal clear. Find out what is expected of you and what you can anticipate in return. Whispers of sweet nothings could amount to just that— nothing. Be imaginative, not gullible. Pisces is involved.

Saturday, October 4 (Moon in Scorpio)   Attention will resolve around power, authority, discovery, and an intense love relationship. This is one Saturday you won't soon forget! Capricorn and another Cancer play major roles, and could have these letters or initials in their names: H, Q, Z. Lucky lottery: 8, 17, 37, 5, 9, 12.

Sunday, October 5 (Moon in Scorpio to Sagittarius 6:43 p.m.)   Stress universality, overcoming distance and language obstacles. You possess magnetic appeal. People will comment on your attractiveness, style, panache, and sophistication. Overseas correspondence results in a telephone call that might lead to future gain. Aries is represented.

Monday, October 6 (Moon in Sagittarius)   Make a fresh start, find different ways of achieving your goal. Employment conditions improve. You'll receive additional compensation for special services. A coworker confides, "I wouldn't be here if it were not for you!" Leo and Aquarius persons play roles, and have these letters or initals in their names: A, S, J.

Tuesday, October 7 (Moon in Sagittarius)   Focus on your marital status, business proposals, the sale or purchase of property, and greater recognition of your product or talent. Once again, your goal is in sight as you get a second chance. Another Cancer figures prominently, and has these letters in a name: B, K. T.

Wednesday, October 8 (Moon in Sagittarius to Capricorn 3:04 a.m.)   At the track: post position special—number 5 p.p, in the seventh race. Pick six: 5, 3, 7, 1, 6, 4. In anticipating winning horses and jockeys, watch for these letters in their names: C, L, U. Speed horses win; these selections apply to all tracks. Hot daily doubles: 5 and 3, 3 and 3, 4 and 8.

Thursday, October 9 (Moon in Capricorn)   Doublecheck references and signatures. The Capricorn moon highlights legal affairs, reputation, credibility, partnership understanding, and marriage. A clash of ideas proves healthy. Express your views in a positive, dynamic way. Taurus, Leo, and Scorpio are involved and have these letters in their names: D, M, V.

Friday, October 10 (Moon in Capricorn to Aquarius 8:29 a.m.)   The key is communication—read and write, learning via the process of teaching others. You'll be at the cutting edge of society—written words prove beneficial. As a result, you might be flirting with fame and fortune. Attention also revolves around your current marital status.

Saturday, October 11 (Moon in Aquarius)   There are compliments galore! What a Saturday! A mystery is solved.

A love relationship resumes and the temperature is hot. A serious discussion involves your home, property, sales and purchases, and marital status. Taurus, Libra, and Scorpio play major roles and have these letters in their names: F, O, X. Lucky lottery: 6, 12, 18, 33, 9, 4.

Sunday, October 12 (Moon in Aquarius to Pisces 10:59 a.m.) The Aquarian moon relates to your eighth house—concerns the occult, arcane literature, and tax and license requirements. Become aware of bookkeeping procedures—figures don't lie, but liars figure. See people, places, and relationships in a more realistic light. A Virgo figures prominently.

Monday, October 13 (Moon in Pisces) The Pisces moon relates to idealism in romance, travel, and communication. You're extra-sensitive, almost psychic. A faraway land soon will not be far away. Someone who is usually aloof will come close, and declare, "I have always adored you!" Capricorn figures prominently.

Tuesday, October 14 (Moon in Pisces to Aries 11:25 a.m.) Let go of the past—move ahead toward the future, where all of us will spend the rest of our lives. Check overseas markets, dine on foreign cuisine, experiment with language. People will be drawn to you with their most intimate questions and problems. Your lucky number is 9.

Wednesday, October 15 (Moon in Aries) Make a fresh start; aim toward your goal; don't settle for hand-me-downs. Emphasize the exclusive, original, unique, and special. Don't follow others; let them follow you. Display inventiveness and the courage of your convictions. Leo and Aquarius are involved, and have these letters in their names: A, S, J. Your lucky number is 1.

Thursday, October 16 (Moon in Aries to Taurus 11:16 a.m.) The full moon in Aries relates to your career, and to the completion of a project that elevates your prestige. Take the initiative in romance, express your feelings, write and recite poetry. Pace yourself, be yourself, and thus guarantee success. An Aries plays an outstanding role, and has these letters in a name: I and R.

Friday, October 17 (Moon in Taurus) Experiment, highlighting versatility, diversity, and different modes of transportation. People consult you on fashion and style—keep your resolutions concerning exercise, diet, and nutrition. It's an excellent day for the purchase of new clothes. You'll be asked to participate in an entertainment committee.

Saturday, October 18 (Moon in Taurus to Gemini 12:26 p.m.) Lucky lottery: 4, 42, 12, 18, 33, 8. Be willing to revise and review, to renovate, and to tear down in order to rebuild on a more solid structure. A wish comes true in a fantastic way—the Taurus moon in your eleventh house spells money, finance and romance, speculation, and career advancement. You'll be saying, "I pinched myself, so I know it's true!"

Sunday, October 19 (Moon in Gemini) Serious discussions evolve around the possibility of survival of the human personality following bodily death. Spiritual interests and values surface. The Gemini moon and Mercury keynote coincide with communication, exchange of ideas, physical attraction, and marital status.

Monday, October 20 (Moon in Gemini to Cancer 4:45 p.m.) The spotlight falls on where you live, your lifestyle, and the obtaining of a lease. A decision made relates to storage, sales and purchases, and transportation. Focus on flowers, music, and a reunion with a loved one. A gift received represents a symbol of love. Taurus and Libra are in the picture, and have these letters in their names: F, O, X.

Tuesday, October 21 (Moon in Cancer) Keep plans flexible—the moon in your sign represents initiative, new experiences, and the revitalization of a relationship. What eluded you 24 hours ago is now available—know it and pounce on an opportunity. Imprint your style, be original and dynamic, and show the courage of your convictions. Pisces is represented.

Wednesday, October 22 (Moon in Cancer)   On this Wednesday, with the moon in your sign, the key word is results. You'll bring order out of chaos, get files in alphabetical order, and communicate with one in authority. An older person, and possibly a Capricorn, lets it be known, "You are our main person!" Your lucky number is 8.

Thursday, October 23 (Moon in Cancer to Leo 1:10 a.m.)   Finish what you start, communicate with someone in a foreign land, get innovative ideas in writing so that you get credit for promotion. Aries and Libra play major roles, and have these letters in their names: I and R. The answer to your question: Break from the past. Begin a new program.

Friday, October 24 (Moon in Leo)   Imprint your style, avoid heavy lifting, and stress originality. Be vulnerable to love, but also protect yourself in clinches. This means that you shouldn't give up the farm for a mere whispered promise of thrills to come. Highlight universal appeal, speak another language, read widely, and communicate in a sophisticated way. Your lucky number is 1.

Saturday, October 25 (Moon in Virgo 12:59 p.m.)   A lost article will be found near water; it was misplaced while participating in a program of entertainment. The Leo moon relates to money, payments, collections, and increased income. Another Cancer becomes your ally, helping you with invoices and files. Lucky lottery: 2, 20, 21, 5, 8, 16.

Sunday, October 26 (Moon in Virgo)   Spiritual values are featured—relatives communicate. Some will tell you, "You are fun to be with and you also provide inspiration!" The emphasis is on trips, visits, intellectual curiosity, and a decision regarding where to go on vacation. Gemini and Sagittarius play meaningful roles.

Monday, October 27 (Moon in Virgo)   This Monday begins with a routine, but could conclude with an exciting discovery. A visiting relative introduces you to someone who could play an important role in your life and could actually become your soul mate. Check basic issues, references, and signatures; be willing to share information.

Tuesday, October 28 (Moon in Virgo to Libra 1:05 a.m.)   A departing relative leaves a note of appreciation—the words play a major role. Do some writing of your own. The current cycle relates to change, travel, and unusual experiences. A flirtation lends spice to your life. Gemini, Virgo, and Sagittarius figure prominently, with these letters in their names: E, N, W.

Wednesday, October 29 (Moon in Libra)   Lucky lottery: 6, 7, 36, 12, 4, 9. Attention revolves around a domestic adjustment, musical instrument, or delicious food as the result of a dinner invitation. Taurus, Libra, and Scorpio play major roles, and have these letters in their names: F, O, X. Furniture will arrive!

Thursday, October 30 (Moon in Libra to Scorpio 1:15 p.m.)   At the track: post position special—number 1 p.p. in the sixth race. Pick six: 6, 4, 3, 8, 4, 1. Apprentice jockeys could make the news. Watch for these letters or initials in the names of potential winning horses or jockeys: G, P, Y. Hot daily doubles: 6 and 4, 1 and 1, 3 and 8.

Friday, October 31 (Moon in Scorpio)   The second new moon of the month is in Scorpio, with a Saturn keynote, on this Halloween. Collect facts, and figures, reunite with a loved one, make a mortgage payment.

Today's lunar position emphasizes love, passion, creativity, style, and variety. Your lucky number is 8.

NOVEMBER 1997

Saturday, November 1 (Moon in Scorpio to Sagittarius 11:27 p.m.)   On the first day of November, there's a Venus keynote and a Scorpio moon. You'll be the center of attention and today's scenario will feature love, creativity, style, and an ability to weather an emotional storm. Attention revolves around partnership, marriage, direction, motivation, and the sale or purchase of property. Lucky lottery: 40, 14, 6, 32, 33, 22.

Sunday, November 2 (Moon in Sagittarius)   On this Sunday, appropriate spiritual values become the subject of attention and discussion. You'll be musing, "It seems it happened before—is this déjà vu?" Define terms, perfect techniques, see people and relationships as they are, not merely as you wish they were.

Monday, November 3 (Moon in Sagittarius)   At the track: post position special—number 9 p.p. in the eighth race. Pick six: 4, 8, 5, 7, 3, 2. Watch for these letters or initials in names of potential winning jockeys or horses: H, Q, Z. Hot daily doubles: 4 and 8, 8 and 5, 7 and 1; these selections apply to all tracks.

Tuesday, November 4 (Moon in Sagittarius to Capricorn 7:31 a.m.)   Complete a project. Reach beyond previous expectations. Work gets done. You'll get more recognition. This might be the day when you meet your soul mate. Aries and Libra figure prominently, and could have these letters or initials in their names: I and R. Your lucky number is 9.

Wednesday, November 5 (Moon in Capricorn)   Take a different approach to legal affairs. Love and marriage dominate. Show the courage of your convictions. Participate in a pioneering project. The answer to your question: Yes, make a fresh start, let go of the past. Leo and Aquarius are in the picture, with these letters or initials in their names: A, S, J. Your lucky number is 1.

Thursday, November 6 (Moon in Capricorn to Aquarius 1:33 p.m.)   The moon keynote blends with your moon significator to emphasize family, home, and security. There's a better relationship with someone who once was your main squeeze. You might be dining on exotic cuisine—another Cancer urges you, "Please stay for dinner!" Capricorn is also involved.

Friday, November 7 (Moon in Aquarius)   Today's Aquarian moon relates to that section of your chart associated with an inheritance, money belonging to another, or information regarding tax and license requirements. Interest in the occult is fanned—step into the unknown and thus gain wisdom. Gemini figures prominently.

Saturday, November 8 (Moon in Aquarius to Pisces 5:35 p.m.)   Do some proofreading—correct errors and check your source material. Someone who once rejected you will now plead, "It is time you forgave me!" A roadblock will be changed within 24 hours into a stepping-stone toward your ultimate goal. Lucky lottery: 4, 40, 48, 13, 19, 22.

Sunday, November 9 (Moon in Pisces)   A project needs time to mature. Check your travel agency. Look beyond the immediate. Investigate a publishing venture. A relationship that went off-track will be restored in an exciting way. You'll benefit from the written word. Gemini, Virgo, and Sagittarius play major roles.

Monday, November 10 (Moon in Pisces to Aries 7:44 p.m.)   Attention revolves around your home, marital status, or participation in a musical event. Remember to keep resolutions concerning diet and nutrition. Control that sweet tooth! The Pisces moon tells of being near water, possibly on a cruise. Trust your psychic impression! Taurus and Libra are involved.

Tuesday, November 11 (Moon in Aries)   Don't back down! Legal double-talk adds up to nothing—refuse to be intimidated. Define terms and clear away emotional debris. Avoid self-deception and perceive a relationship as it actually exists. Pisces and Virgo figure prominently, and could have these letters or initials in their names: G, P, Y.

Wednesday, November 12 (Moon in Aries to Taurus 8:45 p.m.)   The Saturn keynote, plus the Aries moon in your tenth house, equates with authority, promotion, production, and power play. Your marital status grabs the spotlight. There is news about a possible addition to your family. Today's scenario also highlights responsibility, awareness of time limitations. Your lucky number is 8.

Thursday, November 13 (Moon in Taurus)   Communicate with the boss. Higher-ups will be receptive to your written words. If you desire changes, say so in writing. Don't limit communications to the local level—reach beyond, to far-away places, perhaps overseas. A love relationship heats up.

Friday, November 14 (Moon in Taurus to Gemini 10:05 p.m.)   Don't stop now! The full moon in Taurus relates to your ability to win friends among the high and mighty. If you use your charm and talent, many of your wishes will be fulfilled. You'll have good fortune in matters of finance and romance. Your lucky number is 1.

Saturday, November 15 (Moon in Gemini)   Lucky lottery: 2, 22, 4, 8, 7, 16. Today's emphasis is on cooperative efforts, favorable publicity, and decisions relating to partnership, investments, or marriage. Capricorn and another Cancer play important roles, and have these letters or initials in their names: B, K, T.

Sunday, November 16 (Moon in Gemini)   On this Sunday, with the moon in Gemini and a Jupiter keynote, you'll transform humor into profundity. Friends you won 24 hours ago will be with you—this includes Gemini and Sagittarius, who are likely to have these letters or initials in their names: C, L, U. Your lucky number is 3.

Monday, November 17 (Moon in Gemini to Cancer 1:32 a.m.)   Check your source material. Heed the words of a Gemini who helps make valuable contacts. You'll be in a position to repay someone who did you a big favor during the past three weeks. Be willing to tear down in order to rebuild—Taurus, Leo, and Scorpio are represented.

Tuesday, November 18 (Moon in Cancer)   At the track: post position special—number 3 p.p. in the second race. Pick six: 5, 3, 4, 8, 1, 7. Watch for these letters or initials in the names of the potential winning horses or jockeys: E, N, W. Hot daily doubles: 5 and 3, 7 and 1, 6 and 2; these selections apply to all tracks.

Wednesday, November 19 (Moon in Cancer to Leo 8:38 a.m.)   You'll make the right decision at a crucial moment. The Cancer moon coincides with favorable circumstances. Prestige is gained through the written word. Make changes in your domestic environment. Taurus, Libra, and Scorpio play meaningful roles. Lucky lottery: 6, 11, 5, 50, 7, 17.

Thursday, November 20 (Moon in Leo)   At the track: post position special—number 1 p.p. in the sixth race. Pick six: 2, 5, 1, 8, 7, 1. Watch for these letters or initials in the names of potential winning horses or jockeys: G, P, Y. Hot daily doubles: 2 and 5, 3 and 4, 6 and 1; these selections apply to all tracks.

Friday, November 21 (Moon in Leo to Virgo 7:33 p.m.) On this Friday, a decision is reached in connection with a love relationship. Today's scenario highlights money, love, security, offspring, and marital status. What you invested in two months ago will surprise you by immediate advancement or dividends. Capricorn and another Cancer figure prominently.

Saturday, November 22 (Moon in Virgo) Don't stop now! Within hours, you'll be rid of a losing proposition or a negative situation. An assignment will be offered that provides a creative outlet, excitement, and overseas travel. Begin study of a foreign language. Express yourself; let it be known you are open to love. Your lucky number is 9.

Sunday, November 23 (Moon in Virgo) By refusing to quit, you opened doors of opportunity. Get a new start. Be independent. You have a chance to promote a relationship that equates to love and money. Don't follow others; let them follow you. To those who claim you are being arrogant, your reply is, "Too bad for you, because that is the way I feel and will act!"

Monday, November 24 (Moon in Virgo to Libra 8:29 a.m.) Attention revolves around large household products, a sense of quality, and constructive criticism. Close relatives, including your brothers or sisters, might be involved—you'll be surprised by their spirit of cooperation. Tell them, "Yes, I'm glad you're here; climb aboard!" Your fortunate number is 2.

Tuesday, November 25 (Moon in Libra) Family affairs! It's an unusual Tuesday—there's dancing, music, different modes of transportation, and foreign cuisine. Focus on entertainment, diversity, design, and color coordination. Participate in a political or charitable campaign. Gemini and Sagittarius are on hand, with these letters in their names: C, L, U.

Wednesday, November 26 (Moon in Libra to Scorpio 8:43 p.m.)   Lucky lottery: 4, 7, 12, 6, 15, 5. Obstacles will be transformed into stepping-stones—don't quit! Your requests will be granted, including a raise in pay. Offer suggestions which modernize techniques or speed production. Taurus and Scorpio figure in this scenario.

Thursday, November 27 (Moon in Scorpio)   Thanksgiving! There will be freedom of thought, expressions of love, and dealings with relatives who declare, "Your being here makes this holiday really something to be thankful for!" Within a matter of hours, the moon transits Scorpio, which stimulates a variety of sensations, including style, creativity, personal magnetism, and sex appeal.

Friday, November 28 (Moon in Scorpio)   The spotlight is on your home and family. You might invest in a precious gem. Married or single, you'll be thinking seriously about your current status and where you go from here. Be diplomatic and open-minded, but not gullible. Consider costs of remodeling, rebuilding, and decorating. Libra is represented.

Saturday, November 29 (Moon in Scorpio to Sagittarius 6:28 a.m.)   On this Saturday, there is much meditation and inspiration, as well as dealings with sensitive, psychic persons, most of whom were born under Pisces. It's important to define terms, to see situations and relationships as they exist, not merely as you wish they might be. Avoid get-rich-quick schemes. An unsavory situation is uncovered in connection with money. Your lucky number is 7.

Sunday, November 30 (Moon in Sagittarius)   On this last day of November, the new moon in Sagittarius equates to employment, basic issues, diet, and nutrition. The keynote is Saturn, representing solid goods, business, career, promotion, and production. A Capricorn talks about legal rights and permissions. Marriage counseling is involved.

DECEMBER 1997

Monday, December 1 (Moon in Sagittarius to Capricorn 1:38 p.m.)   Today, the moon is in Sagittarius, with an astrological keynote in Neptune. These aspects relate to long ago and far away. What appeared out of reach will become available. Begin early to compile your holiday gift list. Pisces figures prominently.

Tuesday, December 2 (Moon in Capricorn)   Today's Saturn keynote and Capricorn moon relate to partnership, construction, durable goods, cooperative efforts, public relations, and marriage. Stubborn Capricorn does have your best interests at heart. A clash of ideas provides stimulation and stirs your creative juices. Your lucky number is 8.

Wednesday, December 3 (Moon in Capricorn to Aquarius 6:58 p.m.)   Lucky lottery: 9, 10, 28, 40, 33, 7. Stress universality, reaching beyond the immediate and looking for hidden potential. You may be planning an overseas trip. Aries and Libra play significant roles, and could have these letters or initials in their names: I and R.

Thursday, December 4 (Moon in Aquarius)   Don't wait too long! Accept a leadership role. Express love in extraordinary ways. Focus on originality, showing the courage of your convictions. Today's Aquarian moon relates to secret meetings, occult revelations, and the discovery of oil. You might be asking, "Could all this be happening to me?"

Friday, December 5 (Moon in Aquarius to Pisces 11:07 p.m.)   The moon keynote emphasizes family, home, partnership, cooperative efforts, and marital status. You could feel jangled nerves from being pulled in two directions simultaneously by people who claim to have your best interests at heart. The spotlight is on diet, nutrition, and the sale or purchase of property.

Saturday, December 6 (Moon in Pisces)   Relief of pressure! Don't feel guilty about being entertained. Turn on the charm, translate humor into profundity—give full play to your intellectual curiosity. Gemini and Sagittarius play key roles, and have these letters or initials in their names: C, L, U. Lucky lottery: 3, 30, 33, 6, 14, 50.

Sunday, December 7 (Moon in Pisces)   At a commemoration of the "Day of Infamy," remember Pearl Harbor, throughout the day. Check details, read between the lines, and study galleys. Correct mistakes, cooperating with Taurus and Scorpio, who are likely to have these letters or initials in their names: D, M, V.

Monday, December 8 (Moon in Pisces to Aries 2:24 a.m.)   Change, travel, variety! Focus on journeys of the mind. Today's Mercury keynote equates to reading and writing, discovering the joy of learning. The scenario highlights flirtation, a chance meeting that could lead to something serious. Virgo plays a dominant role.

Tuesday, December 9 (Moon in Aries)   Focus on gifts, visits, flowers, music, and the sound of your own voice. The Aries moon relates to promotion, production, initiative, originality, and the spark of love. Money, marriage, redecorating, and remodeling are also part of this scenario. Taurus, Libra, and Scorpio are involved, and have these letters in their names: F, O, X.

Wednesday, December 10 (Moon in Aries to Taurus 5 a.m.)   Someone attempts to fool you, but in turn becomes the victim of his own tricks. Find out what is expected from you and what you can anticipate in return for your efforts and contributions. Don't take anyone for granted, and don't permit people to take you for granted. Insist on explanations, not evasions. Your lucky number is 7.

Thursday, December 11 (Moon in Taurus) Today's Taurus moon relates to friends, hopes, wishes, the fulfillment of desires. Turn on your charm, use your powers of persuasion. Money, romance, love, and marital status are featured. Meet a deadline. Deal gingerly with a Capricorn who has these letters or initials in a name: H, Q, Z.

Friday, December 12 (Moon in Taurus to Gemini 7:35 a.m.) An early invitation is received for a New Year's Eve celebration. Someone of the opposite sex courts you, seeking to please and promote romance. Remember what broke you up in the first place and proceed with caution, especially if the person in question requires a journey. Aries figures in this dynamic scenario.

Saturday, December 13 (Moon in Gemini) Refuse to be the guinea pig in a test case. A supposed secret is revealed; a Gemini attorney is involved. The sun keynote blends with the moon rulership to push you to make a fresh start in a new direction. Do it! Let go of the status quo and get ready for love. Your lucky number is 1.

Sunday, December 14 (Moon in Gemini to Cancer 11:25 a.m.) The full moon highlights mystery, intrigue, institutions, hospitals, galleries, and your possible participation in a motion picture. By getting in touch with someone confined to home or hospital, you could do some important networking. An opportunity exists for you to provide light in darker corners of lives, including your own.

Monday, December 15 (Moon in Cancer) When moving furniture, avoid heavy lifting. Diversify, transforming what seems to be a dull routine into moments of excitement. Discovery of photographs, scrapbooks, and memos jogs your memory, stirs your sentiments. Elements of timing and luck ride with you. Leo plays an outstanding role. Your lucky number is 3.

Tuesday, December 16 (Moon in Cancer to Leo 5:58 p.m.)   On this Tuesday, what seemed to be lost forever makes a dramatic reappearance. This includes a relationship with an old flame. Proceed with caution. The moon in your sign is your high cycle, when your judgment and intuition are on target. Be wary of someone who attempts to sell you a get-rich-quick scheme. Scorpio plays a role.

Wednesday, December 17 (Moon in Leo)   Lucky lottery: 5, 10, 1, 25, 35, 7. Read and write, spread the word, get ready for a surprise, as a relative returns the favor or pays a debt. Today's scenario highlights wit and wisdom, humor blended with profundity. There's spice in your life—you'll be complimented by attempts to seduce. My heart belongs to Daddy!

Thursday, December 18 (Moon in Leo)   Reviewing events of 24 hours ago provides humor, laughter. Your sense of the ridiculous is heightened. Focus on home, security, income potential, music, entertainment, and dining in a posh restaurant. The spotlight also falls on income, royalties, back pay, or a profitable assignment. Libra is involved.

Friday, December 19 (Moon in Leo to Virgo 4 a.m.) On this Friday, you learn plenty about money and how to earn it. A false report can be corrected. Your views are vindicated. Play the waiting game. Don't be cajoled into making a snap decision. Analyze terms, look behind the scenes. See people and situations in a realistic way. Pisces figures prominently.

Saturday, December 20 (Moon in Virgo)   Lucky lottery: 6, 15, 42, 5, 1, 30. Focus on timing, and on dealings with representatives of corporations that spread influence far and wide. Capricorn and another Cancer figure in today's fast action. Look for these letters or initials in their names: H, Q, Z. Order will be restored tonight!

Sunday, December 21 (Moon in Virgo to Libra 4:35 p.m.) A spontaneous discussion with Aries relates to a possible overseas journey. Let go of the status quo. One cycle is ending; another gets under way. Love plays a key role. You no longer will feel you're alone in the world. Highlight universal appeal, foreign cuisine, and acquiescing to Libra's request.

Monday, December 22 (Moon in Libra) Make fresh start. A favor you did for a Libra will be repaid twofold. Strive for balance. Let others know you accept a leadership role. The spotlight is on building material, the sale or purchase of property, or participating in long-term negotiations involving partnership.

Tuesday, December 23 (Moon in Libra) Lessons learned 24 hours ago will be put into use—this involves payments, collections, sturdiness of goods, reliability, and credibility. Another Cancer figures prominently, inviting you to dine. Directions are revealed. You'll know where you are going and why. Your lucky number is 2.

Wednesday, December 24 (Moon in Libra to Scorpio 5:07 a.m.) Christmas spirit! The Jupiter keynote is a "planetary Santa Claus." You'll receive gifts in large, colorful packages. The true values of this holiday will not be ignored—you'll get assurances that you are loved, and this is one Christmas Eve not soon to be forgotten. A Sagittarian is in your life now.

Thursday, December 25 (Moon in Scorpio) What a Christmas! Today's Scorpio moon represents children, challenge, excitement, and an outlet of your creative urge. A roadblock becomes a stepping-stone toward your ultimate goal. Taurus and Leo lend spice to your life. The Taurus native helps make one of your fondest hopes and wishes come true.

Friday, December 26 (Moon in Scorpio to Sagittarius 3:07 p.m.)   Change is in order—this includes an exchange of gifts. Today's Mercury keynote relates to the written word, your ability to articulate feelings, and to reading and writing and disseminating information. Be analytical; take nothing for granted and show your true colors, which are excellent. Virgo is represented.

Saturday, December 27 (Moon in Sagittarius)   Lucky lottery: 6, 9, 19, 3, 30, 8. A significant domestic adjustment takes place. Family members gather, music sounds, and expressions of appreciation and love abound. The key is to be diplomatic; don't force issues, but make an intelligent concession to a family member. Libra is involved.

Sunday, December 28 (Moon in Sagittarius to Capricorn 9:48 p.m.)   Define terms, making your meanings crystal clear. Focus on employment, basic issues, and the responsibility of pet ownership. Pisces and Virgo play meaningful roles, and could have these letters or initials in their names: G, P, Y. See people as they are, avoiding self-deception. Streamline procedures and keep confidences.

Monday, December 29 (Moon in Capricorn)   A serious discussion involves a possible change of name, for professional reasons. The new moon in Capricorn relates to a revival of a project that long lay dormant. Get legal papers in order, protect your rights, make public appearances, and promote your point of view. Your marital status is not ignored.

Tuesday, December 30 (Moon in Capricorn)   The sword of Damocles is removed—a legal hindrance no longer exists. Emphasize universality, develop language skills, plan ahead for a journey that could take you overseas. Capricorn and another Cancer play outstanding roles, and have these letters in their names: I and R. Your lucky number is 9.

Wednesday, December 31 (Moon in Capricorn to Aquarius 1:58 a.m.)   New Year's Eve! On this last day of the year, you apparently have the power of prophesy. Your senses are honed to razor-sharpness—you are in rhythm with the future. The sun keynote means you are proceeding with confidence in the right direction, heading for fulfillment, happiness, and love. Your lucky number is 1. Happy New Year!

HAPPY NEW YEAR!

JANUARY 1998

Thursday, January 1 (Moon in Aquarius)   With a Venus keynote and the moon in Aquarius, you'll be resting comfortably. The rest represents a change of pace and is accompanied by music and the return of domestic sanity. Taurus, Leo, and Scorpio figure prominently, and are likely to have these letters in their names: F, O, X.

Friday, January 2 (Moon in Aquarius to Pisces 4:56 a.m.)   Play the waiting game! Don't be afraid to dabble in the occult, asking questions and finding out more about money. An Aquarian dispenses information previously withheld for no good reason. Define your terms and perceive a relationship as it exists, not merely as you wish it might be.

Saturday, January 3 (Moon in Pisces)   Lucky lottery: 8, 12, 25, 7, 13, 4. Focus on bringing order out of chaos, lining up priorities, and realizing that a relationship, despite frailties, is ultimately durable. Capricorn and Cancer-born persons figure prominently, and are likely to have these letters in their names: H, Q, Z.

Sunday, January 4 (Moon in Pisces to Aries 7:43 a.m.)
What a Sunday! Spiritual values flow with the focus on universal appeal, communication with people overseas, learning more about foreign cuisine, and coming to grips with distance and language barriers. Aries and Libra play memorable roles, and are likely to have these letters in their names: I and R.

Monday, January 5 (Moon in Aries)   Make a fresh start, taking the initiative and exercising independence of thought and action. Today's Aries moon relates to your career, ambitions, and dealings with higher-ups. If you have been waiting for the right time, this is it. Let go of the status quo, for you no longer are a prisoner of preconceived notions or inertia. Your lucky number is 1.

Tuesday, January 6 (Moon in Aries to Taurus 10:52 a.m.)   At the track: post position special—number 6 p.p. in fifth race. Pick six: 2, 2, 4, 8, 6, 5. Watch these letters in the names of potential winning horses or jockeys: B, K, T. Hot daily doubles: 2 and 2, 3 and 2, 5 and 4; these selections apply to all tracks.

Wednesday, January 7 (Moon in Taurus)   Lucky lottery: 3, 25, 2, 26, 13, 22. Social activities accelerate and people ask you to join campaigns, either political or charitable. New clothes improve your body image, but keep your resolutions concerning exercise, diet, and nutrition. Elements of luck rise with you, and this could be the start of a winning streak.

Thursday, January 8 (Moon in Taurus to Gemini 2:42 p.m.)   In a way, you'll be feeling, "This has happened before!" It could indeed be a matter of déjà vu. You'll untie a Gordian Knot, the puzzle pieces will fall into place, and order will evolve from chaos. You'll know what must be done and it will get done! Taurus, Leo, and Scorpio are involved, with these letters in their names: D, M, V.

Friday, January 9 (Moon in Gemini)   Focus on change, travel, variety, and the excitement of discovery. What was held back is now released—you'll read, write, disseminate information, and be romantically involved after a serious flirtation. You'll encounter a character analyst who helps you regain confidence. Sagittarius is involved.

Saturday, January 10 (Moon in Gemini to Cancer 7:43 p.m.)   A musical score is involved as people seek your opinion on sound, rhythm, design, color, and a possible domestic adjustment. Be diplomatic, even if the questions are trite. The spotlight is on antiques, luxury items, art objects, and comfortable chairs. Libra figures in today's dynamic scenario, with these letters in a name: F, O, X.

Sunday, January 11 (Moon in Cancer)   Within 24 hours, your cycle moves up, transforming indecision into progress. For today, define your terms, perceive relationships realistically, perfect your techniques, and practice meditation. Play the waiting game, refusing to be intimidated into making snap decision.

Monday, January 12 (Moon in Cancer)   The full moon is in your sign! Events transpire almost as if by magic to bring you closer to your goal. Circumstances move in your favor, featuring romance and drawing people to you. You could be pointed out as a figure of mystery and regarded as someone who handles responsibility in a cool, dynamic, intense way.

Tuesday, January 13 (Moon in Cancer to Leo 2:45 a.m.) Difficulties are overcome! Help comes from a surprising source, possibly overseas. A relationship that recently (perhaps as recently as yesterday) became serious requires your immediate attention. Do not play games with your life or love. There are thorns among the roses, but the roses outnumber the thorns. Aries plays a role.

Wednesday, January 14 (Moon in Leo)   In matters of speculation, stick with these numbers: 1, 9, 2. Today's Leo moon highlights ideas that eventually become viable and valuable. Focus on relatives, neighbors, and questions that invade your privacy. The answer: Affirmative. Make a fresh start, welcoming new love and leading the way.

Thursday, January 15 (Moon in Leo to Virgo 12:31 p.m.)   Attention suddenly revolves around marriage. Questions involve career, business, investments, and a possible addition to your family. If single, another Cancer extends a dinner invitation. You guessed it—there's an ulterior motive! You're due almost immediately to discover your soulmate. Capricorn is involved.

Friday, January 16 (Moon in Virgo)   Elements of timing and luck figure prominently—this kind of cycle could represent a winning streak. The Virgo moon highlights diversity, versatility, and a nose for news. You'll be pleased with your body image following the purchase of apparel. A long-distance communication from a relative revolves around diet, nutrition, and ways of living a healthy life.

Saturday, January 17 (Moon in Virgo)   It's your kind of day! The cards are on the table face up—a situation or challenge is made crystal clear. It could be a Saturday night you won't soon forget! Taurus, Leo, and Scorpio are involved, and could have these letters in their names: D, M, V. Be willing to tear down in order to rebuild on a more suitable structure.

Sunday, January 18 (Moon in Virgo to Libra 12:44 a.m.)   Focus on structure, design, written material, and communication with a secret ally. Loyalty to your family and principles strictly prohibits a secret lover. It is difficult today to remember that discretion is the better part of valor. A Gemini does plenty of talking, enabling you to know more than you care to know. Your lucky number is 5.

Monday, January 19 (Moon in Libra) Accent moderation! There's an almost overwhelming temptation to overindulge, even to the point of having a sweet tooth. Attention revolves around your home, security, the comforts of life, and your marital status. Before today is over, you'll be engaged in a discussion of your favorite easy chair. Libra figures prominently.

Tuesday, January 20 (Moon in Libra to Scorpio 1:34 p.m.) The pace slows. You'll have time to perfect your techniques, streamline your procedures, and to view a relationship in a rational way. Look behind the scenes for answers, separating fantasy from creative thinking. You'll hear stories concerning things that go bump in the night. Pisces plays a role.

Wednesday, January 21 (Moon in Scorpio) Emotions run rampant! The Scorpio moon represents your fifth house, that section of your solar horoscope relating to style, passion, panache, sensuality, and sex appeal. The Saturn keynote cautions you to be familiar with time—don't attempt to break the bank in one night! Your fortunate number is 8.

Thursday, January 22 (Moon in Scorpio) Focus on creativity, style, and a variety of sensations. You're on the precipice of ending one phase of activity and beginning another—this could also be applied to a relationship. Strive to overcome distance and language obstacles and study methods of communication. Aries is in the picture.

Friday, January 23 (Moon in Scorpio to Sagittarius 12:25 a.m.) Celebrate the fact that you no longer are a prisoner of preconceived notions and inertia! A lingering situation is about to be concluded, so don't permit sentiment to cloud logic. Say goodbye to someone who takes you for granted. Leo and Aquarius figure prominently, and are likely to have these letters in their names: A, S, J.

Saturday, January 24 (Moon in Sagittarius)   What puzzled you will be straightened out. You'll enjoy the weekend by being with people who share your interests and work. Music is featured, domestic harmony is restored, and you'll feel at last that you are dancing to your own tune. Capricorn and another Cancer are involved, and have these letters in their names: B, K, T.

Sunday, January 25 (Moon in Sagittarius to Capricorn 7:39 a.m.)   What a Sunday! Expect exciting company, different food, and discussions of current events and fashion. Confidence soars upward and you'll be pleased with your body image and the compliments that flow your way. The emphasis is also on advertising, publishing, and news of a faraway land. Your lucky number is 3.

Monday, January 26 (Moon in Capricorn)   In matters of speculation, stick with these numbers: 4, 1, 0. Proofreading is necessary. A change of routine could be sudden, so be prepared. Scorpio plunges into the picture, which creates controversy. An emotional involvement dominates; you'll be asked to make almost impossible choices.

Tuesday, January 27 (Moon in Capricorn to Aquarius 11:27 a.m.)   At the track: post position special—number 3 p.p. in the second race. Pick six: 2, 3, 5, 5, 4, 8. Watch for these letters in the names of potential winning horses or jockeys: E, N, W. Hot daily doubles: 2 and 3, 5 and 5, 1 and 1; these selections apply to all tracks.

Wednesday, January 28 (Moon in Aquarius)   The new moon in Aquarius relates to eighth-house matters—inheritance, hidden values, and a serious relationship that temporarily must be kept secret. Attention revolves around your lifestyle and a domestic adjustment that could include a change of residence or marital status.

Thursday, January 29 (Moon in Aquarius to Pisces 1:08 p.m.) Associates tend to change their names, for business reasons or to indicate changes in their marital status. Friends might not mean to do it, but deception prevails with the attitude, "It won't do any harm!" Keep your antenna up and use your psychic capabilities—if something doesn't look good, it probably is not.

Friday, January 30 (Moon in Pisces) Power! A long-distance communication equates to a green light, so proceed with publication, plans, prospects, and original material. You'll be asked to bring order out of chaos. The spotlight is on time, money, budget, and an intense relationship. Capricorn and another Cancer are involved, and have these letters in their names: H, Q, Z.

Saturday, January 31 (Moon in Pisces to Aries 2:21 p.m.) The moon is in Pisces, with a Mars keynote, so you'll be reviewing the past while planning ahead. A project is completed; you're given credit for never giving up. Love is no stranger and you'll be reassured with these words, "You never are and never were far from my heart!" Lucky lottery: 9, 8, 18, 27, 28, 12.

FEBRUARY 1998

Sunday, February 1 (Moon in Aries) With the moon in Aries and a Neptune keynote, you'll know where you are going and why you are here. Spirituality ascends, which is appropriate for a Sunday. You'll be dealing with a Pisces whose search for knowledge is insatiable.

Monday, February 2 (Moon in Aries to Taurus 4:25 p.m.) Today's Aries moon relates to career, ambition, your standing in the community, and leadership. Someone previously indifferent seeks your counsel and perhaps hints of a desire for a more intimate relationship. Capricorn and Cancer are involved, and are likely to have these letters in their names: H, Q, Z.

Tuesday, February 3 (Moon in Taurus)   At the track: post position special—number 8 p.p. in the first race. Pick six: 8, 1, 3, 6, 4, 5. Watch for these letters in the names of potential winning horses or jockeys: I and R. Hot daily doubles: 8 and 1, 4 and 4, 6 and 2; these selections apply to all tracks.

Wednesday, February 4 (Moon in Taurus to Gemini 8:09 p.m.)   In matters of speculation, stick with these numbers: 5, 7, 3. A Taurus neighbor tells of good luck at the casino or racetrack. Offer congratulations, but fight a tendency to be jealous. Your turn is coming—sooner than you anticipated! A wish comes true in a stunning way. Leo and Aquarius are involved.

Thursday, February 5 (Moon in Gemini)   Within 24 hours, a secret that has been haunting you will be made public—this turns out to be nothing of importance, so breathe a sigh of relief! Tonight a family member talks about a private celebration that will include gourmet dining. A Cancer is involved with these letters in a name: B, K, T.

Friday, February 6 (Moon in Gemini)   What a way to start the weekend! There's a Jupiter keynote and a Gemini native whispering sweet nothings. Maintain your perspective and don't believe everything you hear. Your cycle moves up; your timing and intuition are on target. You'll discover a secret relating to creative endeavors, especially writing. Your lucky number is 3.

Saturday, February 7 (Moon in Gemini to Cancer 1:57 a.m.)   Lucky lottery: 4, 34, 7, 16, 17, 48. You'll be asked to bring order out of chaos, straightening files and checking references. Be willing to rewrite and rebuild, to tear down in order to create a more attractive base.

Taurus, Leo, and Scorpio are in the picture, with these letters in their names: D, M, V.

Sunday, February 8 (Moon in Cancer)   Today features good writing and reading, along with communication with a relative who is usually incommunicado. There's gourmet dining tonight, accompanied by music, poetry, and a forecast of the future. A flirtation lends spice and could develop into something serious. Virgo figures prominently.

Monday, February 9 (Moon in Cancer to Leo 9:57 a.m.) Refuse to give up something of value for nothing. Home economics is involved; a gift is received that helps beautify your surroundings. The moon in your sign relates to correct judgment. Accurate information can be gleaned from your intuitive intellect. Aries, Libra, and another Cancer figure in today's dynamic scenario.

Tuesday, February 10 (Moon in Leo)   At the track: post position special—number 1 p.p. in the sixth race. Pick six: 3, 4, 7, 1, 5, 1. Watch for these letters in the names of potential winning horses or jockeys: G, P, Y. Hot daily doubles: 3 and 4, 6 and 1, 4 and 7; these selections apply to all tracks.

Wednesday, February 11 (Moon in Leo to Virgo 8:10 p.m.)   The full moon in Leo relates to your second house, so complete financial deals, get ready for new information, and continue to move forward. The spotlight also falls on romance, creativity, style, panache, and showmanship. Say what you mean; don't play games. Capricorn and another Cancer take you seriously.

Thursday, February 12 (Moon in Virgo)   Prior to midnight, you'll learn where you stand, and whether your love is appreciated, desired, and applauded. Focus on expanding your horizons, possibly planning for an overseas journey. It's an excellent day for promoting your product or talent. On a personal level, you'll overcome distance and language barriers.

Friday, February 13 (Moon in Virgo to Libra 8:17 a.m.) This could be your lucky day. The Virgo moon relates to trips, visits, and a pleasant relationship with your siblings. The sun keynote highlights creativity, the excitement of discovery, and the revival of a love relationship. Leo and Aquarius figure in a dramatic scenario, and are likely to have these letters in their names: A, S, J.

Saturday, February 14 (Moon in Libra) You receive more Valentine's Day cards from your family than in previous years! Dining at home enables free expression, beating restaurant crowds and traffic. Another Cancer not only is loving and affectionate, but could also prepare a sumptuous dinner.

Sunday, February 15 (Moon in Libra) Expect various experiences, perhaps even thrills, on this Sunday. Music and family are involved. There's a major domestic adjustment and some serious consideration of your marital status. Secret: If you're diplomatic, you get everything you desire. If you attempt to force issues, you come up empty. The choice is your own.

Monday, February 16 (Moon in Libra to Scorpio 9:13 p.m.) The Libra moon relates to your home, security, and the value of your property. Tender loving care is featured. Give vent to any desire to write poetry. If the truth be known, you have many hidden talents, so permit the words to flow. Taurus and Scorpio are involved, with these letters in their names: D, M, V.

Tuesday, February 17 (Moon in Scorpio) Within 24 hours, you could meet your soulmate. Be discreet, enjoying the surge of power, but keep a special secret. Disseminate information, ask questions, and deal with Gemini, Virgo, and Sagittarius, who are likely to have these letters in their names: E, N, W. Your fortunate number is 5.

Wednesday, February 18 (Moon in Scorpio)   Lucky lottery: 18, 6, 8, 33, 12, 4. Today's Scorpio moon relates to creativity, style, challenge, change, children, physical attraction, and sex appeal. Refuse to be frightened by a drinker who makes up stories. Attention revolves around your home, security, family, and music. Dance to your own tune!

Thursday, February 19 (Moon in Scorpio to Sagittarius 8:56 a.m.)   Special note: Examine the contents of a message, looking for subtle innuendoes and keeping your antenna up for possible deception. The answers can be found behind the scenes, so remember the aphorism, "All that glitters is not gold!" Pisces and Virgo play roles, and are likely to have these letters in their names: G, P, Y.

Friday, February 20 (Moon in Sagittarius)   Results! No more nebulous material, for what occurs today is solid and real. You can bank on it! The Saturn keynote blends with your moon ruler to bring about added recognition and increased financial security. Work methods are subject to radical change. A new boss upsets the applecart!

Saturday, February 21 (Moon in Sagittarius to Capricorn 5:30 p.m.)   On this Saturday, love finds a way. Someone who shares your interests confides a most intimate problem, but instead of being embarrassed, give your all. Karma is at work—the more you help others, especially this individual, the more your own dilemma will dissolve.

Sunday, February 22 (Moon in Capricorn)   You have a right to be optimistic! Many of your questions answered in a positive way, especially those involving legal matters or marital areas. The spotlight is on independence, courage, children, and being prepared to accept an invitation to love. Leo plays a dramatic role.

Monday, February 23 (Moon in Capricorn to Aquarius 10:10 p.m.)   Gather your forces, backing claims with written material and making a gesture of reconciliation with a family member. Toss aside false pride! Food, basic values, property, and relationships are involved, so make this assertion: "Let us be adult and intelligent. Let us love one another!"

Tuesday, February 24 (Moon in Aquarius)   At the track: post position special—number 5 p.p. in the seventh race. Pick six: 3, 7, 5, 8, 2, 3. Watch for these letters in the names of potential winning horses or jockeys: C, L, U. Hot daily doubles: 3 and 7, 3 and 3, 5 and 7; these selections apply to all tracks.

Wednesday, February 25 (Moon in Aquarius to Pisces 11:42 p.m.)   Down to Earth! Handle details recently neglected due to a family crisis. Get your files in order, check expiration dates on credit cards, and get in touch with a past deadline for keeping a promise. Taurus, Leo, and Scorpio are involved, and likely to have these letters in their names: D, M, V.

Thursday, February 26 (Moon in Pisces, Solar Eclipse 12:37 p.m. EST)   With the new moon, total solar Eclipse in Pisces, postpone a journey, if possible. Today's warlike situation in a foreign land could make a long-distance journey unsafe. A love relationship survives controversy; money and security are involved. A third person gets into the act. Gemini figures prominently.

Friday, February 27 (Moon in Pisces to Aries 11:42 p.m.)   The emphasis is on color coordination, decorating, remodeling, and a foreign import. Finish what you start. Don't be discouraged by someone who knows the price of everything but the value of nothing. Taurus,

233

Leo, and Scorpio are involved, and are likely to have these letters in their names: F, O, X.

Saturday, February 28 (Moon in Aries)   You'll be presented with a package that's either too big or too small. Insist on a suitable size; don't buy a pig in a poke. A Pisces helps clarify indications, and will aid where storage, basic values, and foreign exchange rates are concerned. Virgo offers constructive criticism, and has these letters in a name: G, P, Y.

MARCH 1998

Sunday, March 1 (Moon in Aries)   What a way to start the month! Today's Aries moon, Saturn keynote, reflects on your career. There are serious discussions involving government. A family member who enjoys controversy will insist on talking politics. A love relationship intensifies and, despite thorns, will prove durable. Capricorn plays a role.

Monday, March 2 (Moon in Aries to Taurus 12 a.m.)   You'll seriously consider breaking from the routine. Focus on universal appeal, distance, language, and the possibility of an overseas journey. Keep up with import–export activities. Participation in a humanitarian project could lead to the discovery of your soulmate.

Tuesday, March 3 (Moon in Taurus)   In matters of speculation, stick with these numbers: 1, 0, 1. Today's Taurus moon relates to that section of your horoscope associated with the powers of persuasion and good fortune in matters of finance and romance. Your influence spreads; your responsibilities increase; many people are attracted to you.

Wednesday, March 4 (Moon in Taurus to Gemini 2:15 a.m.)   Lucky lottery: 2, 20, 6, 14, 12, 44. Today's emphasis is on partnership, public relations, and legal trans-

234

actions involving your home and property. Capricorn and another Cancer will play significant roles, and they're likely to have these letters in their names: B, K. T. Check door locks!

Thursday, March 5 (Moon in Gemini)   At the track: post position special—number 5 p.p. in the seventh race. Pick six: 3, 5, 7, 1, 8, 4. Watch for these letters in the names of potential winning horses or jockeys: C, L, U. Hot daily doubles: 3 and 5, 3 and 3, 4 and 7; these selections apply to all tracks.

Friday, March 6 (Moon in Gemini to Cancer 7:27 a.m.)   It's time to do some proofreading! The Gemini moon in your twelfth house equates to the possibility of careless writing. Institutions are involved, along with governmental agencies, so be sure some bureaucrat does not find fault with your reckoning. Scorpio is represented.

Saturday, March 7 (Moon in Cancer)   You could win a popularity contest, for the moon in your sign guarantees a high cycle. You'll be at the right place at a special moment. The emphasis is on words, both spoken and written, so be sure to communicate your ideas. You'll clash with a member of the opposite sex, then possibly fall madly in love. Your lucky number is 5.

Sunday, March 8 (Moon in Cancer to Leo 3:45 p.m.)   The spotlight is on family, music, and the restoration of domestic harmony. Your judgment and intuition can serve as reliable guides. Wear your colors: emerald green and white. A Taurus helps make wishes come true, and Leo helps provide funding. Attention will revolve around beautifying your surroundings, improving your lifestyle, and changing your marital status.

Monday, March 9 (Moon in Leo)   At first, you'll be saying, "I feel blue; nothing ever changes!" Then, like a bolt out of the blue, things do change. The Leo moon relates to money, payments, collections, and the sudden discovery of potential wealth. Pisces and Virgo play dramatic roles.

Tuesday, March 10 (Moon in Leo)   At the track: post position special—number 8 p.p. in the ninth race. Pick six: 4, 4, 8, 7, 1, 3. Watch for these letters in the names of potential winning horses or jockeys: H, Q, Z. Hot daily doubles: 4 and 4, 8 and 7, 3 and 5; these selections apply to all tracks.

Wednesday, March 11 (Moon in Leo to Virgo 2:35 a.m.) Ride with the tide, refusing to be inhibited as a prisoner of inertia. Let go of the status quo as you knock preconceived notions for a loop. One phase of activity is ended while another is on the horizon, which could include a different kind of love. Let go of a burden you should not have carried in the first place. Aries is involved.

Thursday, March 12 (Moon in Virgo, Lunar Eclipse 11:34 p.m.)   Keep your plans flexible, for a relative could arrive from out of town expecting to be wined and dined. Wear bright colors, imprinting your style and emphasizing independence of thought and action. The adventure of discovery is featured, and you'll exude personal magnetism and sex appeal. Your lucky number is 1.

Friday, March 13 (Moon in Virgo to Libra 2:58 p.m.)   A full moon, lunar eclipse in Virgo, means that you should postpone a short trip, take no chances in traffic, and avoid all arguments with your siblings. If you don't know what to do, do nothing; if you need direction, just ask. The spotlight falls on your home and the acquisition of furniture. Another Cancer is involved.

Saturday, March 14 (Moon in Libra)   Attention revolves around home, security, musical innovations, and increasing your sphere of activity. Accent diversity, versatility, and the necessity for experimentation. Accept a social invitation. You'll meet fascinating people who find you the most fascinating of all. Lucky lottery: 3, 30, 4, 2, 12, 1.

Sunday, March 15 (Moon in Libra)   Revamp, revise, review, and rewrite—today is excellent for improving the appearance of a product. Do some mending, sharpen your tools, and check your recipes. Exchange ideas with Taurus, Leo, and Scorpio, who are likely to have these letters in their names: D, M, V. A Scorpio finds you devastatingly attractive.

Monday, March 16 (Moon in Libra to Scorpio 3:51 a.m.)   You feel vibrant, alive, alert, and intent on getting your feelings on paper. Focus on reading, writing, disseminating information, and giving your own interpretation to current events. The spotlight is on flirtation, the excitement of discovery, and your ability to analyze character.

Tuesday, March 17 (Moon in Scorpio)   On this St. Patrick's Day, celebrate at home. The spotlight revolves around where you live, your lifestyle, and the necessity for healing a breach with a loved one. Music is involved. Toss aside false pride, making this kind of statement: "I never want to lose your friendship and your love!"

Wednesday, March 18 (Moon in Scorpio to Sagittarius 3:56 p.m.)   Lucky lottery: 18, 17, 27, 19, 5, 33. Today's Scorpio moon relates to physical attraction, creativity, style, and a sudden change of plans. An element of deception exists, so protect yourself at close quarters. Special note: Your psychic impression is valid! Pisces and Virgo are involved with these letters in their names: G, P, Y.

Thursday, March 19 (Moon in Sagittarius)   It's a powerful Thursday! The Saturn keynote, moon in Sagittarius, equates to responsibility, overtime, and the challenge of bringing order out of a chaotic situation. You'll be dubbed a powerful person. A love relationship is hot and heavy, but it may be too hot not to cool down! Capricorn and another Cancer are represented.

Friday, March 20 (Moon in Sagittarius)   One who dared you withdraws the challenge. Focus on the completion of a project and the ability to reach beyond the immediate to a sense of what the future holds. An aggressive Aries admits, "I had you all wrong!" Stress universality, refusing to be limited by distance and language. Promote your product, advertise, publicize, and check legal rights.

Saturday, March 21 (Moon in Sagittarius to Capricorn) New love on Saturday! The sun keynote blends with your moon significator, helping you to discover your soulmate. The answer to your question: Yes. Make a new start in a different direction, for a new love is on the horizon! Avoid guilty pangs over a situation in which you play a positive, not negative, role. Lucky lottery: 1, 10, 17, 26, 5, 12.

Sunday, March 22 (Moon in Capricorn)   The Capricorn moon relates to your somber appearance, dealings with serious-minded people, and becoming sensitive to your legal rights and permissions. Property value is involved. Direction and motivation also figure prominently. The spotlight shines bright on areas of your life associated with dealings with the public, partnership, and marriage.

Monday, March 23 (Moon in Capricorn to Aquarius 8:02 a.m.)   Wake up and sing! A very unusual Monday—the Jupiter keynote, moon in the seventh sector, makes for a great Monday. You'll be too active to brood, so focus on social activity, fashion, and improving your body image. Gemini and Sagittarius are represented with these letters in their names: C, L, U.

Tuesday, March 24 (Moon in Aquarius)   Routine changes prove to be beneficial. You'll see the need to rebuild on a more solid base. The Aquarian moon relates to a concern associated with a possible inheritance. Some people misunderstand your motives; others accuse you of dabbling in the occult. Scorpio is involved.

Wednesday, March 25 (Moon in Aquarius to Pisces 10:43 a.m.) A written notice concerns financial prospects, the money status of a partner or mate, and information relating to hidden values. Learn more about tax or license requirements, and try to become familiar with accounting procedures. You'll be trusted with confidential information. Someone of the opposite sex says you are a glamorous figure. Your lucky number is 5.

Thursday, March 26 (Moon in Pisces) The pace slows. People express a desire to be with you, to wine and dine you. The Pisces moon relates to your ninth house, which in turn represents distance and language, foreign cuisine, and being with a bilingual person who says, "You could get along in any country!"

Friday, March 27 (Moon in Pisces to Aries 10:49 a.m.) Go slow, playing the waiting game. Important: Do not equate delay with defeat! You are on the right track. A package arrives. A letter proves puzzling, as it seems to be a blend of business and personal. Best counsel: Don't look a gift horse in the mouth! Pisces and Virgo are in this picture, and have these letters in their names: G, P, Y.

Saturday, March 28 (Moon in Aries) On this Saturday, with a Saturn keynote and the new moon in Aries, you get what amounts to a new lease on life. Focus on the pressure of responsibility, the comprehension of time limitation, and your ability to bring order out of chaos. Just 24 hours ago, you appeared to wander aimlessly; tonight, you'll be all business.

Sunday, March 29 (Moon in Aries to Taurus 10:06 a.m.) This could be the perfect Sunday! The Mars

239

keynote blends with your moon significator to bring a blend of romance, style, and creativity. Let go of an unsavory situation or relationship. Open up the lines of communication to let the world know that you are a lover who is not afraid to fight if the cause is right.

Monday, March 30 (Moon in Taurus)   What a Monday! The spotlight revolves around hopes, wishes, desires, fulfillment, sensuality, and sex appeal. The Taurus moon in your eleventh house brings you the gift of knowing how to increase your income. You'll impress those among the high and mighty, as well as ordinary people. Leo is involved.

Tuesday, March 31 (Moon in Taurus to Gemini 10:37 a.m.)   On this Tuesday, the last day of March, the moon keynote blends with your own moon ruler and you will find that family members suddenly rediscover you. You'll be asking yourself, "What is the secret?" Focus on direction, motivation, lifestyle, and your marital status. Another Cancer is involved.

APRIL 1998

Wednesday, April 1 (Moon in Gemini)   You're no fool! Perceive your potential, reaching beyond the immediate for your future prospects. With today's Mars keynote and the moon in Gemini, you'll be up to date with both personal and world affairs. Aries and Libra figure prominently, and are likely to have these letters in their names: I and R.

Thursday, April 2 (Moon in Gemini to Cancer 2:10 p.m.)   You've been waiting for it! Express your personal style; make a new start in a different direction. You'll be dealing with dynamic, talented, temperamental people. Let others know you are no slouch yourself and refuse to be taken for granted. Be sure love is special and that no one can make you feel cheap.

240

Friday, April 3 (Moon in Cancer)   In matters of speculation, stick with these numbers: 2, 2, 3. The moon in your sign highlights independence and your ability to state where and when the action will be. Don't follow others; let them follow you. Focus on glamour, intrigue, personal magnetism, and sex appeal.

Saturday, April 4 (Moon in Cancer to Leo 9:36 p.m.)   Lucky lottery: 3, 4, 12, 27, 18, 33. The cycle continues high so trust your own judgement. Follow through on guidance from your intuitive intellect. The Jupiter keynote relates to diversity, curiosity, fashion, and your improved body image. Yes, there's reason for celebration tonight! A Sagittarian is in the picture.

Sunday, April 5, Daylight Saving Time (Moon in Leo)   Check your invitation list. A relative recently returned from a trip expects to be with you. Don't overlook details. Proofreading could be necessary. Within 24 hours, you could hit the financial jackpot. You most certainly will locate a lost article. Taurus, Leo, and Scorpio are involved, and have these letters in their names: D, M, V.

Monday, April 6 (Moon in Leo)   It's a lively Monday! The moon in your money house and the Mercury keynote all add up to communication, writing, and flirting. Gemini, Virgo, and Sagittarius are represented, and they could have these letters in their names: E, N, W. Take nothing for granted as you explore the possibility of a serious relationship.

Tuesday, April 7 (Moon in Leo to Virgo 9:25 a.m.) The spotlight falls on personal environment and your home. There's serious consideration of where you live, your lifestyle, and marriage. Be diplomatic as you promote art, music, and literature. A question about your income is answered in a positive way, and you'll be happy as a result. Taurus, Libra, and Scorpio are involved, and have these letters in their names: F, O, X.

Wednesday, April 8 (Moon in Virgo)   At the track: post position special—number 1 p.p. in the sixth race. Pick six: 7, 7, 5, 2, 1, 1. Watch for these letters in the names of potential winning horses or jockeys: G, P, Y. Hot daily doubles: 7 and 7, 3 and 4, 1 and 1; these selections apply to all tracks.

Thursday, April 9 (Moon in Virgo to Libra 10:04 p.m.)   The answer to a question: A project is in the works. More capital is required, but your ultimate success is almost guaranteed. The emphasis is on time, deadlines, more responsibility, and an intense relationship. You will not be traveling the road of life alone! Capricorn and another Cancer are featured, with these letters in their names: H, Q, Z.

Friday, April 10 (Moon in Libra)   Finish, rather than start. Let go of a burden you should not have carried in the first place. The aura of confusion will be erased within 24 hours, the spotlight falls on basic values, issues, property, home, and marital prospects. Aries is represented.

Saturday, April 11 (Moon in Libra)   The full moon in Libra equates to long-term negotiations that are finally completed, involving property value, a financial settlement, or your marital status. An overseas journey could be in the planning stage. The sun keynote emphasizes the return of vigor, style, panache, and romance. Special: Avoid heavy lifting! Lucky lottery, 1, 10, 15, 35, 40, 48.

Sunday, April 12 (Moon in Libra to Scorpio 10:56 a.m.) Family members somehow feel they know best how to live your life, but make it crystal clear that you intend to live your own life in your way, for better or for worse. The emphasis is on motivation, direction, and the sale or purchase of a home or other property. Dress up your product, spotlighting entertainment, music, and prizes.

Monday, April 13 (Moon in Scorpio)   This could be your lucky day! The Scorpio moon relates to creative endeavors, challenge, change, variety, children, speculation, and sex appeal. It's an unusual Monday! Focus on celebration, wardrobe, body image, and the remarkable rise in your popularity. You could find yourself involved in a political situation.

Tuesday, April 14 (Moon in Scorpio to Sagittarius 10:52 p.m.)   Maintain your perspective, enjoying flattery, but not allowing yourself to be carried away. The moon in Scorpio in your fifth house tells of intensity, passion, and impulsiveness. Use some self-control, please! Taurus, Leo, and Scorpio play significant roles, and have these letters in their names: D, M, V.

Wednesday, April 15 (Moon in Sagittarius)   Enjoy the moon in the last degrees of Scorpio! It's an excellent day for dining out, entertaining, and being entertained. What begins as a gleam in your eye could develop into a creative, profitable enterprise. Get promises in writing. You'll benefit by writing, reading, and being in the role of teacher.

Thursday, April 16 (Moon in Sagittarius)   What a Thursday! Expect pleasant working conditions at home or in your office, or during a journey where you make valuable contacts and insure your future financial profit. Libra plays a major role.

Friday, April 17 (Moon in Sagittarius to Capricorn 9:05 a.m.)   Make your terms crystal clear, not permitting others to take credit for your work and creativity. You'll learn today to separate the real things from the showy. See people, places, and relationships as they exist, not merely as you wish they might be in a perfect world.

Saturday, April 18 (Moon in Capricorn)   Iron filings fall into place as if drawn by a giant magnet—you'll know what means most to you and what can be discarded. Focus on organization, creativity, style, responsibility, and comprehending time, and meeting a deadline. A relationship is not without thorns, but it proves ultimately durable. Your lucky number is 8.

Sunday, April 19 (Moon in Capricorn to Aquarius 4:41 p.m.)   Today you possess the secret of universal appeal. Realize you can overcome barriers that include distance and language. Someone you helped recently is now out of the woods and willing to repay you for your kindness. Finish what you start, letting go of the status quo and a burden that was not yours to carry in the first place.

Monday, April 20 (Moon in Aquarius)   Your strength returns; you'll also have an abundance of charm and sex appeal. Today's Aquarian moon relates to other people's money, knowledge concerning tax and license requirements, and the possibility of an inheritance. Some people express apprehension, accusing you of dabbling in the occult. Leo is involved.

Tuesday, April 21 (Moon in Aquarius to Pisces 9:06 p.m.)   The dust settles! Some family members, much upset during the past week, will regain their senses. Don't back down from your principles. Stand tall without being arrogant. Your views are verified concerning basic issues, values, property, and home. Capricorn and another Cancer figure in this exciting scenario.

Wednesday, April 22 (Moon in Pisces)   Fun and frolic are featured—focus on diversity, fashion, news reporting, and the dissemination of information. Transportation is also highlighted. You'll be invited to attend a prestigious social affair, but even if you're at home alone you will not be lonely. An aura of intellectuality surrounds you. People call and consult with you. Your lucky number is 3.

Thursday, April 23 (Moon in Pisces to Aries 10:31 p.m.)   At the track: post position special—number 4 p.p. in the fourth race. Pick six: 8, 5, 4, 4, 1, 7. Watch for these letters in the names of potential winning horses or jockeys: D, M, V. Hot daily doubles: 8 and 5, 4 and 4, 7 and 1; these selections apply to all tracks.

Friday, April 24 (Moon in Aries)   As this weekend approaches, with the moon in Aries, expect to rub shoulders with the high and mighty. The Mercury keynote means you gain via contacts with intellectuals, accrue benefits, and add to your prestige via the written word. A flirtation tonight could become serious and lead to an engagement.

Saturday, April 25 (Moon in Aries to Taurus 10:09 p.m.)   Lucky lottery: 50, 51, 6, 13, 16, 12. The emphasis is on what occurs at home. Music and relatives are involved. Gourmet dining is accompanied by a frank discussion concerning money, payments, collections, and interest rates. People will know once and for all that you did not fall off a turnip truck! Taurus is represented.

Sunday, April 26 (Moon in Taurus)   The new moon in Taurus relates to your powers of persuasion. You get almost everything you request, so be sure you know what you want and can handle what you obtain. Focus on being quiet within; try meditation. Have the courage to follow a hunch. Terms will be clearly defined and Pisces will play an outstanding role.

Monday, April 27 (Moon in Taurus to Gemini 9:55 p.m.)   A deal is settled, with money involved. What appeared to be purely speculative turns out to be solid. An overtime assignment is included. Press ahead; don't let up now! An expert at obtaining funding is on your side, and will prove it. Love and marriage are also part of this dynamic scenario.

Tuesday, April 28 (Moon in Gemini)   A secret is revealed involving a family member. It's not quite a double-cross, but it's bordering on sharp practice. A long-distance communication verifies your views. The possibility of an overseas journey becomes more realistic. Let go of a burden and be vulnerable to love. Refuse to be taken for granted by someone who is envious. Aries is involved.

Wednesday, April 29 (Moon in Gemini to Cancer 11:57 p.m.)   The answer to your question: Yes! This is the time for a new start, for putting forth your product or talent and letting people know, "This is the best, real quality. When you see me, you are seeing leadership!" In discussing a product, say these words: "When this you see, remember me!" Lucky lottery: 1, 10, 5, 3, 30, 4.

Thursday, April 30 (Moon in Cancer)   On this last day of April, with the moon in your sign, imprint your style and show the courage of your convictions. The moon keynote relates to your own moon rulership, giving you wide appeal to the public, especially to women. Focus on your home, direction, motivation, family, and marital status.

MAY 1998

Friday, May 1 (Moon in Cancer)   With the moon in Cancer and the sun keynote, you'll have a new lease on life. Some of your major wishes are closer to fulfillment than you originally anticipated. You will not be forgotten where love is concerned! Leo figures prominently.

Saturday, May 2 (Moon in Cancer to Leo 5:49 a.m.)   The moon in the last degree of your sign coincides with time to let go of a situation or relationship that has become tiresome. Attention revolves around your home, security, household appliances, and a decision relating to a business partnership or your marital status. Lucky lottery: 2, 12, 4, 40, 15, 16.

Sunday, May 3 (Moon in Leo)   Keep your plans flexible. A dynamic Aries, Leo, or Sagittarius comes into your life and provides color and excitement. Focus on diversity, versatility, and special attention to your body image. A secret meeting involves a Gemini who proves cooperative and charming. Stake out your territory!

Monday, May 4 (Moon in Leo to Virgo 3:47 p.m.)   Be willing to revise, review, rewrite, remodel, and rebuild. Today's moon in Leo represents your money's worth in connection with showmanship, entertainment, advertising, and promotion. Taurus, Leo, and Scorpio are involved, with these letters or initials in their names: D, M, V.

Tuesday, May 5 (Moon in Virgo)   The spotlight falls on your ability to analyze and to recognize a news story when you encounter it. You'll be dealing with inquisitive people who at first appear nosey, but later prove they have your best interests at heart. Gemini, Virgo, and Sagittarius are involved, and have these letters, initials in their names: E, N, W.

Wednesday, May 6 (Moon in Virgo)   Lucky lottery: 6, 51, 13, 14, 12, 7. Attention revolves around decoration, remodeling, and the beautification of your surroundings. Harmony is restored on the homefront, and music is involved. A relative returns from a trip with good money news. Taurus, Libra, and Scorpio are involved, and have these letters in their names: F, O, X.

Thursday, May 7 (Moon in Virgo to Libra 4:19 a.m.) Define your terms, making your intentions crystal clear. An element of deception could exist, so try to see people and places in a realistic light. Within 24 hours, your property will be evaluated. A decision could be reached in connection with your business, career, or marriage. Pisces figures prominently.

Friday, May 8 (Moon in Libra)   As this weekend gets under way, you're asked to bring order out of chaos. Overtime could be involved. Sparks fly in connection with an intense relationship—stick to your course and be faithful to your principles. Legal matters are involved. The law is on your side. Capricorn and another Cancer figure prominently.

Saturday, May 9 (Moon in Libra to Scorpio 5:10 p.m.) Plan ahead for a possible long-distance journey. A relative, possibly Libran, provides encouragement and boosts your confidence. Stress universal appeal, refusing to balk because of distance and language obstacles. Aries and Libra are represented, and have these letters in their names: I and R.

Sunday, May 10 (Moon in Scorpio) Lost-and-found is featured—you will find your way! The sun keynote relates to enlightenment, recognition of spiritual values, and a scenario that highlights children, challenge, change, and variety. The Scorpio moon coincides with adventure, discovery, personal magnetism, and sex appeal.

Monday, May 11 (Moon in Scorpio) The Scorpio full moon tells the story of love, romance, and physical attraction. You may act first and think about it later. A young person declares, "You are right, and from now on, I will listen!" Focus on direction, motivation, the sale or purchase of property, and a decision associated with marriage.

Tuesday, May 12 (Moon in Scorpio to Sagittarius 4:48 a.m.) Within 24 hours, your employment picture is subject to change. Special care will be required for pets. You'll once again resolve to take better care of yourself and embark on a fitness program. Pay more attention to diet and nutrition. Gemini and Sagittarius are involved, with these letters in their names: C, L, U.

Wednesday, May 13 (Moon in Sagittarius) What goes around comes around! You might be asking, "Is this déjà vu?" Maintain a low-key approach. When a relative who is irritable aches for a fight, don't accommodate! Check details; be aware of source material; do the necessary proofreading. Taurus, Leo, and Scorpio figure in this scenario.

Thursday, May 14 (Moon in Sagittarius to Capricorn 2:39 p.m.)   Today's scenario highlights change, travel, variety, and the adventure of discovery. Show off your ability as a character analyst. Pay attention to hobbies involving the mantic arts, including numerology, graphology, and astrology. Gemini, Virgo, and Sagittarius are represented, and have these letters in their names: E, N, W.

Friday, May 15 (Moon in Capricorn)   At the track: post position special—number 2 p.p. in the fourth race. Pick six: 6, 2, 1, 2, 4, 4. Watch for these letters in the names of potential winning horses or jockeys: F, O, X. Hot daily doubles: 6 and 2, 4 and 4, 2 and 2; these selections apply to all tracks.

Saturday, May 16 (Moon in Capricorn to Aquarius 10:30 a.m.)   What a Saturday night! You could receive proposals, business and marriage, but be sure to get promises in writing and avoid the trap of self-deception. See people, places, and situations as they actually exist, not merely as you wish they were. Someone from a foreign land makes romantic advances. Your lucky number is 7.

Sunday, May 17 (Moon in Aquarius)   People take you seriously. Forego a tendency to make light of problems that are actually heavy. Today's Capricorn moon relates to how the world looks to you and how you appear to others. The spotlight is on public relations, legal rights, partnership, and marriage. Get your priorities in order—pronto!

Monday, May 18 (Moon in Aquarius)   In matters of speculation, stick with these numbers: 1, 9, 11. Finish what you start; don't give up the ship. Circumstances begin to turn in your favor—know it and act accordingly. Let go of a burden you should not have carried in the first place. Explore import–export opportunities.

Tuesday, May 19 (Moon in Aquarius to Pisces 4:03 a.m.) All arrows point to new fields to conquer! You'll be dealing with stubborn, determined, successful people with strong egos. Imprint your own style, overcoming the temptation to be a follower and boldly leading the way. Leo and Aquarius figure prominently, and are likely to have these letters in their names: A, S, J.

Wednesday, May 20 (Moon in Pisces) Today's moon in Pisces relates to travel, publishing, communication, special interest in philosophy, and theology. You'll be near water, perhaps even traveling over water. A long-distance communication involves a chance to promote your product or talent overseas. Capricorn and another Cancer figure in this dynamic scenario.

Thursday, May 21 (Moon in Pisces to Aries 7:06 a.m.) Suddenly your spirits are up as your tendency toward depression is met head on and decisively defeated. You'll be invited to dine out. The focus will be on humor, wit, wisdom, and your ability to make people laugh despite their problems. Gemini and Sagittarius help fill blank spaces. Your fortunate number is 3.

Friday, May 22 (Moon in Aries) Attention revolves around your goal, career, ambition, and ability to favorably impress your superiors. Check the small print and read between the lines. Material needed to complete a project is available in print. The key is to be thorough, checking claims, references, and accounting procedures. Scorpio figures prominently.

Saturday, May 23 (Moon in Aries to Taurus 8:06 a.m.) Restrictions are loosened. People are drawn to you, especially members of the opposite sex. You'll receive compliments regarding your ability to communicate, write, and to analyze character. You'll be told by attractive, intelligent people, "You are not only reliable but also charming and sexy!" Lucky lottery: 5, 50, 16, 17, 22, 33.

Sunday, May 24 (Moon in Taurus)   What you missed yesterday will be obtainable tonight—flowers, music, and gifts are involved. A domestic adjustment is featured. Look beyond the immediate, for a change of address may be necessary. Focus also on decorating, remodeling, and your marital status. Taurus, Aries, and Libra play outstanding roles.

Monday, May 25 (Moon in Taurus to Gemini 8:25 a.m.)   The new moon in Taurus helps prevent any hint of a blue Monday. The lunar position highlights friends, hopes, wishes, the powers of persuasion, and your ability to influence people in different cities. Events synchronize to bring you good fortune in finance and romance. Money delayed will be repaid!

Tuesday, May 26 (Moon in Gemini)   Focus on the element of time in the real and metaphysical sense. You might be musing, "This is my time and I'll prove it!" A relationship is stormy and intense, but durable. Legal decisions lift the load. The sword of Damocles no longer threatens. Capricorn and another Cancer are in the picture, with these letters in their names: H, Q, Z.

Wednesday, May 27 (Moon in Gemini to Cancer 9:58 a.m.)   At the track: post position special—number 8 p.p. in the first race. Pick six: 8, 1, 7, 3, 4, 5. Watch for these letters in the names of potential winning horses or jockeys: I and R. Hot daily doubles: 8 and 1, 4 and 4, 2 and 6; these selections apply to all tracks.

Thursday, May 28 (Moon in Cancer)   The cycle is high. Take the initiative. The answer to your question: Move ahead and take the cold plunge into the future.

New love is featured, vigor returns, and you'll be asked, "What happened—did you discover the Fountain of Youth?" Smile knowingly but don't volunteer information. Emphasize independence of thought and action.

Friday, May 29 (Moon in Cancer to Leo 2:38 p.m.) An appointment you missed yesterday will haunt you unless you take steps to rectify your error. Contact a Leo to present your efforts in the best light. Another Cancer moves closer to your way of looking at events and personalities. Property values are involved. A Capricorn represents your interests.

Saturday, May 30 (Moon in Leo) Diversify, showing that you can laugh at your own foibles and giving full play to your intellectual curiosity. Study language, foreign customs, and cuisines. A Sagittarian declares, "You help make work seem like fun!" A gift adds to your wardrobe and your body image improves. Lucky lottery: 3, 30, 48, 8, 5, 12.

Sunday, May 31 (Moon in Leo to Virgo 11:21 p.m.) With a Pluto keynote and the Moon in Leo, you'll upset your preconceived notions and break free from a prison of inertia. Good news arrives concerning money, and your cash flow resumes. Taurus, Leo, and Scorpio are involved, and are likely to have these letters in their names: D, M, V.

JUNE 1998

Monday, June 1 (Moon in Virgo) With the moon keynote and the moon itself in Leo, your thoughts center around your home, security, income, and marital status. A message from the stars tells you to dress up your product, use showmanship, and repair plumbing and other problems in the home. Another Cancer plays a role.

Tuesday, June 2 (Moon in Virgo)   At the track: post position special—number 6 p.p. in the fifth race. Pick six: 3, 7, 1, 4, 6, 1. Be aware of these letters in the names of potential winning horses or jockeys: C, L, U. Hot daily doubles: 3 and 7, 3 and 3, 4 and 4; these selections apply to all tracks.

Wednesday, June 3 (Moon in Virgo to Libra 11:17 a.m.) People drawn to you will include Taurus, Leo, and Scorpio. A relative provides written material that helps you locate what you need. The emphasis is on intellectual curiosity, trips, visits, and your ability to make people laugh, even through their tears. You'll hear these words, "I don't know what I would have done without you!"

Thursday, June 4 (Moon in Libra)   You'll be dealing with Gemini, Virgo, and Sagittarius, who are likely to have these letters in their names: E, N, W. Written material plays a role. You'll be asked to disseminate information. Special Note: Don't confuse gossip with creative storytelling! Flirtation is involved.

Friday, June 5 (Moon in Libra)   Today's scenario features music, family, home appliances, and improving your body image. The lunar position highlights where you live, your lifestyle, building material, and the completion of long-term negotiations. Go slowly and diplomatically. Don't ignore a sore throat. Libra plays a role.

Saturday, June 6 (Moon in Libra to Scorpio 12:06 a.m.)   You'll know tonight that romance is just around the corner! A past obligation is close to fulfillment—you should not have assumed it in the first place. A chance exists to make your terms and feelings crystal clear, so do so! Pisces and Virgo are involved, and are likely to have these letters in their names: G, P, Y.

Sunday, June 7 (Moon in Scorpio)   All that you ask for—and more! You'll attract powerful people. The emphasis is on your marital status, and in taking on responsibility and meeting and beating a deadline. A Capricorn and another Cancer figure prominently, and are likely to have these letters in their names: H, Q, Z. Your lucky number is 8.

Monday, June 8 (Moon in Sagittarius 11:34 a.m.) Stress universal appeal, looking beyond the immediate to be understood in many languages. You'll be enamoured with the language of love. Aries and Libra play outstanding roles, and they could have these letters in their names: I and R. You'll hear this refrain: "Lover, come home!"

Tuesday, June 9 (Moon in Sagittarius) At last—a fresh start in a new direction! Basic issues, care of pets, employment, and fitness dominate this scenario. A Sagittarian will have much to do with work methods, fixing things at home, and general repairs. Adventure is featured in connection with discovery, revelation, and creative processes involving love.

Wednesday, June 10 (Moon in Sagittarius to Capricorn 8:50 p.m.) The full moon in Sagittarius relates to questions concerning health, work, and dependents. You'll get a lucky break. A relative calls or writes concerning a proposed trip or visit. Don't put aside basics in order to be polite. State your needs frankly, and make clear, without being arrogant, that privacy and time are precious commodities that you don't take for granted.

Thursday, June 11 (Moon in Capricorn) In matters of speculation, stick with these numbers: 3, 6, 9. Focus on diversity, versatility, willingness to experiment with clothes, exercise, diet, and nutrition. Within 24 hours, a legal agreement involving partnership, public relations, or cooperative efforts will become a reality.

Friday, June 12 (Moon in Capricorn) The question of marriage looms large. Taurus, Leo, and Scorpio figure prominently, and are likely to have these letters in their names: D, M, V. Learn rules before breaking them. A Capricorn brooks no interference!

Saturday, June 13 (Moon in Capricorn to Aquarius 4:03 a.m.)   The lunar position continues to emphasize your ability to deal with the public, to protect your image, to verify views, and to let others know you mean what you say. Focus also on your partnerships, legal rights, and marital status. Written words figure prominently. You'll be dealing with Gemini, Virgo, and Sagittarius.

Sunday, June 14 (Moon in Aquarius)   Attention revolves around the home, funding, music, and a special gift representing a token of affection. The Aquarian moon relates to mystery, intrigue, and the financial status of your partner or mate. Dig deep for information, recalling a lesson learned from reading old books. Taurus and Libra figure in this scenario.

Monday, June 15 (Moon in Aquarius to Pisces 9:31 a.m.)   Separate fact from fancy, seeing people, places, and relationships as they exist, not merely as you wish they were. Define your terms, perfect your techniques, and streamline your procedures. A long-distance call from a Pisces helps clarify your agenda and your itinerary. Virgo is also involved.

Tuesday, June 16 (Moon in Pisces)   Take charge of your own destiny! Powerful people are in your corner, so forget being modest, at least for today. You'll be dealing with another Cancer who urges, "Let's break out of our shell; let's let the world be aware that here we come!" Capricorn also plays a role.

Wednesday, June 17 (Moon in Pisces to Aries 1:23 p.m.)   Lucky lottery: 9, 12, 16, 44, 51, 1. Focus on distance, language, correspondence, and opening the lines of communication. You're capable of reaching beyond the immediate, perceiving your potential and having a valid psychic impression of the future. Aries is represented.

Thursday, June 18 (Moon in Aries)   Break free from foolish restrictions and inhibitions. Imprint your style, emphasizing originality, independence, and creativity. Special note: Avoid heavy lifting! Love figures prominently, no matter what your chronological age. If single, you could fall head over heels; if married, you may rediscover your mate in an exciting, physical way.

Friday, June 19 (Moon in Aries to Taurus 3:47 p.m.)   The focus is on partnership and your marital status. Expect a reunion as well as a decision relating to the sale or purchase of your property. Another Cancer figures prominently and extends a dinner invitation; that person is likely to have these letters in a name: B, K, T. Today's Aries moon relates to your career, leadership, and standing in community.

Saturday, June 20 (Moon in Taurus)   Suddenly, puzzle pieces are in place—today's Taurus moon relates to your eleventh sector, and this in turn emphasizes hopes, desires, and attaining what you want through your powers of persuasion. You'll have good fortune in finance or romance. Lucky lottery: 12, 20, 2, 22, 1, 15.

Sunday, June 21 (Moon in Taurus to Gemini 5:26 p.m.)   Before this Sunday is finished, you'll thank your lucky stars in connection with money, payments, and collections. There is reason to celebrate, but don't forget resolutions concerning diet, exercise, and nutrition. A different wardrobe will improve your body image. A Taurus will pledge loyalty.

Monday, June 22 (Moon in Gemini)   Be ready for change and for a variety of sensations and experiences. A Gemini figures prominently, relating to your twelfth house, which involves secrets and a clandestine relationship. Special note: Remember that discretion is the better part of valor. Read and write!

Tuesday, June 23 (Moon in Gemini to Cancer 7:39 p.m.)   Review the notes you took 24 hours ago, for they could play an important role tonight. Focus on gifts, diplomacy, and promises concerning your future financial security. Be kind and diplomatic, but not weak; be generous, but not extravagant. Taurus, Leo, and Scorpio are in the picture, and have these letters in their names: F, O, X.

Wednesday, June 24 (Moon in Cancer)   The new moon in your sign highlights initiative, a pioneering spirit, and elements of timing and luck. Wear the color sea green. Express your views, test your recipes, and prepare a dining experience that helps win friends and love. Don't repeat the mistake of trusting too much, too soon.

Thursday, June 25 (Moon in Cancer)   What went awry in connection with your career or romance will be realigned. Order is brought out of confusion as a chaotic situation is corrected. The focus is on responsibility, an overtime assignment, an intense relationship, durable goods, and commitment to your product or talent. Capricorn plays a role.

Friday, June 26 (Moon in Cancer to Leo 12:06 a.m.) Keep plans flexible, for a long-distance call or letter could transform your agenda or itinerary. Your cycle is high, so circumstances will turn in your favor. You'll overcome obstacles associated with distance and language. Highlight universal appeal; don't give up the search for your soulmate. Aries plays a dominant role.

Saturday, June 27 (Moon in Leo)   On this Saturday, people share their opinions and desires—it will be as if you were designated the expert on love affairs! You'll be told, "You are vibrant and you have such a pleasing personality!" Make a fresh start, wearing bright colors and asserting your views in a positive way. Your lucky number is 1.

Sunday, June 28 (Moon in Leo to Virgo 7:54 a.m.) What a Sunday! The Leo moon relates to the value of your possessions, locating what you need, and being with people who fascinate you without taking you for granted. The focus is also on family, food, shelter, and a gift that adds to your comfort. Capricorn and another Cancer figure prominently, and are likely to have these initials in their names: B, K, T.

Monday, June 29 (Moon in Virgo)   Test your luck! Keep your plans flexible, highlight humor and versatility, and let others know you are capable of laughing at your own foibles. Focus on fashion, style, and different modes of transportation. You'll be told by a member of opposite sex, "I wish this was another time and place!"

Tuesday, June 30 (Moon in Virgo to Libra 7:05 p.m.)   At the track: post position special—number 4 p.p. in the fourth race. Pick six: 1, 4, 2, 4, 6, 8. Watch for these letters in the names of potential winning horses or jockeys: D, M, V. Hot daily doubles: 1 and 4, 5 and 8, 8 and 8; these selections apply to all tracks.

JULY 1998

Wednesday, July 1 (Moon in Libra)   Planning begins for the holiday—stress originality and give thought to decorations and displays relating to Independence Day. Gemini and Sagittarius are involved, and are likely to have these letters in their names: C, L, U. A relative announces plans to shake things up.

Thursday, July 2 (Moon in Libra)   Details unravel in connection with immediate plans—music and entertainment are featured. You might be musing, "Is this déjà vu?" Today's scenario highlights familiar places and faces. A Taurus proves a true friend. Use your charm and your powers of persuasion to win major points.

Friday, July 3 (Moon in Libra to Scorpio 7:45 a.m.)   At the track: post position special—number 3 p.p. in the second race. Pick six: 2, 3, 5, 5, 4, 7. Watch for these letters in the names of potential winning horses or jockeys: E, N, W. Hot daily doubles: 2 and 3, 5 and 5, 4 and 7; these selections apply to all tracks.

Saturday, July 4 (Moon in Scorpio)   It's the fourth of July! Stick close to home, if possible. A family celebration could be the highlight. The Scorpio moon relates to physical attraction, creative energy, children, challenge, and a variety of sensations. Taurus, Libra, and Scorpio figure prominently, and have these letters in their names: F, O, X.

Sunday, July 5 (Moon in Scorpio to Sagittarius 7:24 p.m.)   Define terms, meditate, and look behind the scenes for the answers. Time is on your side so play the waiting game. Don't equate delay with defeat—a mixed-up itinerary is to blame. Pisces and Virgo figure in today's dynamic scenario, and are likely to have these letters in their names: G, P, Y.

Monday, July 6 (Moon in Sagittarius)   What a Monday! Today's Saturn keynote, moon in Sagittarius, focuses on pressure, deadline, responsibility, and complications in connection with a special relationship. While distracted, you possibly made a promise that you cannot keep at this time. Capricorn and another Cancer figure prominently.

Tuesday, July 7 (Moon in Sagittarius)   At last! Results are featured. Universal appeal and communication from a distant land help overcome a language barrier. Focus on import–export opportunities, and on travel in connection with romance, a product, or a talent. Aries and Libra play major roles, and have these letters in their names: I and R.

Wednesday, July 8 (Moon in Sagittarius to Capricorn 4:27 a.m.) Lucky lottery: 1, 9, 18, 12, 40, 51. Make a fresh start, letting go of an obligation you should not have carried in the first place. Imprint your style, refusing to follow others but letting them follow you. A Leo plays a dramatic role and helps plan entertainment, advertising, or publicity for a unique event connected with a political or charity campaign.

Thursday, July 9 (Moon in Capricorn) The full moon in Capricorn relates to romance, legal affairs, special permissions, or your marital status. Become more aware of accounting procedures; check your bankbook; protect collections. A recent acquisition is associated with antiques. Another Cancer trades recipes. Your lucky number is 2.

Friday, July 10 (Moon in Capricorn to Aquarius 10:52 a.m.) In matters of speculation, stick with these numbers: 3, 6, 9. Your forces are scattered, so keep your perspective. Show that you can laugh at your own foibles. New clothes improve your body image; you'll be complimented by people you admire. A Sagittarian plays an important role.

Saturday, July 11 (Moon in Aquarius) Don't neglect your duties, including signing legal documents and checking legal rights in connection with a possible inheritance. Tonight restrictions are lifted. Deal with Scorpio and Capricorn persons, who *do* have your best interests at heart. Lucky lottery: 4, 40, 12, 18, 33, 7.

Sunday, July 12 (Moon in Aquarius to Pisces 3:22 p.m.) What begins as a mild flirtation could become more serious than you originally anticipated. Keep your plans flexible and study written material carefully. Dig deep for information that has been suppressed, which could involve money, relatives, or marital status. Virgo figures prominently.

Monday, July 13 (Moon in Pisces)   Someone in hiding surfaces—this involves home, property, or a family member. Go slow, proofread, and check your source material. The Pisces moon relates to philosophy, travel, publishing, and getting your message across. Tonight, music plays, so dance to your own tune! Libra figures prominently.

Tuesday, July 14 (Moon in Pisces to Aries 6:45 p.m.)   Answers can be found via meditation—so look behind the scenes. Don't be caught off guard by one who plays an innocent role. See situations, relationships, and people as they are, not merely as you wish they were. The answer to your question: Yes, but not now. First, you must play the waiting game.

Wednesday, July 15 (Moon in Aries)   Someone in a decision-making position thinks seriously about a possible promotion—you are involved. A deadline figures in this scenario. There's a need for organizing, for lining up priorities, and for bringing order out of chaos. Capricorn and another Cancer play roles, and are likely to have these letters in their names: H, Q, Z.

Thursday, July 16 (Moon in Aries to Taurus 9:33 p.m.)   Universal appeal! Today's cycle highlights your ability to reach beyond the immediate, to be understood in all walks of life. Meanings will be comprehended despite distance and language barriers. Participate in a humanitarian project. Let go of a burden you should not by carrying—don't confuse gullibility with altruism.

Friday, July 17 (Moon in Taurus)   The answer to your question: Affirmative. Spread influence; win friends; use your powers of persuasion. Highlight independence, creativity, and a willingness to be vulnerable to love. Leo and Aquarius figure in this scenario, and are likely to have these letters in their names: A, S, J.

Saturday, July 18 (Moon in Taurus)   Lucky lottery: 2, 12, 20, 31, 5, 4. Focus on partnership, public relations, and the sale or purchase of property. An important decision involves marriage. Tonight the emphasis is on food and on serious discussions relating to both personal and the national economy. Another Cancer makes an interesting proposal.

Sunday, July 19 (Moon in Taurus to Gemini 12:18 a.m.)   You'll enjoy this Sunday! A Gemini comes up with a surprise, your social life is activated, and relationships improve. The day is excellent for giving full play to your intellectual curiosity. Discussions revolve around fashion, diet and nutrition, your body image, and current events. A Sagittarian figures in this scenario, and has these letters in a name: C, L, U.

Monday, July 20 (Moon in Gemini)   What you've been waiting for happens. The other shoe falls, but not as loud as you thought it would. The entire situation proves to be a tempest in a teapot. Taurus, Leo, and Scorpio are involved, and they could have these letters in their names: D, M, V. Review accounting procedures.

Tuesday, July 21 (Moon in Gemini to Cancer 3:43 a.m.)   On this Tuesday you'll do more writing than you have on previous days. The moon in your sign brings your high point, when events transpire to bring you closer to your goal. Even as you read these words, circumstances turn in your favor. Opportunity knocks, so answer the door! Virgo plays an outstanding role.

Wednesday, July 22 (Moon in Cancer)   Lucky lottery: 6, 20, 12, 2, 7, 9. Today's cycle revolves around music, art objects, luxury items, design, and the beautifying of your surroundings. You'll be concerned with your lifestyle, making a possible change of residence or marital status. The answer to your question: Be diplomatic; don't force issues. Libra is involved.

Thursday, July 23 (Moon in Cancer to Leo 8:48 a.m.)   The new moon in Leo relates to your money house. To put your program and agenda across, emphasize color, showmanship, entertainment, and a spectacular attraction. Define your terms and spotlight an illusion, a romance, or a mirage. Pisces and Virgo figure prominently, and are likely to have these letters in their names: G, P, Y.

Friday, July 24 (Moon in Leo)   At the track: post position special—number 8 p.p. in the ninth race. Pick six: 8, 4, 5, 2, 7, 1. Watch for these letters in the names of potential winning horses or jockeys: H, Q, Z. Hot daily doubles: 8 and 4, 2 and 5, 1 and 7; these selections apply to all tracks.

Saturday, July 25 (Moon in Leo to Virgo 4:34 p.m.)   Finish rather than initiate projects. Money is involved as your cycle moves up, so designate where you want to be and when. This adds up to taking charge of your own fate and destiny. Focus on love and spirituality, letting others know, however, that you will fight when the cause is right. Aries is represented.

Sunday, July 26 (Moon in Virgo)   Speak your piece, then permit a relative to talk. Today's scenario highlights a clash of ideas and the necessity for taking the initiative. The Virgo moon relates to trips, visits, ideas that eventually become viable and valuable. Attention also revolves around passion, romance, and a determination to make a relationship work.

Monday, July 27 (Moon in Virgo)   Regain your sense of direction and motivation. A clash of ideas with a Virgo proves stimulating, but know when to stop. Gourmet dining is indicated tonight. Another Cancer expresses affection, love, and confidence in your ability to succeed. Be discriminating and choose quality.

Tuesday, July 28 (Moon in Virgo to Libra 3:14 a.m.)   In matters of speculation, stick with these numbers: 3, 8, 4. The answer to your question: Be versatile but don't scatter your forces. By attempting to please everyone, you will please no one, least of all yourself. You'll have luck with timing, speculation, and social activities. Sagittarius is involved.

Wednesday, July 29 (Moon in Libra)   The cards are on the table face up, so don't overlook the obvious. Figures tend to be juggled, so watch your accounting methods. Read between the lines, dealing gingerly with Taurus and Scorpio, both of whom tend to be temperamental, stubborn, and pugnacious. Hold the line!

Thursday, July 30 (Moon in Libra in Scorpio 3:44 p.m.)   At the track: post position special—number 3 p.p. in the second race. Pick six: 2, 3, 8, 4, 1, 1. Watch for these letters, in the names of potential winning horses or jockeys: E, N, W. Hot daily doubles: 2 and 3, 5 and 5, 6 and 5; these selections apply to all tracks.

Friday, July 31 (Moon in Scorpio)   With the moon in Scorpio, facts previously hidden come to light. Focus on your home and on family relationships. Explain to someone close to you that your funds are limited. The spotlight is also on music, luxury, art, and the purchase of a gift that marks you as being extravagant.

AUGUST 1998

Saturday, August 1 (Moon in Scorpio)   You do have a right to celebrate! With the moon in Scorpio and a Pluto keynote, the emphasis will be on speculation, emotional responses, and even, perhaps, on falling madly in love. Married or single, male or female, your emotions tend to take over. Be sure to give logic at least a little space!

Sunday, August 2 (Moon in Scorpio to Sagittarius 3:48 a.m.)   On this Sunday, focus on relatives, visits, and trying out ideas. Be analytical; don't be satisfied merely to know something happened—ask questions and find out *why* it happened. Gemini, Virgo, and Sagittarius are involved, and are likely to have these letters in their names: E, N, W.

Monday, August 3 (Moon in Sagittarius)   Today's Venus keynote relates to continuous romantic notions, ideas, and concepts. August for you means money, love, achievement, and an ability to locate a missing link. It is certain you'll be more popular as social activities accelerate and you become involved in political or charitable campaigns.

Tuesday, August 4 (Moon in Sagittarius to Capricorn 1:18 p.m.)   Slow down! Within 24 hours, you'll be dealing with public responses to your efforts and products. Today's Neptune keynote warns that an element of deception might be present, so make your meanings crystal clear. Avoid the trap of self-deception. See people, places, and relationships in a more realistic light.

Wednesday, August 5 (Moon in Capricorn)   Lucky lottery: 8, 18, 16, 10, 1, 5. The Capricorn moon brings you into the public eye. Legal matters are spotlighted. Be aware and sensitive to subtle nuances. Focus also on partnership, cooperative efforts, and your marital status. Capricorn and another Cancer are involved; look for these letter in their names: H, Q, Z.

Thursday, August 6 (Moon in Capricorn to Aquarius 7:31 p.m.)   Elements of timing and luck ride with you. Emphasize language, publishing, getting your message across, corresponding, and communicating with friends in foreign lands. A love relationship is accented, relating to red-hot Mars. Nothing is likely to be tepid or lukewarm! Aries is involved.

Friday, August 7 (Moon in Aquarius) Take a fresh look at your accounts. A telephone bill could be out of kilter. Be aware of bank deposits and withdrawals. Forces are scattered and confusion results. Good news is received from a distant city. Leo and Aquarius figure in today's scenario, with these letters in their names: A, S, J.

Saturday, August 8 (Moon in Aquarius to Pisces 11:04 p.m.) The full moon, lunar eclipse in Aquarius, relates to a mysterious, strange woman, who brings news about a possible inheritance. You'll learn more about the financial status of someone close to you, including your partner or mate. Capricorn and another Cancer play roles, and have these letters in their names: B, K, T.

Sunday, August 9 (Moon in Pisces) You might be asking, "Is this déjà vu?" What happens today seems to be a repeat performance of what happened this past Friday. The focus is on social activity and on sensitivity about your wardrobe or body image. A Sagittarian relates information about exercise, diet, or nutrition.

Monday, August 10 (Moon in Pisces) Be ready for a transformation. The Pisces moon relates to distance and language and combines with the Pluto keynote. Tear down in order to rebuild on a more suitable base. Play your cards close to your chest, protecting confidential information. Taurus, Leo, and Scorpio figure in today's dynamic scenario.

Tuesday, August 11 (Moon in Pisces to Aries 1:10 a.m.) Be ready for change, travel, variety, and a surprise visit by a relative recently returned from a trip. Sharpen your writing skills and report and disseminate information. A liaison with a romantic Pisces lends spice.

Protect yourself at close quarters; don't take every whisper seriously.

Wednesday, August 12 (Moon in Aries)   Lucky lottery: 6, 1, 10, 9, 13, 22. Attention revolves around the necessity to get your house in order. Music figures prominently, with the emphasis on a possible change of address and marital status. Keep resolutions about your diet and nutrition—don't give in to that sweet tooth!

Thursday, August 13 (Moon in Aries to Taurus 3:04 a.m.)   Focus on mystery, intrigue, and the need to protect your privacy. Today's Aries moon relates to your career, ambition, leadership, and standing in the community. The Neptune keynote blends with your moon significator, and if this does not mean poetry, then astrologers will have another guess coming.

Friday, August 14 (Moon in Taurus)   The chips are down! Today's Saturn keynote means awareness of time and deadlines. A strong love relationship carries with it responsibility. Capricorn and another Cancer figure prominently, with these letters in their names: H, Q, Z. Take care that you don't bump your knees in the dark.

Saturday, August 15 (Moon in Taurus to Gemini 5:45 a.m.)   A project that lay dormant will be revived, largely due to your influence. Today's Taurus moon relates to that section of your horoscope associated with your ability to win friends and influence people and to use your power of persuasion. Today, you learn more about how people live in other nations. You'll also become aware that your soulmate might be just around the corner.

Sunday, August 16 (Moon in Gemini)   The answer to your question: You have nothing to fear. Take a cold plunge into the future. A Leo helps dramatize your product and obtain publicity, and becomes your ally in love. Stress independence, originality, and inventiveness; welcome an opportunity for a different kind of love.

Monday, August 17 (Moon in Gemini to Cancer 9:55 a.m.)   Another Cancer figures prominently, helping to review facts and figures and inviting you to dine—for once, you won't be doing the cooking. A Capricorn also plays a role, and is likely to have these letters in a name: B, K, T. Domestic harmony is restored!

Tuesday, August 18 (Moon in Cancer)   At the track: post position special—number 5 p.p. in the fifth race. Pick six: 3, 7, 5, 4, 5, 5. Be aware of these letters in the names of potential winning horses or jockeys: C, L, U. Hot daily doubles: 3 and 7, 5 and 5, 4 and 8; these selections apply to all tracks.

Wednesday, August 19 (Moon in Cancer to Leo 4:01 p.m.)   Lucky lottery: 19, 4, 24, 2, 20, 50. The moon in your sign begins your high cycle, indicating that circumstances are turning in your favor and providing encouragement for making a fresh start in a different direction. Trust your own judgment, because your intuition is honed to razor sharpness. Scorpio plays a role.

Thursday, August 20 (Moon in Leo)   Get your thoughts on paper—read and write and be ready for consultation concerning news and current affairs. A member of the opposite sex, drawn to you, asserts, "I love your mind and I am afraid I can hardly keep my hands off your body!" Gemini and Virgo play memorable roles. Your lucky number is 5.

Friday, August 21 (Moon in Leo)   A reconciliation relates to your family and marital status. The Leo moon tells of the necessity for curbing extravagance. You'll locate what was lost, missing, or stolen—it could be found near a fireplace. Taurus, Libra, and Scorpio figure in this scenario, and are likely to have these letters in their names: F, O, X.

Saturday, August 22 (Moon in Leo in Virgo 12:21 a.m.)   It's a memorable Saturday! The new moon, solar eclipse in Leo, relates to your investments and personal possessions, and to buying and selling. Beware of someone who attempts to buy you a free lunch—you can't get something for nothing. Pisces is in the picture.

Sunday, August 23 (Moon in Virgo)   A serious discussion involves relatives, the element of time, investment, and plans for future organization. Capricorn and another Cancer figure prominently, are likely to have these letters in their names: H, Q, Z. The Virgo moon encourages critical examination of a proposal made by a sibling.

Monday, August 24 (Moon in Virgo to Libra 11:02 a.m.)   Look beyond the immediate to see the picture in its entirety. Give full play to your intellectual curiosity. Maintain your perspective, showing that you can laugh at your own foibles. A surprise social invitation is likely to involve Aries. There's music in your home tonight. A Libra professes more than friendship.

Tuesday, August 25 (Moon in Libra)   In matters of speculation, try these numbers: 1, 7, 6. The emphasis is on having the courage of your convictions, letting go of the status quo, and making a fresh start in a new direction based on original thinking. You could be enamoured of a Leo who opens doors and talks much about music, literature, and art.

Wednesday, August 26 (Moon in Libra to Scorpio 11:25 p.m.)   Focus on your marital status, public appearances, and an invitation to dine gourmet style. Capricorn and another Cancer figure in this scenario, and they could have these letters in their names: B, K, T. Get to the heart of matters, state your case frankly, and be honest with others and expect honesty in return. Your lucky number is 2.

Thursday, August 27 (Moon in Scorpio) At the track: post position special—number 5 p.p. in the ninth race. Pick six: 3, 6, 8, 4, 4, 5. Watch for these letters in the names of potential winning horses or jockeys, C, L, U. Hot daily doubles: 3 and 6, 7 and 2, 3 and 3; these selections apply to all tracks.

Friday, August 28 (Moon in Scorpio) Insist on a square deal. New rules are in order, as today's scenario highlights a willingness to tear down in order to rebuild on a more solid structure. The Scorpio moon relates to your fifth house favoring creative endeavors. Your personal magnetism is highlighted, along with sex appeal. Scorpio plays role.

Saturday, August 29 (Moon in Scorpio to Sagittarius 11:55 a.m.) Flirtation! Male or female, married or single, a clash of ideas is featured and could be interpreted as a flirtation. Gemini, Virgo, and Sagittarius are involved, and they could have these letters in their names: E, N, W. You'll be complimented on your appearance and your writing talent. Lucky lottery: 5, 50, 7, 16, 22, 13.

Sunday, August 30 (Moon in Sagittarius) What threatened to erupt into a family quarrel relating to money, or a possible inheritance cools down. Be diplomatic without being subservient, and make an intelligent concession without watering down your principles. Today's scenario highlights music, art, a serious consideration of your lifestyle, residence, and marital status.

Monday, August 31 (Moon in Sagittarius to Capricorn 10:23 p.m.) With the moon in Sagittarius and a Neptune keynote, you learn where you stand and with whom. Your psychic faculties are honed to razor sharpness. You obtain a behind-the-scenes view as coworkers show their hands despite themselves. Play your cards close to your chest. Virgo is in the picture.

Tuesday, September 1 (Moon in Capricorn)   The moon is in Sagittarius and astrological keynote is Mercury. Synchronizing these factors, it becomes evident that you should be alert to sudden change of plans or itinerary. Words, both spoken and written, play significant roles, as an intriguing love note lends spice and elevates your morale.

Wednesday, September 2 (Moon in Capricorn)   Attention revolves around responsibility for the renovation of your home. Focus on a domestic adjustment, lifestyle, income and potential. A gift represents a token of love. Music figures prominently, so dance to your own tune. Lucky lottery: 50, 7, 3, 13, 6, 51.

Thursday, September 3 (Moon in Capricorn to Aquarius 5:21 a.m.)   Today's moon position highlights public appearances, publicity, and a greater awareness of your legal rights, partnership, or marriage. You'll be saying, "What a Thursday! I couldn't stand much more activity!" Pisces and Virgo figure prominently, and are likely to have these letters in their names: G, P, Y.

Friday, September 4 (Moon in Aquarius)   At the track: post position special—number 8 p.p. in the ninth race. Pick six: 4, 6, 2, 5, 3, 3. Keep your antenna up for these letters in the names of potential winning horses or jockeys: H, Q, Z. Hot daily doubles: 4 and 6, 8 and 8, 7 and 1; these selections apply to all tracks.

Saturday, September 5 (Moon in Aquarius to Pisces 8:48 a.m.)   In matters of speculation, stick with these numbers: 3, 6, 9. You'll have reason to celebrate, for you get recognition and could meet a soulmate. Let go of an obligation you should not have carried in the first place. Focus on freedom to travel, explore, read, advertise, and publish.

Sunday, September 6 (Moon in Pisces)   The full moon, lunar eclipse in Pisces, relates to travel, philosophy, theology, making a new start, and revising old plans to fit with modern concepts. Leo and Aquarius play significant roles, and they could have these letters in their names: A, S, J. The answer to a question: Yes. Make a fresh start, then take the cold plunge into the future.

Monday, September 7 (Moon in Pisces to Aries 9:53 a.m.)   The moon remains in your ninth house, relating to idealism in romance, travel, and correspondence with someone residing overseas. Food plays a paramount role. It is likely you will be dining on foreign cuisine or your dinner companion will be bilingual.

Tuesday, September 8 (Moon in Aries)   You'll be saying, "This is possibly the most social Tuesday I've experienced in a long time!" Focus on fun, frivolity, experimentation, and keeping up to date in fashion. A recent addition to your wardrobe improves your image. Your fortunate number is 3.

Wednesday, September 9 (Moon in Aries to Taurus 10:16 a.m.)   Lucky lottery: 4, 40, 1, 10, 9, 51. Check references and source material. Investigate any accounting methods and unorthodox procedures that may have caused worry among friends and associates. Taurus, Leo, and Scorpio figure in this scenario, and could have these letters in their names: D, M, V.

Thursday, September 10 (Moon in Taurus)   You've been waiting for the right time to make changes that could relate to where you live, your lifestyle, or your marriage—today is the time! Gemini, Virgo, and Sagittarius figure in this scenario, and could have these letters in their names: E, N, W. Today's moon promotes the ability to win friends and influence people.

Friday, September 11 (Moon in Taurus to Gemini 11:40 a.m.)   Gifts, music, and flowers are part of today's exciting, romantic drama. As the weekend gets under way, you might be musing in disbelief, "Life can be beautiful after all!" Attention revolves around a love relationship and a decision relating to marriage.

Saturday, September 12 (Moon in Gemini)   Lucky lottery: 12, 3, 5, 50, 7, 8. The moon in Gemini relates to your fourth house, involving negotiations concerning your home or property that are due to be completed. Real estate figures prominently; circumstances move in your favor; you'll be at the right place at an exciting moment.

Sunday, September 13 (Moon in Gemini to Cancer 3:20 p.m.)   With the Saturn keynote and the moon in Gemini, you'll have the ability to bring order out of chaos. The moon in your twelfth house coincides with a secret hiding place, dining in a secluded area, and learning once and for all that discretion truly is the better part of valor.

Monday, September 14 (Moon in Cancer)   Emphasize universal appeal, relating to people in foreign lands and overcoming distance and language barriers. Promote your product and seize the opportunity to travel. You'll be rid of a burden you had no right to assume in the first place. Aries and Libra are involved, and could have these letters in their names: I and R.

Tuesday, September 15 (Moon in Cancer to Leo 9:48 p.m.)   Make a fresh start in a new direction. The moon in your sign begins your high cycle. Don't wait to be told what to do—do your own thing. A love relationship is stimulated; if married, you can rediscover your mate in an exciting, physical way. Married or single, you could be madly in love. Leo plays a role.

Wednesday, September 16 (Moon in Leo)   Lucky lottery: 2, 12, 20, 4, 13, 40. The moon transits your sign and gets ready to enter Leo, which goes well for you in

273

connection with your income. Get an estimate of the value of your possessions and attend an auction, if possible. Luck rides with you in connection with a legitimate bargain.

Thursday, September 17 (Moon in Leo) At the track: post position special—number 5 p.p. in the seventh race. Pick six: 3, 2, 5, 7, 7, 8. Watch for these letters in the names of potential winning horses or jockeys: C, L, U. Hot daily doubles: 3 and 2, 5 and 5, 3 and 7; these selections apply to all tracks.

Friday, September 18 (Moon in Leo to Virgo 6:52 a.m.) Slow down! The emphasis is on money, payments, collections, and investments. Locate a missing link. Your cycle is high, despite a temporary delay in achieving your goal. Tax and license requirements command attention. Taurus, Leo, and Scorpio figure in today's scenario and could have these letters in their names: D, M, V.

Saturday, September 19 (Moon in Virgo) Movement! Astrological and numerical symbols points to moving from one place to another and to involvement with the lively arts. Disseminate information, record your dreams, and write of your experiences. A flirtation lends spice, and could lead to something important. Lucky lottery: 5, 6, 7, 12, 9, 8.

Sunday, September 20 (Moon in Virgo to Libra 5:57 p.m.) On this Sunday, with the Venus keynote and the new moon in Virgo, you have another opportunity to restore harmony to family relationships. Do not permit false pride to deter your progress. Focus on flowers, gifts, music, and discussions concerning your lifestyle and marriage. Libra is represented.

Monday, September 21 (Moon in Libra) An element of deception is present. Play the waiting game, seeing people and relationships as they actually exist. Focus on property value and the necessity for being on familiar ground. There's music in your home tonight—be receptive without being gullible. Pisces and Virgo figure prominently, and are likely to have these letters in their names: G, P, Y.

Tuesday, September 22 (Moon in Libra)   Break free from preconceived notions—create your own tradition! You'll be dealing with time, both actual and metaphysical. A deadline exists, so meet it and beat it. An older person lends the benefit of experience, talking about life and times and love. Capricorn figures in a meaningful way.

Wednesday, September 23 (Moon in Libra to Scorpio 6:22 a.m.)   Don't hold back! The moon is entering that section of your horoscope relating to creativity, challenge, change, personal magnetism, and sex appeal. Overcome your apprehension concerning distance and language. Reach beyond the immediate and use your ability to see tomorrow. Your lucky number is 9.

Thursday, September 24 (Moon in Scorpio)   It's time for a new start! The Scorpio moon relates to creativity, children, challenge, fresh concepts, and your ability to imprint your own style. Be receptive to new love, stressing universal appeal and originality. Show the courage of your convictions. Leo and Aquarius play memorable roles, and are likely to have these letters in their names: A, S, J.

Friday, September 25 (Moon in Scorpio to Sagittarius 7:05 p.m.)   You might be asked to work overtime. Keep your plans flexible, realizing that a family member has something special planned. The emphasis is on the comforts of home. Capricorn and another Cancer figure in today's dynamic scenario, and they could have these letters in their names: B, K, T.

Saturday, September 26 (Moon in Sagittarius)   A lively Saturday night! Social functions dominate; you'll be invited to join charitable or political activities. Your popularity soars and you're looking great in new clothes. Laugh at your own foibles and transform humor into profundity. Your lucky number is 3.

Sunday, September 27 (Moon in Sagittarius)   At the track: post position special—number 4 p.p. in the fourth race. Pick six: 8, 8, 3, 4, 2, 5. Keep your antenna up for these letters in the names of potential winning horses or jockeys: D, M, V. Hot daily doubles: 8 and 8, 4 and 4, 6 and 2; these selections apply to all tracks.

Monday, September 28 (Moon in Sagittarius to Capricorn 6:30 a.m.)   It's an exciting Monday! Learn through the process of teaching. Start a diary, making note of your experiences and relationships. Within 24 hours, a legal problem comes to a conclusion, and it will favor you. The focus is also on partnership, public relations, reputation, credibility, and your marital status. A Sagittarian is in the picture.

Tuesday, September 29 (Moon in Capricorn)   Today's Venus keynote relates to music, romance, style, gifts, and decisions relating to where you live, your lifestyle, or your marriage. The good news is that your cash flow resumes. The business of being a day late and a dollar short is finished. Taurus, Libra, and Scorpio figure in today's dynamic scenario, and are likely to have these letters in their names: F, O, X.

Wednesday, September 30 (Moon in Capricorn to Aquarius 2:53 p.m.)   Your efforts receive more attention than you originally anticipated. The Capricorn moon is associated with public response to your contributions. The spotlight also falls on cooperative efforts and a clash of ideas in a constructive, exciting way. Questions about marriage continue to loom large.

OCTOBER 1998

Thursday, October 1 (Moon in Aquarius)   With the moon in Aquarius and a Venus keynote, expect a pleasurable evening that could include music and dining out. Focus on harmony, rhythm, and a domestic adjustment that could bring feuding family members together for peace talks. Libra is involved.

Friday, October 2 (Moon in Aquarius to Pisces 7:23 p.m.)   Check your social calendar and your invitation list. People, including relatives, tend to be ultra-sensitive. Money is involved; discussions include finances and a possible inheritance. Pisces and Virgo figure prominently, and they could have these letters in their names: G, P, Y.

Saturday, October 3 (Moon in Pisces)   Saturday night special! Capricorn and another Cancer play outstanding roles, and could have these letters in their names: H, Q, Z. You'll be handed responsibility for healing a family rift and for bringing order out of chaos. Today's Pisces moon relates to a long-distance communication, or to a possible journey.

Sunday, October 4 (Moon in Pisces to Aries 8:32 p.m.)   Reach beyond the immediate, stressing universal appeal and refusing to worry about distance and language obstacles—you'll overcome them! Questions surface concerning romance, love, marriage, and future plans. Aries and Libra figure prominently, and could have these letters in their names: I and R.

Monday, October 5 (Moon in Aries)   The full moon in Aries relates to the tenth sector of your horoscope, affecting your ambitions, goals, career, and standing in community. The Aries moon tells of aggressiveness, initiative, originality, controversy, and ideas that disturb the complacent.

Tuesday, October 6 (Moon in Aries to Taurus 7:57 p.m.)   Concentrate on direction, motivation, and a family relationship. Someone in a position of authority seems to be aching for a fight. Realize you have backing and don't water down your principles. Before the day is finished, you'll be invited for gourmet dining. Another Cancer is in the picture.

Wednesday, October 7 (Moon in Taurus) On this Wednesday, your mood turns from gloom to frivolity. The Taurus moon relates to your eleventh house, that section of your horoscope associated with your ability to win friends and influence people. A wish is fulfilled, so fast that you'll be musing, "When it rains, it pours!" Lucky lottery: 3, 36, 50, 4, 17, 22.

Thursday, October 8 (Moon in Taurus to Gemini 7:44 p.m.) What was supposed to happen yesterday will take place today. It's a blessing in disguise! An opportunity exists to correct mechanical defects, so check the batteries in your automobile and your home. Taurus, Leo, and Scorpio play significant roles, and are likely to have these letters or initials in their names: D, M, V.

Friday, October 9 (Moon in Gemini) At the track: post position special—number 3 p.p. in the second race. Pick six: 2, 3, 5, 1, 3, 3. Have your antenna up for these letters in the names of potential winning horses or jockeys: E, N, W. Hot daily doubles: 2 and 3, 5 and 5, 3 and 3; these selections apply to all tracks.

Saturday, October 10 (Moon in Gemini to Cancer 9:48 p.m.) The dust settles! Secrets surface and you will learn where you stand and why. Music is involved as harmony is restored on the home front. Special: Remember resolutions relating to diet, exercise, and nutrition. Overcome a tendency to give in to your sweet tooth. Also, be moderate with alcoholic beverages.

Sunday, October 11 (Moon in Cancer) The moon gets ready to enter your sign—by tomorrow, you'll be in charge of your own destiny. Tonight, a Gemini spills the beans. Be receptive but not gullible. Define your terms, watching out for an element of deception. It's important to see people, places, and relationships in a realistic light.

Monday, October 12 (Moon in Cancer) The emphasis is on organization, responsibility, and dealing with the element of time—meet and beat a deadline! A former teacher or employer lends the benefit of experience. The moon in your sign coincides with accurate judgment and intuition. The action will be where you designate as circumstances turn in your favor.

Tuesday, October 13 (Moon in Cancer to Leo 3:25 a.m.) Your lucky numbers: 3, 6, 9. Finish what you start, for your worth and your product will be judged—you might be on the precipice of fame and fortune. Extricate yourself from a situation, proposition, or relationship that is draining you financially or emotionally. Be open to an opportunity for romance and travel, or to promoting your product in new markets, including those overseas.

Wednesday, October 14 (Moon in Leo) It's the day you've been waiting for! The Leo moon means money and the sun keynote means enlightenment and a fresh start in a new direction. Expect a heated romance. Leo and Aquarius figure in today's action, and could have these letters in their names: A, S, J. Lucky number is 1.

Thursday, October 15 (Moon in Leo to Virgo 12:32 p.m.) The answer to your question: You need more information about structure, design, and past performance. Check the budget, as well as lease and rental documents. Food is involved; restaurant management could play a role. Another Cancer figures in this scenario, and is likely to have these letters in a name: B, K, T.

Friday, October 16 (Moon in Virgo) Don't feel guilty about celebrating! A Virgo tends to be critical and advocates self-denial. But the Jupiter keynote, moon in Virgo, highlights joyful exuberance. Focus on curiosity, transportation, fashion, and being up to date on news events. Gemini and Sagittarius figure prominently, and have these letters in their names: C, L, U.

Saturday, October 17 (Moon in Virgo) What appears to be an upset actually proves beneficial. Know it and respond accordingly. Proofread material for implications between the lines. What begins as a subtle innuendo could come crashing down with hammer force. Taurus, Leo, and Scorpio are involved, and these letters stand out: D, M. V.

Sunday, October 18 (Moon in Virgo to Libra 12:02 a.m.) Get ready for change, travel, variety, and a surprising admission by a relative who once said, "I have nothing to hide!" A trip may be necessary in order to reestablish legal precedence—a document is involved and it will be located promptly. By tomorrow, a decision will be made in connection with the sale or purchase of your property or home.

Monday, October 19 (Moon in Libra) The emphasis is on familiar ground. A dilemma involving the sale or purchase of property is solved. The spotlight is on getting together with those whose ideas clash—be diplomatic but refuse to be the umpire. Today's Libra moon relates to entertaining at home, music, and delicious hors d'oeuvres. Your lucky number is 6.

Tuesday, October 20 (Moon in Libra to Scorpio 12:36 p.m.) Mirage! Your five senses could be fooled, but not your extrasensory perception. Make your terms crystal clear. Discover exactly what is expected of you and what you may anticipate in return for your contributions, both creative and financial. Pisces and Virgo are involved, and have these initials in their names: G, P, Y.

Wednesday, October 21 (Moon in Scorpio)   Lucky lottery: 8, 16, 4, 40, 22, 19. You'll be trusted with other people's money—accept this challenge, but make clear, "This time and this time only!" The emphasis is also on a stormy relationship. Capricorn and another Cancer play featured roles, and are likely to have these letters in their names: H, Q, Z.

Thursday, October 22 (Moon in Scorpio)   Creative activities and endeavors grab the spotlight. By giving of yourself, you receive rewards, including love. Reach beyond previous limitations to accent distance and language, and to restore your belief in finding a soulmate. Aries and Libra play featured roles, and are likely to have these letters in their names: I and R.

Friday, October 23 (Moon in Scorpio to Sagittarius 1:16 a.m.)   The answer: Affirmative. Stress your independence and originality. Don't be a doormat for someone who takes you for granted. A different, exciting kind of romance is on the horizon—be confident, dynamic, try a different wardrobe. Special: Avoid heavy lifting! Leo and Aquarius figure prominently.

Saturday, October 24 (Moon in Sagittarius)   Two directions! You reach a crossroads—go backward and an old flame will be there. So move forward, take a cold plunge into the future, to be refreshed, alive, and vibrant. The choice is your own. Another Cancer is involved, and likely to have these letters in a name: B, K, T.

Sunday, October 25, Daylight Saving Time ends (Moon in Sagittarius to Capricorn 12:05 p.m.)   On this Sunday, family differences can be straightened out. Be diplomatic but firm, speaking frankly concerning money without creating panic. A Taurus expresses deep appreciation for your talent and advice. Social activities follow spiritual involvement. Gifts are received. You'll be happy and will be able to laugh at yourself.

Monday, October 26 (Moon in Capricorn)   Have your antenna up in connection with legal matters, copyright infringements, and proposals that include business or marriage. A clash of ideas stimulates, assuring that you are intellectually alive. Taurus, Leo, and Scorpio figure in this scenario, and have these letters in their names: D, M, V.

Tuesday, October 27 (Moon in Capricorn to Aquarius 9:44 p.m.)   Write your way in and out of anything! The lunar position highlights public attention, added recognition, a review of legal rights, and the spotlight on your marital status. Gemini, Virgo, and Sagittarius play outstanding roles, and are likely to have these letters in their names: E, N, W. Your lucky number is 5.

Wednesday, October 28 (Moon in Aquarius)   Your lucky numbers: 2, 8, 6. A Libra confides, "When I'm near you, I hear music!" Protect your property, and feel good concerning flattery and expressions of affection. But don't give up the farm for mere whispered romantic words. Taurus, Libra, and Scorpio are involved, and have these letters in their names: F, O, X.

Thursday, October 29 (Moon in Aquarius)   At the track: post position special—number 1 p.p. in the sixth race. Pick six: 7, 6, 4, 2, 1, 1. Be alert for these letters, initials in names of potential winning horses or jockeys: G, P, Y. Hot daily doubles: 7 and 6, 4 and 7, 1 and 1; these selections apply to all tracks.

Friday, October 30 (Moon in Aquarius to Pisces 3:58 a.m.)   The Aquarian moon relates to secrets, hiding places, arcane literature, and the financial worth of your mate or partner. The emphasis is on the pressure of time limitation, an intense relationship, thorns among roses, and durable goods. Capricorn and another Cancer figure in this scenario. Your lucky number is 8.

Saturday, October 31 (Moon in Pisces)   Halloween! The moon is in mysterious Pisces, so focus on spiritualism, ghosts, goblins, and eternal mysteries—you could be directly involved! Share your research findings, and relate anecdotes concerning Houdini and whether or not he appeared at seances. Hold hands in the dark! Lucky lottery: 1, 9, 18, 7, 12, 33.

NOVEMBER 1998

Sunday, November 1 (Moon in Pisces to Aries 6:27 a.m.)   The moon is in Pisces, with a Neptune keynote, so be cautious—you don't know the complete story. Look backstage, for someone could attempt to pull the wool over your eyes while pulling the rabbit out of a hat. Long-distance communication relates to the current situation. Pisces is involved.

Monday, November 2 (Moon in Aries)   The Aries moon represents your career, your standing in the community, and your business relationships. The Saturn keynote is associated with discipline, deadlines, and the restoration of confidence. If you're frivolous about a relationship, it's best to move on. People today take you seriously, noting your words and actions.

Tuesday, November 3 (Moon in Aries to Taurus 6:12 a.m.)   Reach beyond the immediate to communicate with the boss. You'll be given extra responsibility, which might include an assignment that takes you on a journey and involve advertising, publicity, or additional written material. Aries and Libra are in the picture, and have these letters in their names: I and R.

Wednesday, November 4 (Moon in Taurus)   The full moon in Taurus, plus the sun keynote, means you have a rare chance to highlight independence, originality, personal magnetism, and sex appeal. Focus on a fresh start in a new direction. Avoid heavy lifting. Don't follow others, but let them follow you. Lucky lottery: 1, 50, 5, 10, 12, 32.

Thursday, November 5 (Moon in Taurus to Gemini 5:11 a.m.)   At the track: post position special—number 6 p.p. in the fifth race. Pick six: 2, 2, 4, 1, 6, 7. Hot daily doubles: 2 and 2, 6 and 5, 1 and 7. Watch for these letters in the names of potential winning horses or jockeys: B, K, T; these selections apply to all tracks.

Friday, November 6 (Moon in Gemini)   Your lucky numbers: 6, 3, 3. The Gemini moon relates to secrets, clandestine arrangements, drama, theater, glamour, and intrigue. Keep your aura on mystery—if you tell all you'll lose your audience, and even, perhaps, love. Gemini and Sagittarius are featured, with these letters in their names: C, L, U.

Saturday, November 7 (Moon in Gemini to Cancer 5:39 a.m.)   On this Saturday, you could be called to work overtime. Revise your source material. Proofread, keeping aware of subtle innuendos between the lines. Taurus, Leo, and Scorpio are involved, and are likely to have these letters in their names: D, M, V. Lucky lottery: 4, 40, 12, 17, 1, 19.

Sunday, November 8 (Moon in Cancer)   Be ready for change, travel, and variety—read and write, teach and learn, and always keep one step ahead of the class. The moon in your sign signals your high cycle, so take the initiative, trusting in your own judgment and intuition. The action will be where you designate, as you exude personal magnetism, sensuality, and sex appeal.

Monday, November 9 (Moon in Cancer to Leo 9:33 a.m.)   Attention revolves around decoration, remodeling, beautifying your surroundings, your lifestyle, and your marital status. Keep recent resolutions concerning exercise, diet, and nutrition—and don't give in to your sweet tooth! Taurus, Libra, and Scorpio figure prominently, and are likely to have these letters in their names: F, O, X.

Tuesday, November 10 (Moon in Leo)   A financial transaction requires caution—play the waiting game, for the second offer is much better than the first one. Find out exactly what is expected of you and what you might anticipate in return for your efforts and contributions. The Leo moon tells of your ability to earn money by a display of showmanship.

Wednesday, November 11 (Moon in Leo to Virgo 5:37 p.m.)   The emphasis is on unique studies, unorthodox procedures, and taking charge of your own destiny. Bright, attractive Leo will become your valuable ally— you'll learn that tonight. Capricorn and another Cancer figure in this scenario, and they could have these letters in their names: H, Q, Z.

Thursday, November 12 (Moon in Virgo)   Your lucky numbers: 3, 6, 9. A project is completed earlier than you anticipated. A relative is involved. There's a possibility of an overseas journey. Promote your product or talent to a wider audience. A burden you had no right to carry in first place is finally removed, much to your relief.

Friday, November 13 (Moon in Virgo)   No bad luck today! Begin a project, take the initiative, and stress independence of thought and action. Break from the everyday routine to create your own tradition. Today's Virgo moon highlights perceptiveness, writing, and a reunion with a relative who once declared, "I don't suppose we'll ever see each other again!" Leo is involved.

Saturday, November 14 (Moon in Virgo to Libra 4:58 a.m.)   Share Saturday night activities with a relative who is an excellent cook, and is very likely a Cancer. Focus on direction, motivation, and the serious consideration of partnership and marital status. Within 24 hours, a decision will be reached concerning your home or property. Lucky lottery: 1, 11, 12, 14, 19, 48.

Sunday, November 15 (Moon in Libra)   Spiritual values surface. Blend fun and frolic with versatility and curiosity about how the other half lives. Gemini and Sagittarius play roles, and are likely to have these letters in their names: C, L, U. Keep resolutions about improving your fashion, body image, diet, and nutrition.

Monday, November 16 (Moon in Libra to Scorpio 5:41 p.m.)   An opportunity will exist to do things your way. A family member brings joy to your home, including music. Your views are vindicated. You'll be told, "You really do strive for justice!" Taurus, Leo, and Scorpio play significant roles, and are likely to have these letters in their names: D, M, V.

Tuesday, November 17 (Moon in Scorpio)   At the track: post position special—number 3 p.p. in the second race. Pick six: 2, 3, 4, 4, 5, 8. Look for these letters in the names of potential winning horses or jockeys: E, N, W. Hot daily doubles: 2 and 3, 5 and 5, 1 and 3; these selections apply to all tracks.

Wednesday, November 18 (Moon in Scorpio)   Your lucky numbers: 6, 1, 2. Attention revolves around domestic issues that include a possible change of residence or marital status. Today's lunar aspect highlights creativity, style, personal magnetism, and sex appeal. Emotional responses are intense, so give logic equal time and protect yourself in close quarters.

Thursday, November 19 (Moon in Scorpio to Sagittarius 6:13 a.m.)   The new moon in Scorpio relates to your fifth house, that section of your horoscope representing children, challenge, change, and variety. Since Scorpio is involved, hormones swirl, and despite chronological age, you could find yourself madly in love. Pisces and Virgo play roles, and have these letters in their names: G, P, Y.

Friday, November 20 (Moon in Sagittarius)   Conditions settle. You'll be instrumental in bringing order out of a chaotic situation. The time factor figures prominently—a deadline exists and you're called upon to meet time requirements with your budget in mind. Capricorn and another Cancer play roles, and are likely to have these letters in their names: H, Q, Z.

Saturday, November 21 (Moon in Sagittarius to Capricorn 5:45 p.m.)   You'll encounter people from foreign lands and participate in bilingual discussions about humanitarian projects. You could meet your soulmate. Your outlook changes and your curiosity is aroused. This could be the precursor to an overseas journey. Aries and Libra are represented, and could have these letters in their names: I and R.

Sunday, November 22 (Moon in Capricorn)   Thanksgiving preparations loom large, as the moon in your seventh house relates to an invitation list, public relations, and marital status. Highlight originality, refusing to follow others and being willing to take risks. You win if you are yourself; conversely, you lose by imitating others.

Monday, November 23 (Moon in Capricorn)   You might be musing, "I wish this had happened yesterday!" Focus on family harmony and good news concerning your financial security. Attention revolves around your home, property, and sales and purchases adding up to profit. Capricorn and another Cancer are featured, with these letters in their names: B, K, T.

Tuesday, November 24 (Moon in Capricorn to Aquarius 3:43 a.m.)   At the track: post position special—number 5 p.p. in the seventh race. Pick six: 3, 5, 3, 7, 2, 1. Have your antenna up for these letters in the names of potential winning horses or jockeys: C, L, U. Hot daily doubles: 3 and 5, 3 and 3, 6 and 4; these selections apply to all tracks.

Wednesday, November 25 (Moon in Aquarius)   Your lucky numbers: 4, 1, 7. The Aquarian moon relates to the solution of a mystery regarding ownership and inheritance. The true financial status of someone close to you is revealed, possibly in an embarrassing way. Maintain your perspective, poise, and panache. Scorpio plays a role.

Thursday, November 26 (Moon in Aquarius to Pisces 11:14 a.m.)   It's Thanksgiving! An exchange of ideas is featured. A family member previously distant will reappear. You'll reflect on the meaning of this day and conclude, "I do have much to be thankful for, and I'm becoming more aware of it." Gemini, Virgo, and Sagittarius are involved, with these letters in their names: E, N, W.

Friday, November 27 (Moon in Pisces)   It's a Friday night to remember! A long-distance communication involves a planned reunion with a loved one. Focus on publishing, advertising, and getting your message across. A study of language figures prominently; you'll be idealistic in romance; you'll feel that life is worth living. Libra figures prominently.

Saturday, November 28 (Moon in Pisces to Aries 3:34 p.m.)   "Glamour kid!" You'll be referred to that way, so revel in it and don't be overly modest. Define your terms, looking behind the scenes for answers and refusing to tell all. The Pisces moon relates to travel, publishing, advertising, and the recognition of spiritual values. A romance tonight could involve the discussion of a future journey—together!

Sunday, November 29 (Moon in Aries)   A parental authority is challenged, and people in charge tend to battle for rights, position, and financial gain. Be responsible for your own actions. The element of time is involved, and a budget and deadline can be met. Capricorn and another Cancer are featured, and are likely to have these letters in their names: H, Q, Z.

Monday, November 30 (Moon in Aries to Taurus 4:53 p.m.) The moon in Aries relates to fate, destiny, promotion, and your ability to accept the responsibility of leadership. An aggressive coworker, associate, or superior tests your mettle. Maintain your equilibrium, refusing to be drawn into a foolish argument. Reach beyond the immediate to perceive your potential. Be open to a strong love relationship. Aries is involved.

DECEMBER 1998

Tuesday, December 1 (Moon in Taurus) You'll be contemplating added responsibility and an intense relationship. Capricorn and another Cancer figure in today's complicated, exciting scenario; they're likely to have these letters in their names: H, Q, Z.

Wednesday, December 2 (Moon in Taurus to Gemini 4:30 p.m.) What a Wednesday! You exude the aura of universal appeal, appealing to all segments and overcoming distance and language barriers. As you peruse this situation, you'll be musing, "I wish every Wednesday and maybe every day could be this way!" Lucky lottery: 9, 19, 29, 1, 10, 12.

Thursday, December 3 (Moon in Gemini) With a full moon in Gemini in your twelfth house, this could be the night of love and laughter! The emphasis is on style, creativity, originality, and sex appeal. A new, exciting relationship is on the horizon or a current affair of the heart is revitalized. Leo and Aquarius are featured, with these letters in their names: A, S, J.

Friday, December 4 (Moon in Gemini to Cancer 4:28 p.m.) Much that occurs is secret, clandestine, and subtle, rather than out in the open. Face the fact that some references will not be valid and that your source material must be brought up to date. Proofread, for glaring errors can be exposed by you. Be familiar with tax and license requirements. Scorpio is involved.

Saturday, December 5 (Moon in Cancer)   The cycle is high, with the moon in your sign and a Jupiter keynote. This is your lucky day, and it could be the start of a winning streak. Focus on popularity and on political and charitable activities. You'll have that rare talent of making people laugh even through their tears. Pisces and Virgo play dramatic roles. Lucky lottery: 17, 6, 51, 22, 33, 18.

Sunday, December 6 (Moon in Cancer to Leo 6:55 p.m.)   Your lucky numbers: 4, 4, 8. Stress your personality, excellent food, and alcoholic beverages. A family gathering won't be all sweetness and light, but much can be accomplished. Taurus, Leo, and Scorpio figure in today's scenario, and are likely to have these letters in their names: D, M, V. Files require review—do it!

Monday, December 7 (Moon in Leo)   The moon in Leo, Mercury keynote, adds up to analytical perceptiveness in connection with an unusual relationship. Focus on written material, communication, and an invitation to travel. If you're single, you'll be pressured into making a decision that could affect your life years from now. Gemini is represented.

Tuesday, December 8 (Moon in Leo)   Get your invitation list and your holiday cards ready early—what's wrong with starting today? Attention revolves around music, theater, voice, and a domestic adjustment that might include where you live or your marital status. Taurus, Libra, and Scorpio are represented, with these letters in their names: F, O, X.

Wednesday, December 9 (Moon in Leo to Virgo 1:21 a.m.)   Your lucky numbers: 2, 5, 9. Within 24 hours, your employment picture changes. Get proposals in writing to avoid self-deception. Define your terms and be ready for a surprise tonight involving what amounts to a broken promise. Maintain your emotional equilibrium, protecting yourself in close quarters and playing your cards close to your chest.

Thursday, December 10 (Moon in Virgo)   At the track, post position special—number 8 p.p. in the eighth race. Pick six: 4, 2, 8, 1, 7, 6. Be alert for these letters in the names of potential winning horses or jockeys: H, Q, Z. Hot daily doubles: 4 and 2, 8 and 8, 6 and 5; these selections apply to all tracks.

Friday, December 11 (Moon in Virgo to Libra 11:43 a.m.)   Your cycle highlights this restoration of credit. Reach beyond the immediate; don't put aside the possibility of overseas travel. Focus on distance, language, and idealism in romance—your soulmate could be closer than you anticipate. Aries and Libra are involved, with these letters in their names: I and R.

Saturday, December 12 (Moon in Libra)   Make a fresh start. Don't push holiday preparations aside; instead, review your gift list. This will be one of your most exciting Saturday nights, featuring emotional encounters that lend spice and elevate your morale and your pride. Leo and Aquarius are represented with these letters in their names: A, S, J.

Sunday, December 13 (Moon in Libra)   Partnership and marriage signs are all over the place! The emphasis is also on special collections, silverware, home improvement, and a reunion with someone who once meant much to you. Capricorn and another Cancer are involved, and they could have these letters in their names: B, K, T.

Monday, December 14 (Moon in Libra to Scorpio 12:16 a.m.)   Within 24 hours, your creative juices flow! Finish with the details today. Get your files in order and bring source material up to date. You'll be dealing with a dynamic Scorpio who hints, "I want to take over!" Your response: "Thank you much, but no thanks!" A Sagittarian is also in picture, with these letters in a name: C, L, U.

Tuesday, December 15 (Moon in Scorpio)   Be scrupulous in checking details, including references, directions, and motivations. The moon in Scorpio relates to your style, panache, creativity, and sex appeal. Restrictions and inhibitions are tossed aside—have fun, but remember, there is a tomorrow! Taurus, Leo, and Scorpio play major roles. Look for these letters in their names: D, M, V.

Wednesday, December 16 (Moon in Scorpio to Sagittarius 12:46 p.m.)   Lucky lottery: 5, 22, 33, 8, 6, 30. Your popularity surges upward and people express the desire to wine-and-dine you. The Scorpio moon stirs your creative juices—it accents children, challenge, change, a variety of sensations. Read, write, disseminate information. Gemini, Virgo, Sagittarius are involved, with these letters in their names: E, N, W.

Thursday, December 17 (Moon in Sagittarius)   At the track: post position special—number 2 p.p. in the fourth race. Pick six: 1, 4, 2, 2, 5, 7. Have your antenna up for these letters in the names of potential winning horses or jockeys: F, O, X. Hot daily doubles: 1 and 4, 6 and 6, 3 and 2; these selections apply to all tracks.

Friday, December 18 (Moon in Sagittarius to Capricorn 11:55 p.m.)   The new moon in Sagittarius relates to health, basic issues, pets, dependents, and employment. Travel might be necessary for an interview concerning a possible executive position. Define your terms, perceive your potential, and look behind the scenes for answers. A Pisces corresponds, calling and saying in effect, "I wish you were not so far away."

Saturday, December 19 (Moon in Capricorn)   Within 24 hours, proposals are received, concerning either your career or marital status. Use this day to prepare, to take care of basic issues, and to respond to a request made by one who constantly seems to have a hand out. Let it be known in no uncertain terms that you no longer are giving up something of value for nothing.

Sunday, December 20 (Moon in Capricorn)   You'll be reunited with someone who once felt you were the most important person in the world. The emphasis is on universal appeal and the ability to deal with distance and language obstacles. Idealism in romance is also featured, along with the recognition of your spiritual values. Aries is involved.

Monday, December 21 (Moon in Capricorn to Aquarius 9:15 a.m.)   It's a bright Monday! The sun keynote and the Capricorn moon indicates this will be anything but a blue Monday. Today's scenario highlights independence, originality, and a strong love relationship. Let go of the status quo, making room for the new and finishing with people who take you for granted. Streamline procedures to get rid of clutter.

Tuesday, December 22 (Moon in Aquarius)   The Aquarian moon relates to hidden values, out-of-the-way dining places, and contacts with people concerned with the occult. You'll learn more about tax and license requirements and the financial status of someone who wants to be your partner or mate. Capricorn and another Cancer native figure prominently.

Wednesday, December 23 (Moon in Aquarius to Pisces 4:45 p.m.)   Deal gingerly with Gemini, making inquiries relating to answers or requests. Reject the superficial. Highlight social activity and knowledge concerning fashion, politics, and current events. Ignore a person who knows the price of everything and the value of nothing. Lucky lottery: 33, 13, 8, 5, 6, 26.

Thursday, December 24 (Moon in Pisces) It's Christmas Eve! The Pisces moon relates to a special holiday significance, as spiritual values are emphasized and stories are told relating to the uniqueness of what occurs tonight. Gifts you receive concern reading material, biographies, travel luggage, coupons, and displays of affection. Taurus and Scorpio are featured.

Friday, December 25 (Moon in Pisces to Aries 10:04 p.m.) On Christmas Day there is much activity in connection with spirituality, travel, visits, and a review of the past year. Important written material involves Gemini, Virgo, and Sagittarius with these letters in their names: E, N, W. Be analytical, taking nothing for granted. Merry Christmas!

Saturday, December 26 (Moon in Aries) You'll be testing, trying gifts, improving conditions at home, and accepting the need for a domestic adjustment relating to your lifestyle, residence, or marital status. You'll recoup enough energy to make this a memorable Saturday night. Music figures prominently and it is important that you dance to your own tune.

Sunday, December 27 (Moon in Aries) It's an ideal Sunday! An opportunity is present in connection with your future prospects and your ability to take charge of your own destiny. People will be drawn to you and confide the most intimate problems. As you help others, you'll also be helping yourself. Pisces and Virgo are involved, with these letters in their names: G, P, Y.

Monday, December 28 (Moon in Aries to Taurus 1:05 a.m.) How about New Year's Eve preparation? The Aries moon relates to your ninth house, which means concern with visitors from distant cities or even overseas. The upcoming celebration could be your most unique New Year's Eve. Focus today on persons who are on the brink of prosperity, which includes another Cancer and a Capricorn with these letters in their names: H, Q, Z.

Tuesday, December 29 (Moon in Taurus)   People talk about changing names. You'll feel ever so good! The Taurus moon is in that section of your horoscope associated with hopes, wishes, and your ability to win friends and influence people. The Taurus moon also means money and luck in matters of finance and romance. Libra plays a stimulating role.

Wednesday, December 30 (Moon in Taurus to Gemini 2:22 a.m.)   Make a fresh start; realize your own power; exude personal magnetism and sex appeal. Special note: Avoid heavy lifting! Your love relationship requires tender loving care. You attract to you determined, talented, stubborn people who seem to expect to be spoiled. Lucky lottery: 1, 50, 11, 12, 33, 22.

Thursday, December 31 (Moon in Gemini)   The last day of 1998—Happy New Year! The moon in Gemini relates to surprises, secret plans, clandestine arrangements, and activities associated with mystery, glamour, and intrigue. A family reunion is featured. Capricorn and another Cancer continue to figure prominently. A marriage proposal might happen at midnight!

Happy New Year!

ABOUT THE SERIES

This is one of a series
of twelve Day-to-Day Astrological Guides
for the signs of 1998
by Sydney Omarr

ABOUT THE AUTHOR

Born on August 5, 1926, in Philadelphia, Omarr was the
only person ever given full-time duty in the U.S. Army
as an astrologer. He also is regarded as the most erudite
astrologer of our time and the best known, through his
syndicated column (300 newspapers) and his radio and
television programs (he is Merv Griffin's "resident astrologer"). Omarr has been called the most "knowledge-
able astrologer since Evangeline Adams." His forecasts
of Nixon's downfall, the end of World War II in mid-
August of 1945, the assassination of John F. Kennedy,
Roosevelt's election to the fourth term and his death in
office . . . these and many others are on record and
quoted enough to be considered "legendary."

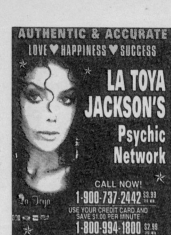

FREE Love Advice

Does he really love me?
Will I ever get married?
Is he being faithful?

FREE
sample
psychic reading
answers any
question!

1-800-743-6130

WIN A PERSONALIZED HOROSCOPE FROM SYDNEY OMARR!
ENTER THE SYDNEY OMARR HOROSCOPE SWEEPSTAKES!

No purchase necessary. Details below.

Name_____

Address_____

City_____State_____Zip _____

Mail to:
SYDNEY OMARR HOROSCOPE SWEEPSTAKES
P.O. Box 9232
Medford, NY, 11763-9232

Offer expires September 30, 1997.

OFFICIAL RULES

1. NO PURCHASE NECESSARY TO ENTER OR WIN A PRIZE. To enter the SYDNEY OMARR HOROSCOPE SWEEPSTAKES, complete this official entry form (original or photocopy), or, on a 3" x 5" piece of paper, print your name and complete address. Mail your entry to: SYDNEY OMARR HOROSCOPE SWEEPSTAKES, P.O. Box 9232, Medford, NY, 11763-9232. Enter as often as you wish, but mail each entry in a separate envelope. All entries must be received by September 30, 1997, to be eligible. Not responsible for illegible entries, lost or misdirected mail.

2. Winners will be selected from all valid entries in a random drawing on or about October 15, 1997, by Marden-Kane, Inc., an independent judging organization whose decisions are final and binding. Odds of winning are dependent upon the number of entries received. Winners will be notified by mail and may be required to execute an affidavit of eligibility and release which must be returned within 14 days of notification or an alternate winner will be selected.

3. One (1) Grand Prize winner will receive a personalized prediction for one (1) year from Sydney Omarr. One (1) Second Prize winner will receive a personalized prediction for one (1) month from Sydney Omarr. Twenty-five (25) Third Prize winners will receive a free phone call to Sydney Omarr's 1-900 number to hear a personal prediction. No transfer or substitution for prize offered. Estimated value of all prizes: $250.

4. Sweepstakes open to residents of the U.S. and Canada 18 years of age or older, except employees and the immediate families of Penguin Putnam, Inc., its affiliated companies, advertising and promotion agencies. Void in the Province of Quebec and wherever else prohibited by law. All Federal, State, Local, and Provincial laws apply. Taxes, if any, are the sole responsibility of the prize winners. Canadian winners will be required to answer an arithmetical skill testing question administered by mail. Winners consent to the use of their name and/or photos or likenesses for advertising purposes without additional compensation (except where prohibited).

5. For the names of the major prize winners, send a self-addressed, stamped envelope after October 15, 1997, to: SYDNEY OMARR HOROSCOPE SWEEPSTAKES WINNERS, P.O. Box 4320, Manhasset, NY, 11030-4320.

Ⓩ Signet

Penguin Putnam, Inc. ✦ Mass Market